Adolescence and Community
the Youth Service in Britain

John Eggleston
with the assistance of Patricia Allatt

Edward Arnold

First published 1976 by
Edward Arnold (Publishers) Ltd
25 Hill Street, London W1X 8LL

ISBN   cloth: 0 7131 5886 7
       paper: 0 7131 5887 5

Set IBM by Zee Graphics, London S E 20. Printed in Great Britain by
The Pitman Press Bath.

Acknowledgements

The author and publishers wish to thank the following for permission to use the photographs reproduced in this volume:

Miss Mary Hall for plate 5; S.H. Bath for plate 6; Laurence D. Curtis for plate 8; and Collins Melvin Ward & Partners for plate 10.

Plates 1, 2, 4 and 7 were supplied by the National Association of Youth Clubs; plates 3 and 8 by the Publicity Department of the Scout Association; plates 5 and 9 by the Public Relations Department of the Girl Guide Association and plate 10 is from the Good Youth Centre Guide, *Education*, 5 July, 1974 (supplement). To all of these our thanks for their most generous cooperation.

Contents

Preface

The research project on the organization and purpose of the Youth and Community Service in England and Wales reported in this volume was commissioned by the Department of Education and Science in 1967. Work commenced in 1968 and was completed in 1974. The generous participation of members of all parts of the Youth and Community Service is gratefully acknowledged as is the interest and support of officers of the Department of Education and Science, Local Authorities and the Inspectorate. In particular the Research Consultative Group, Mr G. Bourne, Miss M. Bone, Mr S. Rowe, Mr J. D. Ridge and Mr A. Griffiths provided a continuing source of help and advice as did Dr D. H. Gibson. Acknowledgement is also due to the research staff of the project, in particular to Mrs P. Allat who carried an especially heavy responsibility in the final stages of the project. For varying periods the team also included Mr D. Case, Dr M. Jordan, Mr M.J. Proctor, Mrs S.M. Ridgway and Mr E. Ring. The perceptive secretarial work of Mrs P.V. Barfield, Mrs S. Chandler, Mrs G.K. Hope, Mrs B.I. Deane and Mrs B. Wiggins has been a major contribution. The Keele Computer Centre responded regularly and effectively to our requirements. But, as is proper in a service dedicated to the development of individual initiative and responsibility, I must make it clear that responsibility for the inevitable errors and omissions rests solely with me.

John Eggleston

University of Keele

1 Grass roots

'One night at the club the phone rang for Susan. After I'd asked her to take the call I wondered a bit. It's unusual for members to have calls at the club and the voice at the other end was that of an older man and sounded very anxious. When Susan left the phone she was almost in tears, so later on I asked her what was up. After a bit she explained that her dad had left home three weeks ago and that Susan had been sick with worry about where he was but her mother had forbidden Susan to try to find him or even to ask about him, telling Susan that she was better off without him. Susan, who didn't like her mother's new friend, hadn't been home much herself it turned out; in fact she hadn't slept at home for the past four nights. If it hadn't been for the club her dad might not have been able to contact Susan and probably nobody would have ever been able to help. Anyway to cut a long story short, I was able to get Susan's mum and dad together again and to line up several things to help them sort out their problems and Susan's.'

'He was a good lad, the star forward of the club football team. He was really keen, turned out twice a week regularly for training with our part-time leader. When he left the club he signed on for the local Working Men's team. But he was always a bit wild like and one Saturday night a few weeks ago he got really tanked up and thumped a copper. He was in dead trouble. First thing on Sunday morning he was down outside our part-time leader's house, the first person he turned to. Together we were able to put in a good word with the probation people and he was let down lightly. But it could have been a very different story.'

Stories like these abound as one visits youth clubs throughout Britain; they are part of the culture of the Youth and Community Service. There are many others that are almost classic in their generality. There is Albert, the rather grotesque and socially ostracized boy who almost in desperation starts 'touching up' the girls in the club. And there is Sandra,

1

the girl who displays an astonishing talent for art and who, belatedly, wants to move to Art College. Alas, she has no O levels or even CSE passes. Almost always the stories end with an indication of the way in which the adults in the club have in some way been able to identify and alleviate the problems and respond to the needs of the young people concerned. Situations such as these regularly dispel beyond doubt suggestions that there may not be useful work for the clubs to under-take. There will always be problems as long as there are young people and there will always be a need for adults outside the home and the school to respond to them. And it is important to realise that the young people mentioned in these examples are neither deviant nor deprived nor indeed in any other category for which special provision normally exists.

One of the encouraging features of the Youth and Community Service is the competence and effectiveness of the response of adults to the needs of their members. Though frequently lacking in advanced training in the range of interpersonal and guidance skills that could often be most appropriate to their work, many nonetheless display a capacity, even a flair, for making sound and appropriate judgements and acting accordingly. More than once it was impressive to see the way in which leaders in a busy club were keenly aware, for example, of the dangers of building up a 'dependency relationship' among their members (as one of them perceptively put it, 'I don't come here each evening on an ego trip'). More than one leader showed his ability to handle not only the creative potential of adolescents but also their equally powerful negativism with an understanding that has regularly escaped many of the theoreticians in the field.

Here we have already reached what is probably the heart of the Youth and Community Service — responsiveness and caring for the needs of the individual in an open and unstructured way. Yet it is precisely this openness that presents the service with its most fundamental difficulties. For the service, if only because it is a recipient of public funds, has to have a structure and an organization[1]. It has to have expressed aims, a constitution of a sort, even recognized procedures and spheres of activity. However loosely conceptualized each of the major sections of the Youth and Community Service, both statutory and voluntary, may be, each has its own bureaucracy with its own hierarchy of responsibility and decision making. And in order to maintain its existence and to substantiate its claims for further finance it has in some way to justify itself in quantitative terms by the measure-ment of its activities, its membership roles, its attendance figures, its provision of courses and the like.

[1] The various criteria for eligibility to receive public funds are detailed in Chapter II of the PEP report (Thomas and Perry, 1975).

Yet, as we have already suggested, the central areas of achievement of the service are often non-quantifiable. In this the dilemma of the Youth and Community Service is similar to, yet greater than, that of other comparable services. Social workers have, at the very least, means of precise identification of clients and have established ways of treating them; schools enrol their pupils and exercise some compulsion over them; even the churches have baptism and confirmation of their members. But in many branches of the Youth and Community Service membership itself is so loose a term as to be almost meaningless. Records may of necessity be incomplete and sporadic and, not surprisingly, may be seen to be unimportant by many adults and young people in the service. Yet the problem of evaluation, however elusive, is a central one for all who work in the Youth and Community Service if only because it offers them the prospect of some reassurance that their work is of value and consequence. Often this need leads workers to seek 'symbolic' indicators of their worth such as building extensions, furniture and titles which, though unquestionably important, are at best secondary instruments of evaluation.

Certainly it is very clear that the detailed administrative requirements of the service are in many cases seen as a distraction, even an inhibition. Some variation of the recurring phrase 'let us get on with the real job' sums up the feelings of many workers when faced with 'office' work. Yet if administration is a nightmare for many workers in the service it is even clearer that for many administrators the Youth and Community Service is an executive nightmare, for the very openness and unstructured nature of the service presents fundamental administrative problems. How are activities to be costed? By what criteria may provision of resources and staffing be judged? In what circumstances and by what criteria should the service be expanded, diminished or modified?

Possibly the only generally acceptable definition of the Youth and Community Service is that it serves the needs of young people insofar as they are not catered for by some other service (although as we shall discuss later there are a number of areas where the Youth and Community Service overlaps and even competes with other providing agencies). But as all young people have needs and all human needs are virtually infinite the definition allows of no effective boundaries. 'Water into the sand' was the not entirely cynical resumé of more than one administrator.

In consequence the administrator has few effective guidelines to tell him what is within the realm of the Youth and Community Service and what is not. Lacking such guidance he is daily faced with the new proposals for growth that are a recurring feature of the Youth and Community Service. From all sides there come proposals for new extensions of activity and service. These may be for the appointment of unattached workers, the development of counselling and guidance

services, new involvement in community action and the establishment of 'shop-front' clubs, to name but a few. The range of potential new commitments is unlimited. Not only does this present the administrator with a situation of almost unlimited demand which, once it has been articulated, he may be under considerable obligation to satisfy; it also presents him with the problems of organizing, providing and costing these new extensions without the aid of previous guidelines. In consequence he is likely to turn with some relief to the long established organizations where at least he is on firmer ground and where there are long established criteria for funding. Something of the difficulties of the administrator were expressed by Lord Belstead, at the time Parliamentary Under Secretary of State for Education, in a speech in September 1972. He was reported as saying, 'But I have to say that few of the problems which come forward for our consideration seem to be designed to get to the heart of the problems of national significance, either because they are set in a limited local context with little obvious prospect for wider application, or because they seem to lack a clear plan of campaign. It may be that our definitions are too exact, our conditions too inhibiting. Perhaps we should be thinking less in terms of self-contained, isolated projects, and rather more of an extension of headquarters' activity.' (Belstead, 1972.) It is not perhaps too great an exaggeration to say that the long established organizations survive, are even protected, by the sheer amorphousness of the service as a whole. They stand out like firm footsteps in a morass.

But in turn this leads us to yet another major paradox of the Youth and Community Service — the conservatism and traditionalism of the structure, much of it almost untouched for a century, which stands in striking contrast to the fluidity, responsiveness and spontaneity that is often alluded to by the practitioners within the service, not least of all by those in the longest established organizations.

The conflict, however, is but one of the many that characterize the Youth and Community Service in Britain. We have already mentioned that which exists between the informality of the club and the necessary bureaucracy of the organization. There are various conflicts between the needs of the organization and the needs of the members; between the lay committees and the professionals. There are conflicts between the clubs and organizations themselves and between the members and the adults. There are particular conflicts between the schools and the service even to the point where the work of one is diagnosed as 'useless' by the other — a conflict not always resolved by common training courses or joint appointments.

It is at least arguable that these conflicts are far greater than those in other branches of our social and educational services. Yet the Youth and Community Service survives. Perhaps the key to its survival in the face of conflict lies in the central 'absorbing' role of the leaders in the individual clubs and units. The strain is often considerable. Leaders speak frequently of their uncertainty and anxiety, understandably because their existence depends upon their capacity to resolve the conflicts almost on a day to day basis. For many leaders there is an almost daily possibility that they will lose the credibility and confidence of either their management committee or their members or even both. Leaders frequently speak with considerable feeling:

I was told to keep the girls out of the place . . . Another member of the management said I was only to let in the 'nice young people', those who would behave themselves and treat the centre properly. When he does not even live in the district and only comes into the club infrequently, how can he say who these are? . . . With the membership dropping off to only a few per evening because of having to implement these policies I feel I cannot remain. I find it difficult answering the young people when they ask why they can no longer come in. (Bristow, 1970)

It quickly became clear that the conflicts inherent in the provision of the Youth and Community Service and the ways in which they are contained or resolved were to be a central theme in the research project on the organization and practice of the Youth and Community Service in England and Wales that is reported here. The research project was envisaged by the Youth Service Development Council towards the end of its existence and was financed by the Department of Education and Science and continued from late 1968 to 1974.

The planning and research strategies of the project are described and the results are presented in subsequent chapters of this volume. The work took place in a representative range of areas in England and Wales and was organized on two levels. There was the 'macro' level in which an attempt was made to look at the organizations overall with special attention to their structure, there values and their operation. There was also the 'micro' level where extensive and detailed work was undertaken in a very limited range of clubs and similar units in which intensive studies of the behaviours of members and their relationships with adults were mounted. The project was conducted alongside and in liaison with a number of other studies discussed in chapter 3, the most notable of these being that of the Survey of the Office of Population Censuses, Social Survey Division, which was published under the title *The Youth Service and Similar Provision for Young People* (Bone and Ross, 1972). Together the studies were intended to provide a considerably more comprehensive picture than heretofore available of the complex group of organizations within the service. It is hoped that this document, read in conjunction with the others, will serve its part in this purpose and provide a source of information that is of value not only to practitioners in the service but also to the very large number of individuals who, at various levels, are charged with the duty of making decisions in this important area of social service. In particular, it is hoped that the present work will allow some of the conflicts inherent in the service to be seen and understood more clearly and to be resolved or at least accommodated more readily. The report draws heavily for its evidence upon the experiences of practitioners in the field as well as on the work of the 'theoreticians' of the service. An important by-product of the work may be the diminution of the gap that often appears to separate them — which itself regularly threatens to be yet another of the symptomatic conflicts of the service.

2 Structure and practice of the Youth and Community Service

The Scope of the Service

What is the Youth Service? An essential prelude to deciding upon a research strategy was an attempt to define what actually constituted the structure and practice of the Youth and Community Service. Not only was it necessary to do so in order to delineate the research field; it was also clear that there were likely to be close links between the practices and the organizational structures of the various components of the service, as several researchers had already demonstrated (for example, Zald, 1970, in a study of the YMCA). In deciding to undertake such a preliminary exploration we reached, almost at our first step, one of our most difficult and intractable problems. This chronicle of our attempts at definition serves two purposes. It shows the structural problems of the Youth and Community Service which led us to conduct our researches in the way we did and it also provides an introduction to readers who lack a detailed knowledge of the British Youth and Community Service through first hand experience. *Youth and Community Work in the 70s* (Youth Service Development Council, 1969) noted that 'few prople outside the Youth Service are aware of a unified service. Our experience quickly led us to suggest that few people, even within the service, were aware of a unified service.

We took as a starting point the simple parameters of the service we were initially offered. The age range of the Youth and Community Service, fourteen to twenty, is in some ways the firmest boundary of the service insofar as only members within these ages count for official records and in calculations for grant and other administrative purposes. Yet we found many clubs had an 'unofficial' attendance of under fourteens usually with the full knowledge of the leader, who saw them as a welcome source of recruitment for the future and even found them very useful in giving the club a more populated appearance.[1] Similarly

---

[1] Indeed, *Youth and Community Work in the 70s* (Youth Service Development Council, 1969) has a chapter devoted to 'The Youth Service and the Under Fourteens'.

7

there were a number of 'senior members' in many clubs whose presence was justified by the leader for a variety of reasons either in the interests of the club or of the individuals concerned.

The broad definition of the purpose of the Youth and Community Service, which is generally seen as 'leisure time education and recreation', again offers a useful parameter though one that is inevitably loose at the edges. For example, the close links between the provision of further education and youth service in a number of local authority areas leads to many vocational and quasi-vocational programmes being associated with youth service provisions. Likewise the experimental projects for unemployed adolescents and those involving community service activities are frequently difficult to categorize as being of a leisure or a recreational nature.

Another parameter commonly offered was the institutional form of the service. Characteristically this is the Youth Club, the Scout Troop, the unit of the pre-service organization, the Young Farmers' Club or the group of young church members. Each is characterized by an explicit organizational structure, a hierarchy of membership, defined roles for members and adults and established rules and financial arrangements. But there are many other groupings that may or may not be officially part of the Youth and Community Service. They include local youth orchestras, choirs, and theatre groups, a range of special interest groups ranging from aero modellers to young zoologists, and a whole gamut of experimental projects that may be particularly designed to cater for 'unattached' or 'unclubbable' young people and which may deliberately play down the institutional nature of the group and even the very concept of membership.

It is important to note that some categories of young people's organizations are not included in the Youth and Community Service and are not fundable through the normal official channels. Chief among these are student unions and the youth wings of the political parties, although *Youth and Community Work in the 70s* recommends closer links between such organizations and the Youth and Community Service. They are not specifically studied in this book but their existence and their importance both for society as a whole and for the Youth and Community Service in particular have not been ignored.

It soon became clear not only that these parameters are difficult to apply rigorously but also that their effectiveness is diminishing in the 'de-structuring' of the Youth and Community Service that is taking place following the dissemination of the ideas of *Youth and Community Work in the 70s*. Here the emphases are on the integration of the Youth and Community Service into a broader community context with a diminished 'segregation' of the young into separate sectors of society. Among its recommendations are that 'the Youth Service should be re-designated the Youth and Community Service' and that 'the existing age limits of fourteen to twenty should disappear'. These recommendations and the current pattern of development, visible in both the more traditional and the more experimental areas of the service, reveal close parallels with a similar 'de-structuring' of the social services following the *Seebohm Report* (1968); of local government following the *Skeffington Report* (1969); and in the schools following the moves towards comprehensive reorganization, de-streaming, integrated curricula and increased student choice of programmes. Indeed, such moves seem to be central to contemporary thinking about the organizational structure of our society. In the face of these difficulties we turned, as have so many others, to the most clearly visible distinction of the Youth and Community Service, the administrative division between the statutory and the voluntary wings.

The Voluntary Sector

Firmly rooted in a century of history, the boundaries of the voluntary sector are among the most secure within the Youth and Community Service; certainly they have remained virtually unchallenged throughout the policy statements of the last decade. There are some obvious reasons for this, among them the high esteem in which many of the voluntary organizations are held — an important feature in a service where high status is in short supply and difficult to generate. But another reason for the intact condition of the voluntary organizations is their unquestioned link with powerful elite groups in business, commerce, the professions and politics: links that are effectively maintained through appointments to committees, consultantships and honorary officerships. Members of the organizations may often be surprised and occasionally resentful at the apparent irrelevance to the day-to-day life of the clubs of the back-grounds and even involvements of some of the senior officers of their movements (Lowe, 1973). Yet from a detached point of view there can be little question of the wisdom of the voluntary organizations in following such policies. The active and visible response of the voluntary organizations to the proposed Private Member's legislation on the Youth and Community Service in 1974 was but one illuminating example of how effective and powerful a 'pressure group' the voluntary organizations represent. But another and perhaps even greater reason for the survival of the voluntary organizations, in many cases for a century or more, lies probably in their immense capacity for adaptation and development.

The organizations vary widely in character but most provide a range of educational and religious activities that are usually closely linked with social, sporting and other recreational programmes. All endeavour to inculcate some agreed and demanding standards of personal conduct. Most have religious objectives, some of an international nature. A minority, notably the uniformed organizations have more specific aims, for example, training in first aid or service activities. But all share wider aims concerned with character training, citizenship and personal development. The programmes of the majority of the voluntary organizations are similar to those of the statutory organizations. Characteristically they include outdoor activities, camping, dramatics, music, dancing, crafts and a range of diverse physical activities. Most voluntary boys' clubs and some of the statutory groups are affiliated to the National Association of Boys' Clubs; mixed clubs are usually in membership with the National Association of Youth Clubs. Most of the voluntary organizations operating in Wales have distinctive Welsh features but there is only one specifically Welsh national youth movement — the Welsh League of Youth — established in 1922.

The contemporary range of voluntary organizations may broadly be seen to be covered by the following six categories:[2]

(1) federations of clubs
(2) uniformed organizations
(3) church coordinating bodies for youth
(4) other bodies where the principal interest is not in young people but where there is a level of national support to youth activity
(5) voluntary service organizations
(6) 'one-off' organizations organizing a specific activity on one or more sites with a national catchment area.

Some organizations could, of course, be placed in more than one of these categories — many, for example, encourage their members to undertake voluntary service — but taking their predominant characteristics many organizations can be grouped as follows:

(1) National Association of Youth Clubs; Welsh Association of Youth Clubs; National Association of Boys' Clubs; Boys' Clubs of Wales; Methodist Association of Youth Clubs; National Federation of Young Farmers' Clubs; Welsh League of Youth; National Federation of Eighteen Plus Groups; Anglican Young People's Association; Association for Jewish Youth; Docklands Settlements; Young Christian Workers.
(2) Scout Association; Girl Guides' Association; Boys' Brigade; Girls' Brigade; Army Cadet Force Association; Girls' Venture Corps; Sea Cadet Corps and Girls' Nautical Training Corps; Girls' Friendly Society: Church Lads' Brigade; The Campaigners.
(3) British Council of Churches; Church of England Youth Council. Catholic Youth Service Council; United Reform Church; Baptist Union of Great Britain and Ireland; Provincial Youth Council of the Church in Wales; Presbyterian Church of Wales.

[2] We are grateful to Political and Economic Planning for suggesting this categorization.

(4) Young Men's Christian Association; Young Women's Christian
     Association; Salvation Army; British Red Cross Society; St John
     Ambulance Brigade; Cooperative Union.
(5) Community Service Volunteers; International Voluntary Services;
     Task Force.
(6) The Foudroyant Trust; Ocean Youth Club. Sailing Training
     Association; Outward Bound; National Youth Theatre; Duke of
     Edinburgh's Award.

The essential difference between the voluntary organizations and the
statutory organizations which we shall discuss later, appears to lie in their
administrative structures. Bristow (1970) devised organizational diagrams
of the structure of a typical voluntary organization and contrasted it
with diagrams of a typical statutory organization. His findings suggested
that the voluntary organizations tend to be semi-autonomous units
linked to a national headquarters in a concentric pattern, while the
statutory organizations tend to take a pyramidal bureaucratic form.

Figure 1 **VOLUNTARY ORGANIZATIONS: Concentric Structure**

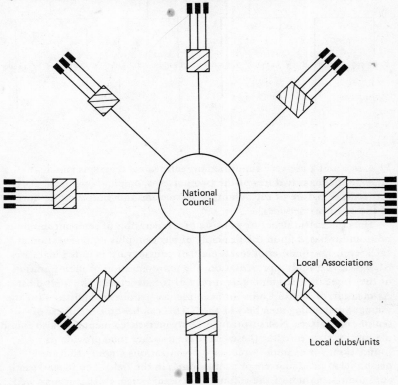

Figure 2 **STATUTORY ORGANIZATIONS: Pyramidal Structure**

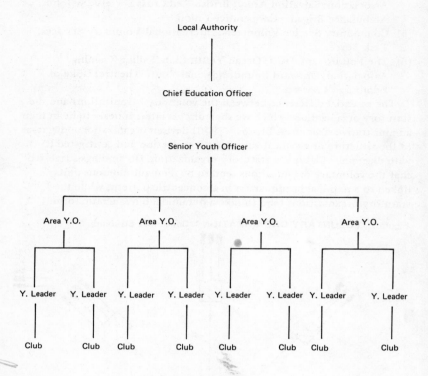

Figures 1 and 2 are very simplified organizational diagrams which indicate the main features of the two patterns, emphasizing particularly the 'federal' nature of the voluntary service and the 'bureaucratic' form of the statutory services.

The concentric structure consists of a federation of semi-autonomous units and is based upon the principle of election plus representation at each level. The number of levels may, of course, vary in individual cases. Alongside the adult representation, the representation or incorporation of the clients is often an inherent part of the structure: The Methodist Association of Youth Clubs for example, has parallel committees for the young; outstanding members of the NABC can become members of senior committees. Not surprisingly, bureaucratic elements are also found within this structure but these elaborate it rather than provide its foundation: for example, voluntary organizations employ fulltime personnel at headquarters or professionals in the field. The federal semi-autonomous nature of the voluntary structure suggests that it may well

be able to adapt to new and localised needs despite the constraints of
tradition and finance that characterize long established organizations.

Until after the 1939/45 period: the voluntary service was, to all
intents and purposes, the Youth Service. The gradual development of a
statutory service during the war years made little significant change and,
indeed, in the years that followed the war it was widely believed that it
would be possible to rely substantially on the traditional voluntary
bodies to satisfy the needs of youth. The organizations were well known
and well trusted. If the statutory local authorities were to have any
involvement at all it was largely seen to lie in administrative and financial
support or in arranging the occasional sports day, gala or tournament to
bring the various organizations together. Even in the 1950s the voluntary
bodies continued to dominate the scene in many areas, notably big cities
such as Birmingham, Liverpool and London; with the local authorities
assisting them in their efforts and supplementing them with care to avoid
resentment — a situation not without its parallel to the relationships
between church and state in the school system a century previously.
(Cruickshank, 1963). Only in a few areas such as Essex did voluntary
provision run at a lower level than the statutory parts of the Youth
Service.

But during the 1960s, in the aftermath of the *Albemarle Report*
(1960) it emerged that the traditional youth organizations were not

always adequately equipped to cope with changing demands and expectations of both young people and society. The need for more trained and
professional youth workers and for new experimental approaches and
adequate buildings was emphasized sharply by the Albemarle Committee.
Its recommendations were at once approved by the then Minister of
Education with immediate consequences for both the voluntary and the
statutory sides of the service. During the 1960s most of the voluntary
bodies re-examined their aims, organization and programmes. A number,
notably the Scouts, Guides, NAYC, Boys' Brigade, the YMCA and the
YWCA set up commissions of enquiry and published reports.[3] . A number
of them made fundamental changes, others made more modest adaptations to meet the post-Albemarle situation. The emphasis on professionalism in the Albemarle Report led to considerable debate between the lay
committees and the newly recognized and qualified professional workers
who were beginning to be appointed to the voluntary organizations. This
period also saw the beginnings of the arguments concerning 'client
determination' in the service, and, indeed, a number of the experimental
projects in which this has developed most fully were initiated in the
voluntary sector. The NABC was particularly active in experimental
projects, notably in the treatment of work with young offenders. The
NAYC initiated major developments in unattached work as well as in
work with the physically handicapped and with unemployed young
people. The Scouts and Guides modified not only their appearance but
also their traditional programmes and badge systems in fundamental
ways, while the YMCA and the YWCA made substantial changes in their
provision of hostel accommodation and in the field of industrial youth
work. There were also a number of local enquiries, investigations and
reports, often spanning the work of both the statutory and voluntary
organizations. A useful recent example of such a study is the report of the
Cheltenham Youth Trust (1972).

Since 1970 the Standing Conference of National Voluntary Youth
Organizations, now the National Council for Voluntary Youth Services,
the coordinating body for the voluntary organizations, has also undertaken a review. The Council now includes representation from local
conferences as well as national representatives from the voluntary bodies
and is, in consequence, likely to be more closely represented by its grass
roots. It is not yet certain whether the range of organizations will widen
in membership to embrace political and student groups. At the moment
the main link between the Youth and Community Service and the young
political groups and students is the British Youth Council, formerly the

[3] See for example the report of the YMCA National Commission (1970), or the
Anniversary Report on Methodist Association of Youth Clubs' Development in the
1970s (1970).

British Committee of the World Assembly of Youth, an international
coordinating body formed for democratic youth movements and funded
by the Foreign and Commonwealth Office. Since 1969 the Council has
established its own local Youth Councils consisting of representatives of
young people from youth organizations in local areas. National gather-
ings of these local Youth Councils led to the National Youth Assembly
launched in 1971 by the then Secretary of State for the Environment.

The Statutory Sector

The statutory side of the Youth Service, with a number of notable
exceptions, dates from November 1939, when the disruption of family
and social life caused by the war was seen to call for a more
comprehensive provision of facilities for young people in all parts of the
country. However, since the establishment of the National Fitness
Council earlier in the 1930s there had in fact been an emergent national
policy to encourage fitness and recreation, especially amongst the young.
Towards the end of the war, indeed, the concern was so great that a
system of registration of sixteen to eighteen year olds was instituted to
help them to find an appropriate role in youth organizations, particularly
the youth service corps. Introduced under the Defence Regulations, the
system of registration was justified by the Prime Minister with the words,
'We must be careful that our boys and girls do not run loose during this
time of stress.'[4] The main administrative changes however were effected
by the Board of Education Circular 1486 *Service of Youth*, issued in
1939 to all local education authorities. The circular recorded the board's
decision to take direct responsibility for youth welfare as part of the
national system of education, defining youth as those between school
leaving age and twenty years. It indicated that a National Youth
Committee, later to become the Youth Advisory Council, had been
established to advise the minister and that a special branch of the board
had been organized to administer grants. It urged that all local education
authorities should take immediate steps to establish youth committees
in their areas and to seek the cooperation of voluntary organizations in
providing a comprehensive youth service. In this way the Youth Service
was established as a partnership of voluntary organizations, local
authorities and central government. The response was enthusiastic and
immediate. Youth organizers and youth committees were appointed
forthwith and the voluntary organizations increased their staffs. A new
pattern of provision including a number of new establishments, notably
the local education authority sponsored Youth Centres, came to exist.

[4] For an interesting brief account of the events of this time see Lindsey, 1975.

The development of the statutory system was reaffirmed by the 1944 Education Act in the following terms:

> Subject as hereinafter provided, it shall be the duty of every local education authority to secure the provision for their area of adequate facilities for further education . . . [including] . . . leisure-time occupation . . . for any persons over compulsory school age who are able and willing to profit by the facilities provided for that purpose . . . [and] . . . to secure that the facilities for primary, secondary and further education provided for their area include adequate facilities for recreation and social training . . . [having] regard to the expediency of cooperation with any voluntary societies or bodies whose objects include the provision of facilities or the organization of activities of a similar character.

Through the fifties the development of the statutory service continued, often in association with a parallel development of further education facilities, though, as with all other educational development, progress varied with the prevailing economic conditions. Nonetheless, the statutory service was still considered in many areas to serve a gap-filling role: certainly it was not in any sense in competition with the established voluntary organizations, though the very existence of an alternative set of provisions had an unquestionable effect on the voluntary bodies.

The characteristic form of the local education authority provision was the Youth Centre, many of which came to have distinctive characters as a result of their size, range of activities and the increasing professionalism of the adult staff. But others were remarkably similar to the voluntary general purpose clubs and, as we have already noticed, were indeed members of national bodies of the voluntary movement (NABC and NAYC). In recent years, however, the emphasis of local authority provision has tended to change. At first strong emphasis was placed on the instructional purpose of the service; many local authorities now recognize more clearly the social needs of young people and have come to accept that their school building may be used in the evenings for purely social purposes. Many local authority schools now have purpose-built youth wings that emphasize the social and recreational rather than the instructional role of the youth club. But local authority provision is by no means confined to work in school premises; a considerable number of the statutory organizations are in separate purpose-built establishments and the range of provision is at least as diverse as that of the voluntary sector ranging from the clubs through unattached workers, shop-front clubs and outdoor activity centres that may be beyond the geographical confines of a local authority. A particular advantage of the statutory provision is the general availability of the local authority's sports ground facilities though facilities are usually generously granted to the voluntary bodies as well.

It is in the statutory sector that the initiative in new building in the Albemarle-inspired 'bricks and mortar era' can be most clearly seen (though the voluntary sector also obtained very considerable aid for building during this period). Projects in both the statutory and voluntary sectors had secured a total funding of some forty million pounds between the publication of the *Albemarle Report* and the end of 1972. Speaking in April 1972 the then Minister of Education, Mrs Margaret Thatcher, announced that capital building programmes amounting to forty-one million pounds had been approved. The 1960s concept of the purpose-built youth centre was initiated with the local education authority centre at Withywood in Bristol, closely associated with the publication of the DES Building Bulletin No 20 (DES, 1961). This incorporated a coffee bar, lounge area, activity and sports area, workshop, quiet room and, by the Youth Service standards of the day, luxurious toilet facilities.

The pioneering of the statutory sector in the development of purpose-built club areas caused it to bear the brunt of the unforeseen difficulties in designing for the fourteen to twenty age group. An attempt was made at Withywood, and subsequently elsewhere, to provide a sophisticated decor in part to match the commercial provision becoming available to the upper end of the age range. Yet, as many surveys confirm, the majority of the active members of the service tend to belong to the fourteen to sixteen age group; less mature and sophisticated than those for whom the premises had been primarily designed, their leisure needs were often far more for a lively area in which they could 'let off steam'. In consequence there have been severe maintenance problems in a number of purpose-built and school-based clubs, often leading to accusations of vandalism and destructiveness. More recent LEA provision has tended to overcome some of these problems and the voluntary bodies, being somewhat later into the field of purpose-built buildings, have tended to benefit from the experience of the statutory sector.

In the seventies indications are that the statutory sector is re-establishing its focus more closely on school-based youth work linked with adult provision following the lead of *Youth and Community Work in the 70s* (1 SDC 1969). The various initiatives were reflected in a variety of LEA memoranda made available to us (unfortunately undated and unpublished in most cases). They included the Kent Education Committee's *Focus on Youth*, the ILEA's *Review of Youth and Adult Services* and the Sheffield Education Committee's Policy Development Groups' *Report on ROSLA* with an appendix devoted to 'Social Centres and Links with the Youth Service'. The link between school and Youth Service activity in Sheffield is also described, interestingly, in an anonymous article in *Forum* (anon. 1973a). One of the more notable pioneering experiments with a school-based youth and community service has been the Minsthorpe High School and Community College in the former West

Riding area of Yorkshire. An unpublished report of the early experience at Minsthorpe reads:

> The West Riding Authority and the National Association of Youth Clubs worked in partnership, with the support of a financial grant from the Carnegie United Kingdom Trust, which enabled a total of 6,000 square feet to be added to the normal building allocation for school purposes. Beyond this point, however, the distinction of space ceased and the total building was designed as a single enterprise. In design terms, the attempt was to give employment, which may be used either to recompense additionally members of the full-time staff for work beyond their normal full-time programme or to employ part-time staff for specific classes or activities. At present more than half the full-time staff of 60 have programmes which involve their working within the school curriculum and in the evenings with groups of young people or adults, or both. A proportion of the staff have a programme which is made up of a combination of morning, afternoon and evening sessions.

In concluding this note on the statutory sector it is important to emphasize once again the concept of partnership between the two parts of the service. In the original establishment of the statutory sector the Board of Education memorandum stated that 'any attempt at a state-controlled uniformity or regimentation would be both stupid and perilous; more than that, it would be wholly alien to the spirit of this country. The function of the state in this work is to focus and lead the efforts of all engaged in youth welfare; to supplement the resources of existing national organizations without impairing their independence; and to ensure through cooperation that the ground is covered in a way never so far attained.'

The Development of Policy

We have already glimpsed some of the important landmarks of the official policy in the period commencing in 1939 and the ensuing growth in the confidence and permanence of the Youth Service. It is important, however, to identify two major recent reports on the service.

The Albemarle Report

The most notable reinforcement of the role of the Youth Service was perhaps that given by the *Albemarle Report* (1960) which has already been discussed at several points. As we have noted, it was accepted at once and fully by Her Majesty's government. Among its recommendations were:

> that the Youth Service should be made available to all young people aged fourteen to twenty [that is, lowering the minimum age to include some in their last year at school as a step towards easing the transition between school and work] ; that a national committee, a Youth Service Development Council, should be set up to advise the Minister on a ten year development programme;
>
> that a building programme should be started which should provide, besides new buildings, more attactive furniture and decorations and better equipment;
>
> that expenditure by local education authorities should be enough to 'sustain the momentum of development.;
>
> that the Ministry of Education should make larger grants to national voluntary youth organizations;
>
> that arrangements for training part-time youth leaders should be improved;
>
> that a long-term scheme for training full-time youth leaders should be started and that there should be an emergency scheme for a big increase in the number of leaders by 1966;
>
> that a representative committee should be appointed to negotiate salary scales and conditions of service for full-time youth leaders;
>
> that a national campaign for more voluntary helpers and the development of the voluntary principle at every level of activity should be organised;
>
> that there should also be opportunities for young people to participate as 'partners' in the Youth Service.'

The Youth Service Development Council was set up to oversee the new arrangements; the National College for the Training of Youth Leaders was established in Leicester to provide a one year training course for adult wokers and other training agencies — Swansea University, Westhill College, the National Association of Boys' Clubs and the YMCA were encouraged to extend their professional training programmes. A Youth Service building programme was announced; grants were made available for experimental projects. Locally, many education authorities elevated their youth committees to be sub-committees of the Education Committee and most of those authorities that had not previously appointed Youth Officers established such posts.

The professional structure of the Youth Service running from youth officer through area youth officer to full-time youth worker became general, with important implications for the career structures of the professional workers. The *Albemarle Report* urged experimentation and new projects particularly with the unattached: two thirds of all young people in 1960 were not connected with any part of the service.

Subsequent to the report some thirty projects were supported from a special Department of Education and Science experimental fund during the sixties and many more were established by the statutory and voluntary bodies. At first most of these were of the 'low commitment' coffee-bar type of establishment where little of the demands of membership were made but where, it was hoped, good relationships between adult worker and young people could be established. From these followed the detached worker projects where trained workers met young people in a variety of extra-club settings both indoor and outdoor. A further Albemarle-inspired development was that of youth counselling to help and guide young people in making decisions about social, occupational and personal issues. At present there are upwards of sixty workers with training in counselling operating generally within a number of statutory and voluntary bodies with access to appropriate vocational social work, medical, legal and psychiatric service. Again, the development of counselling is parellel to that in the schools and the by now well known conflict between the school counsellor and the teacher is met in the clubs as a conflict between the youth counsellor and the youth worker. Understandably the youth worker, like the teacher, feels that as a professional worker he himself has counselling functions and indeed counselling skills. However, the comparative rarity of counsellors in the Youth and Community Service has, as yet, prevented this conflict from becoming a major issue.

Another consequence of the *Albemarle Report* was the initiative of the Youth Service Development Council in establishing a central information service, the Youth Service Information Centre, in conjunction with the training function of Leicester College. This was seen as essentially an information retrieval and dissemination service with particular emphasis on experiment and new development. In April 1972 the Department of Education and Science agreed to support a change in the structure and functions of the YSIC which resulted in its being absorbed in 1973, into the new wider agency, the National Youth Bureau, co-ordinating information, training and research services to the broad field of youth affairs, while maintaining its services to the Youth Service. Other government departments now also financially support the Bureau; its anticipated budget for 1975/76 was £140,000. Currently the NYB, directed by Mr J. Ewen, has a staff of some 35. It already issues a range of publications including a well regarded glossy magazine *Youth in Society* and is widely recognized as a reliable and comprehensive source of information on a national and an international level.

Youth and Community Work in the 70s.

In 1967 the Youth Service Development Council established two study groups, one on the relationships between the Youth Service and the

schools under the chairmanship of Mr A. Fairbairn of the Leicestershire
Education Authority and one on the relationship between Youth
Service and the community under the chairmanship of Dr F. Milson,
Head of Youth Work at Westhill College of Education. The reports
of the two committees were subsumed, along with a DES consideration
of training, in the report *Youth and Community Work in the 70s*,
published in 1969,[5] to which extensive reference has already been made
in this chapter. The report acknowledged many of the problems of the
service, not least that of the separate age groups, the under fourteens,
who were for the first time recognized as spending part of their time
within the facilities of the Youth Service, the fourteen to sixteens and
the over sixteens. But the most striking feature of the report was the new
philosophy outlined for the Youth Service, which went considerably
beyond the view of the Albemarle committee. The main role of the
service was seen to be education and experience for membership of the
active society, a society in which all people had the opportunity and the
right to be involved in the decision-making processes affecting their lives,
particularly those of their immediate social and occupational context.
The Youth Service was seen to be a body that was to augment the role of
the schools in educating them for this participative role and giving them
experience of 'contracting in' to the decision-making process.

The implications of the report, not by any means fully spelt out in its
pages, were for a strong increase in 'client participation' not only in the
Youth Service but in society. A central phrase was, 'young people must
be encouraged to play an active part in a society which they themselves
will help to mould.' There was particularly strong emphasis on political
education: 'few young people have any political education at all; with
the lowering of the voting age this vacuum is more noticeable and needs
filling. One way of doing this is to consider how youth groups of the
political parties can be associated with the new service.'

The radicalism of the report led to a predictable lack of consensus in
the Youth Service. On the one hand there was considerable enthusiasm
for the 'new dynamism', many seeing it as a way in which the 'alienation
of youth' in a technological society may be alleviated if not overcome.
But many others saw the de-structuring, and amorphousness of the
structure that could emerge, as fundamentally threatening to the established patterns of the service in the past and cited the wilder excesses
that at the time appeared to be springing from student autonomy in the
universities as evidence to support their views. Certainly the implementation of the report was likely to be administratively even more difficult
than heretofore in the service and even the immediate consequences

[5] *Youth and Community work in the 70s* was specifically concerned
with developments in England and Wales. A Scottish report *Community of
Interests,* published in 1968, indicated many areas that were also of common
concern in Scotland.

were not at all clearly set out. For example, the report recommended the abandonment of the existing age limits of fourteen and twenty but offered no alternative. The committee suggested that over eighteens should be able to purchase alcoholic drinks in clubs, yet offered little consideration of the complex difficulties that this would provide for most existing institutions with a predominance of younger members. The report was presented in 1969 and the government of the day left office in June 1970 without having taken a decision. The subsequent government rejected in March 1971 the concept of a Youth and Community Service on the lines envisaged and at the same time discontinued the Youth Service Development Council on the grounds that adequate alternative lines of communication between government and the service were by then available.

But *Youth and Community Work in the 70s* has by no means been without influence. Many of the statutory and voluntary bodies have responded to it and many local statutory provisions have been renamed Youth and Community Services even though few yet operate fully with the radical brief envisaged by the report. The segregation of the Youth Service from the adult community has undoubtedly diminished and, in particular, the concept of the school as a community resource which young and adult utilise (following the early model of the Cambridgeshire Village Colleges subsequently developed by Leicestershire and other authorities) appears to have reduced some of the unacceptability of the school as a location ('because it's a school') by the adolescent population.

Youth and Community Work in the 70s also made proposals for work with 'young people at risk', an initiative that came to be strongly reinforced by the Children and Young Persons Act of 1969. The intermediate treatment that has been established as a consequence of the Act envisages many young people taking part in some form of youth club and group activity, essentially within the context of a 'normal' club. In this specific field the potential links with the social services rather than specifically educational services that were envisaged in *Youth and Community Work in the 70s* came to be taken considerably further and, indeed, there are already a number of professional youth workers on the staffs of the new Social Services Departments in various local authorities. Another important issue within the service at the time of *Youth and Community Work in the 70s* was the integration of immigrant adolescents. The report endorsed the findings of the Hunt Committee of the YSDC (1967) and recommended a range of initiatives in this field with integration as an important goal of community activity.

The de-structuring, even fragmentation, of the Youth Service that currently appears to be taking place has led to many anxieties and uncertainties and a speculation that future DES responsibilities may come to be restricted to the educationally based aspect of the Youth Service with community service activities under the responsibility of the

Home Office, and the Department of Health and Social Security in control of 'youth at risk' services. As always at such times, there have been suggestions for new methods of coordination, notably the suggestion by Ewen and others that a co-ordinating office for youth affairs be attached to the Cabinet Office. These issues are discussed in the concluding chapter in the light of the results of our enquiries.

Training

Between 1961 and 1970 the National College at Leicester produced 1,000 one-year trained youth workers (Watkins, 1972). In the same period the total number of professional workers rose from 700 to over 2,000. In 1970 the National College was closed following the decision that the training of youth workers should take place in the context of more broadly based training establishments. Six courses were set up to maintain the supply of trained personnel (at City of Leicester College of Education, Westhill College of Education, Manchester Polytechnic and Goldsmiths' College, in addition to two course run by voluntary bodies — the YMCA in association with North East London Polytechnic and the NABC in association with the extra-mural department of Liverpool University). All courses were at the same time extended to two years' duration. Following *Youth and Community Work in the 70s* all courses were renamed Youth and Community Work courses. Despite the DES insistence that this phrase should be restricted to the training of youth workers and community centre wardens, in all cases the content and the range of the courses appears to extend far beyond such a definition and many of the workers qualified by the courses are now working in Social Service Departments, community development teams, neighbourhood projects and the like. In addition to these specialized courses some 53 Colleges of Education offer programmes at various levels in youth and community work and it is estimated that some 750 students each year follow such courses.[6] In the light of the current reorganization of the Colleges of Education and tertiary education generally, further changes in the arrangements for the training of youth workers are likely, possibly involving a year's specialist training after successful completion of a two year Diploma in Higher Education course in relevant subjects. (DES White Paper 'Education: A Framework for Expansion; 1972). However, the supply does not meet the demand and even by the beginning of 1972 there were 500 vacancies for professional youth workers in England and Wales. A number of authorities, notably the ILEA, have appointed unqualified workers to fill some of their many vacancies.

One of the first acts of the Youth Service Development Council was to set up a working party on the training of part-time youth workers

---

[6] The role of youth work in teacher training is usefully reviewed by Clérnans (1966).

under the chairmanship of Mr G. Bessey, Chief Education Officer of
Cumberland. The Committee's report (1962), followed by a further
report three years later (1965), suggested joint training committees
bringing together those responsible for training volunteer and part-time
workers in both the voluntary and statutory sectors. Such joint provision
took a range of different forms in different areas but in most parts of the
country 'Bessey' courses were established wherein all participants joined
together for common elements of training in areas such as sociology and
adolescent psychology and returned to their own organizations for
training specific to them. Some 5,000 part-time workers followed these
courses in the period 1962 to 1972 and a majority of all adults now in
the Youth Service have had some training.[7]

Finance

The financing of the Youth Service is a particularly intractable subject
for investigation and we were more than pleased when the responsibility
for detailed investigations of the finances of the voluntary sector at the
national level was entrusted to Political and Economic Planning, whose
report is now available (1975).[8] The legislation for the financial
provision and support of most of the activities of the Youth Service is
brought together under the Further Education Regulations 1969.
However, Acts and Regulations only define in very broad terms the
powers and duties of central and local government towards provision for
youth, and details of policy and administrative strategies are dealt with
by Departmental Circulars and memoranda. Basically financial provision
for the statutory sector is made through the local education authority
block grant arrangements; the provision for the voluntary sector is more
complex. The powers of the central government to provide direct aid to
voluntary youth organizations derived originally from the Social and
Physical Training Grant Regulations 1939 and the Physical Training and
Recreation Act 1937. The former set of regulations covered headquarters
grants to national voluntary youth organizations, grants to local
voluntary bodies in respect of the capital cost of premises and equipment for youth clubs and centres, experimental or special grants to
voluntary youth organizations for particular projects and annual grants
for the training of youth leaders. The 1937 Act covered grants offered to
national voluntary organizations which provided services (especially

---

[7] The uniformed groups have tended to pursue their own training arrangements.

[8] The difficulties clearly exist not only at a national level but also at a personal
one. The problems of the Treasurer of the Neverbroke Youth Club are described in
detail in an NAYC publication (Bailey, 1962).

coaching in physical pursuits) for young people as well as adults, and grants in aid of the capital expenditure incurred by local voluntary bodies on village halls, community centres, swimming baths, playing fields and equipment for them. It is these provisions, together with the provisions of the Further Education (Local Education Authorities) Regulations 1959 and the Further Education (Grant) Regulations 1959, which were combined in the Further Education Regulations 1969, under which headquarters grants are now made. Central government grants to sporting bodies are still made under the Physical Training and Recreation Act 1937.

The Further Education Regulations 1969 give the DES broad powers to grant-aid voluntary youth organizations but do not make it a duty for the DES to do so. Section 29 states that

The Secretary of State for Education and Science may pay grants to any other voluntary organization, and in particular to any youth organization in respect of expenditure incurred by them, whether as part of wider activities or not, in providing or in connection with the provision of, facilities for further education within the meaning of Section 41(b) of the Education Act 1944.

The further education provisions of the Education Act 1944 are important in this context in that they largely determine the lower age limit of statutory Youth Service provision. As before the details of adminstration are dealt with mainly by means of official circulars and memoranda. Under these powers conferred upon it by the Further Education Regulations 1969, the DES gives the following grants to voluntary youth organizations:

1. Headquarters' grants to national voluntary youth organizations
2. Capital grants to local voluntary youth organizations
3. Experimental grants to voluntary youth organizations
4. Grants towards the costs of training full-time youth leaders
5. Capital grants to local voluntary bodies in aid of the costs of providing village halls, community centres, etc.

The DES gives no direct grant aid to LEAs in respect of the statutory Youth Service which is their responsibility nor does it aid the training of part-time youth leaders which is also the responsibility of LEAs. Local education authorities have also facilities to make grants to the voluntary organizations as follows:

1. Grants towards, or the full payment of, the salaries of full-time or part-time youth leaders working for voluntary bodies
2. Grants towards the running and administrative costs of local voluntary clubs and centres, district headquarters, etc., special non-recurring grants for redecoration and equipment
3. Grants towards the costs of training full and part-time leaders
4. Capital grants to local voluntary bodies in connection with the provision of Youth Service facilities.

There are many examples of ministerial intervention. For example, in March 1971, the then Minister of Education announced that the 'system of capital and recurrent grants made by the Department needs to be simplified. The balance of the programmes will in future be shifted towards the provision of assistance to less prosperous areas. Plans will shortly be put to the local authority associations and voluntary bodies to introduce new financial and administrative arrangemnts which will provide for the supervision of individual capital projects to be undertaken locally. Some of the funds currently devoted to capital aid will be released to give greater assistance to experimental work in the youth field, and some will be diverted, by means of the Urban Programme, to areas of high social need. Voluntary bodies should be able to benefit from both these kinds of provision'. (Thatcher, 1971.)

The same Minister, in April 1972, said 'New arrangements for capital grants for the Youth Service announced last year had been a success and the response for 1972/73 showed that fears expressed at the time were unfounded'. She went on to say, doubts were expressed about the wisdom of devolving on local authorities responsibility for determining which voluntary capital projects should receive assistance within resources at the Department's disposal. Two main objections were raised. First, that to be successful there would need to be a degree of cooperation between local authorities and voluntary agencies in determining local priorities, which was unlikely to be achieved. Secondly, making grant aid from local authorities a pre requisite to grant from the Department would lead to a significant reduction in the value of new building provided with assistance from public funds. Compared with the bids received for the last building programme under the old arrangements (1970-71), the total value of voluntary youth projects for which local education authorities have said they are prepared to grant aid is half as much again. The new arrangements would foster cooperation among all local interests and lead to wiser planning and a greater joint use of premises. (Thatcher, 1972). The statement is an illuminating one — not only throwing light on the complex balance of financial arrangements between the statutory and voluntary sectors but also on the very concept of partnership that underlies the Youth Service.

Summary

How can the structure and practice of a service that, as we have seen, is becoming ever more open, diverse and disparate be summarized? Its recent history shows several phases:
1. The 'establishment phase' where the Youth Service became a recognized feature of our educational and social arrangemnts in the period 1939-1944
2. The 'reconstruction and development phase' in the period 1944-1960
3. The expansionist 'buildings and training' era in the 'post-Albemarle' period 1960-1965
4. The 'experimental phase' in which the experimental initiatives of Albemarle were regarded as more urgent and more viable: 1965-1972
5. The 'community phase' commencing in 1972 inspired, somewhat diffusely, by the *Youth and Community Work in the 70s* report.
   In our attempt to establish a sharper research focus it proved useful to add a further dimension to the voluntary/statutory dichotomy that is of a somewhat more sociological nature. The evidence shows a pronounced move towards a 'client-centred' approach and away from an 'organizational centred' one. The client-centred approach may be strongly localized, rooted in the needs of the local community as well as in the needs of the individual himself. Conversely, the more traditional approach which gave all members a similar 'organizational treatment' tended to be national or at least regional in its forms. To use Gouldner's (1957-1958) terms it was 'cosmopolitan' rather than 'local' to use the models of Bernstein, Elvin and Peters (1966) it was 'institutionalized' rather than 'personalized'. Using both the dimensions of voluntary/statutory and organisation-centred/client-centred, figure 3 is an attempt to place on a grid the various organizational forms that have been cited in this brief review of the service.

Figure 3 **Organizational forms within the Youth Service**

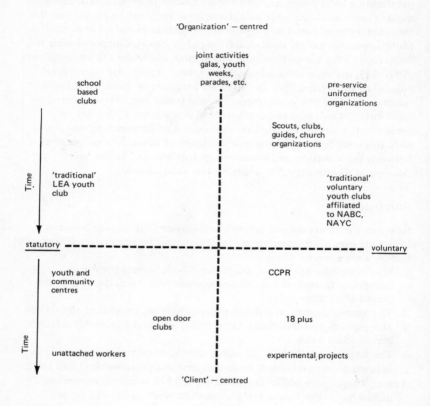

'Organization' — centred

joint activities
galas, youth
weeks,
parades, etc.

school
based
clubs

pre-service
uniformed
organizations

Scouts, clubs,
guides, church
organizations

Time

'traditional'
LEA youth
club

'traditional'
voluntary
youth clubs
affiliated
to NABC,
NAYC

statutory   voluntary

youth and
community
centres

CCPR

open door
clubs

18 plus

Time

unattached workers

experimental projects

'Client' — centred

The diagram has a compelling simplicity, though at the price of an arbitrariness that will be apparent to many readers. Yet it provides a useful starting point for the consideration of the theoretical orientations of the next chapter, which presents the still finely balanced equilibrium between the statutory and the voluntary sectors of the Youth Service but also indicates the tendency to move from organizational to client-centred orientations. In the discussion of the ideology of the Youth Service in Chapter 4 a similar summary of the ideological divisions of the service will be presented as a prelude to the detailed accounts of our field work.

3 The design of the study

The Context of Research

Youth has been of major concern to the adult population of all known societies. Through the centuries, from Aristotle's perceptive and enduring comments on the manners of the young onwards, the study of each new generation has been compounded of anxiety and sympathy, prejudice and empathy, introspection and intuition. Frequently the resulting statements have been either patronizing or obsequious; occasionally they have shown a remarkable, unmistakeable degree of perception and understanding. The writings of the young themselves, though less frequent, have tended to display a similar range of orientations. More recently the emergence of the social sciences have held out the promise of a new and higher level of understanding of the young in human soceites, and in the present century a vast literature of studies of youth and its characteristics has been assembled. It is not possible and fortunately not necessary to review this literature exhaustively in this report. However, a brief glance at the field may serve a useful purpose in providing a context for the subsequent discussion.

Overall the writing displays an overwhelmingly 'positive' orientation. Not only is 'youth' taken as a given category by almost all writers (Musgrove being a notable exception) but it is also accepted that youth 'has problems' and that these problems should be 'solved'. Such an orientation is in marked contrast to the 'interpretative orientations' currently being developed by sociologists who seek to explore why and how such problems are given. Though the theoretical basis of our research embraces interpretative approaches we were unable to develop them from the established literature in the same way as was possible with the more functional positive approaches and had to break new ground in order to do so.

Some of the classic early studies of the place of youth in human societies and of its behaviour, roles and transistion to full adult status have been presented by social anthropologists. Of the many studies two of the best known and most representative of this *genre* are Margaret

Mead's *Growing Up in New Guinea* (1942) and *Coming of Age in Samoa* (1943). Also in this category is Hollingshead's (1949) study of adolescent behaviours in a rural American community *Elmtown's Youth.*

The anthropological literature was followed by the extensive development of psychological studies, many of which took the form of explorations of the behavour and motivation of adolescents. Fleming (1963) provides a useful resumé of these in *Adolescence: its Social Psychology* There is also a wide range of studies of adolescent group behaviour, classic examples here being the work of Thrasher (1927) and Whyte (1955). Specifically sociological investigation came somewhat later but has more than compensated in volume since its arrival. An early and central figure in the field was Parsons (1961). He saw adolescence as a time in which two important developments take place:

> One of course is the emergence of more positive cross-sex relationships outside the classroom, through dances, dating and the like. The other is the much sharper prestige-stratification of informal peer groupings, with indeed an element of snobbery which often exceeds that of the adult community in which the school exists. Here it is important that though there is a broad correspondence between the prestige of friendship groups and the family status of their members, this, like the achievement order of the elementary school, is by no means a simple 'mirroring' of the community stratification scale, for a considerable number of the lower status children get accepted into groups including members with higher family status than themselves. This stratified youth system operates as a genuinely assortive mechanism; it does not simply reinforce ascribed status.

Parsons's analysis brings us face to face with the social group of the adolescent. Its members may be equal in age and in other important characteristics, but they are differentiated in status. These differences in status are often based on differences in role — individual members become associated with the performance of special tasks in the group for which they seem well fitted, and these tasks may be of high or low status. As a result the adolescent group comes to have some of the stratification of the adult world. And as Parsons points out, this stratification does not just reflect the status of the members' parents in the adult community, it may be on an entirely independent basis.

There are other important features of the social behaviour of this age group. One is its universality. A casual observer in Sidcup, Swansea or Stockport would not find it difficult to detect similarities in the dress, speech, leisure and spending patterns of adolescents in all these places which override many of the regional sub-cultural variations of these areas. But of even greater significance is the fact that he would almost certainly remember that the distinctive behaviour he was examining was as distinctive as the behaviour of adolescents some years previously —

even though the individual membership of the groups may have changed completely. True, he may have seen changes in fashion between the areas and over time, but he could hardly have failed to notice underlying common patterns of values, attitudes and behaviour.

To summarize, adolescent social behaviour is seen to be a shared and identifiable way of life transmitted to each new generation of adolescents and to have its own established norms reinforced by its own sanctions, sub-cultural features which we have noticed in embryonic form in the primary school group. But it also has independent stratification systems and universality which show it to be nearer to a genuine sub-culture in contemporary society.

In America the separation of the culture of adult society from that of the adolescents has been stressed by many writers. Coleman speaks of distinctive 'adolescent social systems' with ways of life which are not only different from but largely opposed to those of the adult world. He suggests that the separation springs largely from the increasing length of school life and the increasing breadth of school-based activities in modern society. As a result the adolescent is 'cut off from the rest of society, forced inwards towards his own age group, made to carry out his whole social life with others of his own age. With his fellows he comes to constitute a small society, one that has most of its main interactions *within* itself, and maintains only a few threads of connection with the outside adult society . . . To put it simply these young people speak a different language. What is more relevant to the present point, the language they speak is becoming more and more different.' (Coleman, 1961.) The strongly worded views of Coleman have been challenged by other writers who suggest that the dramatic contrasts in the behaviour of adults and adolescents may at times be superficial and not always related to fundamental differences in value systems. The regularity with which adolescents successfully adapt to membership of the adult community is cited as evidence for these views, which are usefully presented in an article entitled 'The Myth of Youth' (Jahoda and Warren, 1965). Despite reservations such as those of Jahoda and Warren the 'segregation hypothesis' is still dominant in the American sociology of youth and is indeed enhanced by the current preoccupation of American sociologists with 'the student movement', commonly analysed as a separate phenomenon distinct from the rest of society. Three recently published collections of papers offer a useful guide to the present state of study (Clark and Clark, 1972; Cottle, 1972 and Silverstein, 1973.)

Another recurring theme of contemporary sociological literature, well reflected in the readings mentioned, is the 'polarization hypothesis'. As Murdock and Phelps (1972) put it:

The central argument of previous studies is that adolescents are caught between two fundamentally opposed cultures; the culture of the school based on deferred gratification, cognitive skill, individual achievement and deference to authority, and the out-of-school 'youth culture' based on immediate gratification, physical skill, group solidarity and the equality of group members. Hence, they are forced to choose either one or the other, and consequently low commitment to school will tend to be associated with high involvement in 'youth culture'.

But as with the segregation hypothesis, there is considerable uncertainty about the polarization hypothesis. Murdock and Phelps conclude:

. . . that there is not one 'youth culture' but several and that, consequently, research in this area should abandon the simplistic conceptualization of the problem employed in the past and explore instead the emerging complexity of the triangular relationships between school culture, 'street culture' and 'pop media culture' together with the various sub-patterns of meaning which exist within each of these general cultural constellations.

There are hopeful signs that European research on youth and adolescence is less committed to these somewhat oversimplified and suspect hypotheses, certainly the extensive list of studies issued by the Council of Europe (1970) is reassuring if only for its diversity of approach.

An important sub-group of mainstream research into youth and adolescence has had a strongly 'applied' orientation. A group of research studies that may be broadly described as 'policy oriented studies' have characterized much of the work of the applied social sciences of the 1960s. The studies have been most strongly in evidence in the field of education where major enquiries by social scientists have been commissioned by policy makers. Perhaps the prototypes were the various enquiries commissioned by the Crowther Committee (Crowther, 1959). A considerably more ambitious enterprise was undertaken four years later in connection with the Robbins Committee's *Report on Higher Education* (1963) and a very large amount of evidence was assembled and presented, evidence that was eventually published in four substantial volumes that accompanied the Committee's Report. Outside of education, applied social science investigations of the relevant age groups have figured less prominently. The 1969 Children and Young Person's Act, which brought about major changes in the definition and treatment of young offenders, particularly in the field of treatment by social workers, was based upon somewhat sporadic evidence, notwithstanding a major involvement of the Home Office in direct and sponsored research in the field, while the report of the Latey Committee (1967) on the age of majority sought little evidence from social scientists.

A not entirely dissimilar situation is to be seen in the exercise of policy making within the Youth Service itself. As we have seen, the Albemarle Committee (1960) made its recommendations on a range of matters, including the development of purpose-built youth clubs and the training of professional youth leaders, largely on the evidence brought by the members of the Committee and those expert witnesses invited by the Committee. We have also noted how The Youth Service Development Council commissioned two enquiries under the chairmanship of Fairbairn and Milson. Towards the end of its life, however, the Youth Service Development Council put in train several major enquiries to be under- taken by researchers who were regarded as being free from major current involvements or commitments in the Youth Service. The first of these was a 'macro' study undertaken by the Government Social Survey, subsequently renamed the Social Survey Division of the Office of Pop- ulation Censuses and Surveys. The ensuing report (1972) explored the nature of the demand and response for Youth Service activities across a representative sample of the relevant age groups of England and Wales and also sought evidence from parents, employers and other interested adults. For the first time a major enquiry explored not only the partici- pants of the Youth Service but also the non-participants and the results are of major importance, representing a substantial contribution to our understanding of the expressed needs of young people in contemporary British society.

The study reported in this book was commissioned concurrently; it is in essence a 'micro' study to accompany the 'macro' study of the Social Survey Division. Its purpose is to look in detail at the behaviour within the various organizations that constitute the Youth Service and to consider the purposes and values of the various providing bodies constituting the service and of the young people and adult workers within them, and to explore the day-to-day interactions in the running of the wide range of clubs, groups and other units that make up the Service.

Alongside these macro and micro studies, a smaller scale study of the relationships between the statutory and voluntary bodies within the Youth Service was also commissioned, based upon field work conducted predominantly in the West Riding area by a group of workers in the University of Leeds Institute of Education. Somewhat earlier the Schools Council commissioned an enquiry on youth work in the schools which was undertaken at the University of Aston, Birmingham, under the direction of Joselyn. This has now been published as *Schools Council Working Paper 28* (1970). More recently the Department of Education and Science invited Political and Economic Planning to explore the financing of the Youth Service with particular reference to the determin- ation of central grants to the various voluntary organizations. (Thomas and Perry, 1975). These reports, published and unpublished, have been of considerable value to the research reported here. Not only

have they provided relevant information that has augmented the
enquiries undertaken within the present study, they have also
provided a parameter. By covering adjacent fields they have allowed
the focus of the present enquiry to be considerably sharper than would
have been possible in their absence. This then is the context in which the
present study was planned and conducted. The picture is, of course,
incomplete — it will be amplified during the presentation of the process,
analysis and results of the research. However, it is now possible to
describe the development of the research design and the strategy that has
been employed.

The Emergence of the Research Perspective

The problems of research design have indeed already been hinted at in
the preceding chapters. With a view to arriving at as objective an account
as possible, the research team was selected from candidates who were,
intentionally, unfamiliar with the full spread of complex institutions that
constitute the Youth Service. This is not of course to say that they were
uninformed, or still less to suggest that they were unsympathetic. An
important prerequisite of all appointments was an interest in and an
awareness of work with young people, but essentially candidates were
sought who saw their identity as research workers rather than as committed members of the Youth Service.

Our initial reaction after the first month of exploratory field work
was one of astonishment, even bewilderment. Two of our analogies from
the difficult early period when we were trying to establish a research
design and strategy are perhaps worth recalling. The first was the analogy
of the ants' nest. The myriad members, workers, youth officers, management committee members and the vast periphery of other 'involved
people' seemed at first glance to lack pattern and structure. Yet in much
the same way as with the ant's nest, careful observation indicated
recurrent patterns of purposeful and intensive activity. At first however,
it was astonishingly difficult to formulate any overall explanatory
hypothesis to explain the movements we observed.

The second analogy concerned the research process itself. Here we
found ourselves thinking of a long-established coal seam in which many
colliers have mined for many years. We discovered (perhaps 'unearthed'
would be a better word) a vast range of 'researches' ranging from the one-
man enquiry conducted by a single worker seeking information with
which to run his club more effectively, to ambitious studies set up by
national organizations or groups of senior workers in the Service.
Frequently however this research had been conducted in order to substantiate some point of view, opinion or belief that was held by the
researchers. Seldom was the point of view itself subject to scrutiny. In a

number of cases the disregard for evidence that conflicted with the required point of view was striking. But from our standpoint, the major problem was that such researches had been opportunist and uncharted. They had sunk shafts in any area which seemed promising, mined what they needed and departed without leaving clear records. In consequence we discovered in our own research that we frequently uncovered old un-mapped workings which at times threatened to produce a major research hazard in that the field had already been 'contaminated' by previous workers. When the existence of previous research was known in advance this presented no problem — it could be allowed for and even made use of, or else avoided. A far greater difficulty occurred when we fell into old workings unsuspectingly. On a few occasions this led to considerable waste of time and effort.

Another, and this time very welcome, feature was the generous willing-ness of all sectors of the Youth Service to be 'researched upon'. Whatever the reasons for it, the accessibility and responsiveness that it generated greatly facilitated the whole project and, in large measure, compensated for the difficulties mentioned above. Yet there were times when the enthusiasm of the volunteers to be researched upon was almost overwhelming. On such occasions we felt very much in the position of the film producer who was making a documentary of the probable situation after the explosion of a hydrogen bomb. His call for volunteer 'victims' provided him, to his astonishment and consternation, with a whole London street full of prostrate bodies at dawn on a Sunday morning.

The warmth of the response also brought other problems. Many members of the service, accustomed to the 'quick fire' results that had characterized some of the previous researches, expected a rapid output and within six months requests were being received for the researchers to address meetings and conferences to present their results. Our inability to respond was occasionally met with disbelief and in a few cases criticism.

How then did we organize the research? As a preliminary we first scrutinized the structure that the Youth Service itself presented to us for examination. We were concerned here with the administrative structure of the service and we explored a wide range of the organizational patterns of the statutory and voluntary sectors. At this stage much of our work was descriptive, recording the organization structures and administration. Our findings have been presented in Chapter 2. But the exploration of the structure and practice of the service was, at best, a preparatory exercise. It quickly became clear that the way forward was to explore in detail the aims and motivating forces that we were already beginning to glimpse behind the structural patterns we had surveyed. At this stage we began the task of setting up a theoretical perspective for our work.

The functional theory

Our preliminary study had alerted us to the major perspectives of the adult members of the Youth Service concerning their purposes in contemporary society. We were able to identify a number of 'social roles' that most, if not all, the sectors of the service saw themselves as performing. Most notable among these was the task of adolescent *socialization* involving the assimilation of cultural patterns both of the society as a whole and of the local communities in which the young were likely to spend their adult lives. At both levels the Youth Service was seen to be assisting the young to internalize relevant behaviours, values, norms and patterns of interaction of a kind that were considered to be appropriate for life in adult society, and in so doing enable them to 'become adult' in a way that will allow society to continue without economic difficulty or social upheaval.

In particular it was widely believed that they must be aided in joining the economic system, making the transition from school to work and becoming part of the world of work. An important part of the ideology of most societies is that 'young people must get a job and hold it down'. The importance of this belief rests not only on its economic implications but also on the fact that work is the central means of involvement in the value system of society. It was also believed that the young must learn the areas of permitted variation of social living and their boundaries — areas where difference turns into 'deviance' and even punishable 'delinquency'. Knowledge of the system of rewards and punishment that reinforce the social system was seen to be a central part of learning. There are not only the legal and economic rewards and punishments of society as a whole but also those less well defined but powerful rewards and punishments that relate to the individual's behaviour in work, home, community and leisure. An important feature of such socialization is usually an attempt to switch the young on to certain reward and punishment systems defined as 'conscientious worker', 'loyal wife and mother', 'responsible member of the community' and the like. Conversely, it endeavours to switch the young off 'deviant' and 'undesirable' systems such as delinquency, the drug culture and 'dropping out' generally.

How is such socialization attempted? Strategies range from fundamental attempts to inculcate a commitment to values that were seen to be appropriate for occupational roles, life in the family and approved patterns of leisure, down to more detailed but no less important patterns of behaviour in the dance hall or the workshop. Different sectors of the service had, of course, different models of the desired adult they sought to produce: in some it was not difficult to detect the vision of the deferential workman willing to obey orders and submit to discipline from those above him; in others a somewhat clearer view of the adult in a participatory democracy seemed apparent. But an important feature of the socialization in virtually all sectors of the Youth Service appears to be the legitimation of social differences in that young people not only came to know of the existence of differences in social position, power and status but also came to accept that such differences were legitimate. It became clear at an early stage that the Youth Service was playing an important part in this process of legitimation. This, of course, is not to say that the service was able to make its members enthusiastic about social differences. Members were often critical about the way in which power was exercised by foremen, managers or simply by 'them'. But their challenge was usually to the *individual* who exercised power or rank unfairly rather than to the *system* that allowed them to exercise these roles. For the most part the system was taken as given, even where it affected the member intimately. In this area then it is possible to see the Youth Service as an important instrument of social control — an agency for preserving the existing social order, whether this be identified as the class system, family life or some specific value system.

Yet although the Youth Service is clearly an instrument of social control it may also be defined as an agency that is helping to bring about certain agreed forms of social change. It was notable, for instance, that a number of clubs, particularly those with mixed racial memberships, were making strenuous efforts to modify traditional attitudes to ethnic minorities. Certainly there was considerable evidence that the various sectors of the Youth Service were playing an important part in helping their members to adjust to some of the fundamental social changes that were affecting their lives. These included such changes as the raising of the school leaving age and voluntary staying on in the schools; the lowering of the age of majority and the minimum voting age; changes in industrial training and day release schemes; the changing economic situation of young people. All these changes have been facilitated, in part, by the Youth Service. In considering them we come to a further important social aspiration of the Youth Service — one that appears to be gaining increasing emphasis in recent years. This is the welfare role of the service: the provision of personal services for all young people but particularly for those in some kind of defined need, the under-privileged, the socially handicapped, the potential delinquent and the young immigrant.

Mention of the welfare role of the service alerts us to a realization that there are problems in the socialization process that we have outlined. Two in particular were seen to be common to most sectors of the Youth Service. The first is that society may not always deliver the goods. Poor housing and homelessness, unemployment and financial hardship may still be the lot of those who conform; affluence and apparent success may greet those who do not. Young people are, of course, not unaware of such problems, as Webb (1962) reminded us:

What sort of person would the boy become who accepted the standards the teacher tries to impose? In himself he would be neat, orderly, polite and servile. With the arithmetic and English he absorbed at school, and after further training, he might become a meticulous clerk, sustained by a routine laid down by someone else, and piously accepting his station in life. Or, if he got a trade, we can see him later in life clutching a well scrubbed lunch-tin and resentful at having to pay union dues, because the boss, being a gentleman, knows best. To grow up like this a lad has to be really cut-off from the pull of social class and gang, which luckily few of the boys at Black School are, because both of these types are becoming more and more redundant as mechanization increases and job content decreases.

The second problem may present even greater ideological difficulties for the Youth Service. Many of the rewards that society offers for conformity to its value systems are those that are incompatible with the ideology of the club or unit. The management committee or the leader may emphasize individual leisure, creative hobbies, discrimination in entertainment and food. Yet the rewards of society may be the provision of unthinking passive leisure, beer and bingo, coke and crisps. Can society offer all its young the experiences the service envisages or are its resources insufficient to provide more than 'mass' facilities for the masses? Does the service present an essentially elite pattern of living to its members, failing to realise that it is unattainable for most of them, and it could be argued, unsought by many? Many youth leaders feel constrained to provide 'activities' whereas members prefer discos and darts.

Questions of this nature alert us to the need to look more rigorously at the theoretical issues implicit in our discussion of the Youth Service. The predominantly functional perspective described so far is one in which society is taken to be imposing certain needs upon its members, needs which the Youth Service, like other institutions, is established to satisfy. The theoretical basis of functionalism can be seen most clearly in the writings of Durkheim who saw society as creating, in each individual, a 'social being' comprised of the appropriate values, behaviours and traditions of the society into which he is born (Durkheim, 1956). Such a functionalist approach is of particular importance in the Youth Service; it can be seen to dominate the thinking of substantial sectors, underlying objectives and practice of the clubs and organizations. The reasons are not difficult to surmise.

From the beginnings of nineteenth-century industrial society the informal socialization procedures of the community could no longer be relied on. When the long-established settled communities of town and village with their own norms and social controls were augmented and, in many cases, supplanted by the new industrial communities, the processes

whereby the young came to know and conform to the accepted patterns
of social behaviour — the written and unwritten laws of church,
community and family that existed in the old communities — were not
re-established in the new.[1] Indeed, conditions of *anomie* prevailed in
many of them — most notably in the transitory settlements set up by the
railway navvies and other itinerant workers (Coleman, 1969). The
anxiety caused by this state of affairs, particularly at a time when
revolution was widespread in other European countries, led to new
attempts to impose the rule of law on a national basis. At first the way
was seen to lie in external imposition — Peel's uniformed police force in
the 1840s. But the realization grew that a more effective method of
achieving social consensus and conformity could lie in the social
education of the young. Yet schools for all their successes in achieving
basic literacy and numeracy, were not always conspicuously successful in
the task of moral socialization and, almost from the start of compulsory
schooling, were augmented by the work of new national voluntary
youth organizations, essentially concerned to ensure the acceptance and
internalization of approved values and social behaviour by the young. To
paraphrase Musgrove's aphorism, 'youth, like the steam engine, is a
Victorian invention' (Musgrove, 1964), we may say with some certainty
that the Youth Service like the school system, is a late nineteenth-
century invention.

With such a background the functionalist orientations of the Youth
Service are hardly surprising — indeed, it would be astonishing if they
were less in evidence. But functionalism provides a further attraction that
is of particular interest to a service that may, at times, lack confidence
in the general evaluation and esteem in which its work is held by the
public at large and even by its members. Bourdieu has suggested that
structural looseness leads to demands for precision, and uncertainty leads
to even greater demands for certainty. (Bourdieu, 1971.) If the providers
of the service can feel that 'society' is requiring them to undertake
specific services that are necessary to ensure its continuance, then they
are likely to feel confident and even assured in their role. And if the
enthusiasm of society for the service can be made manifest in such
forms as new buildings, extensions and facilities, or even in enhanced
titles or status for its adult workers, then it is likely that a secure, even
though potentially static, set of provisions for Youth Service work will
exist.

Yet, as we have already indicated, there are fundamental problems in
the functionalist approach despite its attraction for many practitioners.
In the last analysis society is not and cannot be saying that it *needs*

---

[1] A striking feature of the new communities was that the young, like their parents,
could leave them and settle elsewhere — in marked contrast to the earlier state of
affairs when geographical mobility, for the majority, was impossible.

young people to respect persons and property, practice Christianity or build their character by experiencing mountain rescue programmes. All these activities, however self-evidently desirable they appear to be, are decisions that are made by individuals or groups of individuals and not by some collective societal wisdom. Their objective is to bring young people to conform to a model of our choosing — not infrequently to a model that is remarkably similar to the adult's view of himself. More generally, the social control of which we have spoken is no more than a need experienced by individuals which may, to a greater or lesser extent, be satisfied by individual decisions in the context of a Youth Service. To attribute these objectives to the authority of 'society' is, in the last analysis, spurious.

The Conflict Theory[2]

The uncertainties inherent in functionalist perspectives have led many theoreticians to seek alternative perspectives that may approximate more closely to social reality. Of these the most common is the conflict frame of reference, which has considerable relevance to the analysis of the Youth Service. It suggests that consensus is an illusory goal; that social living is the working out of a continuing series of conflicts which may be marked by a transitory truce situation between groups of participants at any time (Rex, 1961).

Mannheim (1952) has drawn attention to the particular nature of intergenerational conflicts, seeing them as a product not only of biological differences but also of social and cultural change. Davis (1940) saw conflict as an inevitable consequence of three factors:

1. the basic birth-cycle differences between parent and child
2. the decreasing rate of socialization with the coming of maturity
3. the ensuing differences between parents and children in the psychological, sociological and psychological planes of behaviour.

However, he suggested that the extent to which they do so depends on a number of variables including the rate of social changes, the extent of the complexity of the social structure, the degree of integration of the culture, and the velocity of movement within the culture. For Bettelheim (1963) however, generational conflict was economic in origin. He suggests that, in the past, parents relied on their children for the continuation of the family's economic resource base and for emotional fulfilment. The result was generational equilibrium: youth and age were able to live in relative harmony. Bettelheim points out that the two

[2] The discussion that follows has been usefully illuminated by a paper by Chekki (1973).

generations needed one another 'not only for their economic, but even more for their moral survival. This makes youth secure — if not in its present position, at least in its self-respect.' Now, however, age no longer relies on youth for economic reasons: 'what little expectation a parent may have had that his children would support him in old age becomes superfluous with greater social security.' Youth, no longer required on economic grounds, evokes the suspicion and hostility of the old: the former now constitute an economic threat to the economic status of the latter. In turn, the young are insecure and without positive direction. Bettelheim goes on to suggest that it is because parents 'still have an emotional need for children, but not for an independent youth, that they often show strenuous resistance when youth fights for its independence.'

Keniston (1963) develops the conflict argument with special reference to youth in a society that has been characterized not only by social innovation but also a rapid pace of technological development. He suggests that from this increased rate of change have come both alienation from the past and uncertainty about the future: the solutions provided by the older generations are no longer of value to contemporary youth, while youth continues to adhere to the traditional patterns of social interactions. The outcome has been a 'split consciousness': the young come to participate in the world of their parents while at the same time remaining detached from it. This theme of social conflict, augmented or even brought about by industrialization and bearing particularly heavily upon the young, is a familiar one in comtemporary sociological analysis. Birnbaum (1970) has suggested that the split in the dominant culture of Western society occurred during the industrial revolution. One of the more striking statements however is that of Feuer (1969) in his description of 'generational disequilibrium': 'The young . . . feel oppressed and blocked in their ambitions; the traumas of unemployment, the humiliation of the diploma without a job nurture a sense of "generational exploitation".'

Sociological literature is by no means the only source of documentation of social conflict theory. It abounds in popular culture, particularly in the contemporary folk music which many adolescents see as oppressing their philosophy of life.

Within the Youth Service there is a widespread awareness of the incidence of conflict despite the dominance of functionalist perspectives. Alongside it there is a group of organizations who publicly espouse the conflict orientations — most notably the young political organizations and the student unions. Within the Youth Service organizations there must, of necessity, also be an awareness of the kind of generational conflict that has been noted and the roles of both adults and of members can be seen to take account of it in many of the interrelationships within the club.

Yet it is less certain that the conflicts that underly the expressed

functional aims of the clubs and organizations are always clearly
understood. As we have already suggested the clubs, possibily even more
than the schools, contain a high proportion of members that, for sheer
statistical reasons alone, are unlikely to 'make it' in society. In schools
they are the students who will not achieve 'good examination results' and
in consequence have considerably diminished prospects of high
occupational and social status. For them school is a failure system, a
prelude to a life on the 'receiving end' of society, taking instructions
from the foreman, the housing manager and the social welfare officer;
in short, an adult life in which effective power is unavailable to them —
at least in 'legitimate' areas of society. Yet frequently the assumptions of
the club or organization are that power will be available to all its
members. In consequence they are offered a socialization relevant to
adult roles in which decision making is taken as given and leadership
is seen to be a real possibility for all. But perhaps a more potent reason
for the intergenerational conflict may be the acute problem, for the
young, of reconciling a socialization in both school and club that assumes
the availablility of power — with the member's clear perception of his
own prospectively powerless role. Certainly such an explanation could
account for the widespread attempt by some of the young to 'count
for something' by at least exacerbating conflict in vandalism, crowd
disturbances at football matches and similar manifestations.

An alternative reaction, only slightly less disturbing to the mainstream
social system, is the formation of separate cultural groups that can, to
their members, accord a degree of esteem and social status that is denied
them outside the group. An obvious example is the motor cycle group
with the 'Hell's Angels' identification; other examples are readily
provided by the drug culture. It is probably not too great an exaggeration
to say that, in part, 'deviant' behaviour of this kind may be seen as a
consequence not just of the social system in general but specifically of
the Youth Service, the schools and other institutionalized arrangements
designed to 'serve' young people.

Clearly the conflict perspective is likely to be relevant to the Youth
Service and is potentially capable of throwing useful light on the social
behaviour of its adult and membership population in a manner that, by
its nature, the functional perspective cannot provide.[3] Yet the conflict
perspective is itself open to many of the same criticisms as the
functionalist approaches. Like them it assumes that human behaviour in

[3] All this is not, of course, to suggest that functionalist and conflict perspectives are
entirely separate and without relationship. For example, a number of writers,
notably Eisenstadt, (1956; 1971) have drawn attention to the functional utility of
certain kinds of institutionalized conflict and to the existence of culturally involved
conflict — such as inter-club rivalry or inter-denominational frontiers. Such institutionalized conflict is, however, somewhat peripheral to the more fundamental
conflict we have been discussing here.

any social system is largely determined outside the individual by the
'system'. Its message is equally depressing for the individual — his
behaviour is largely determined externally and he has to learn to comply
with the system or else escape through deviant or private behaviour.
Though the roles it outlines for the individual may be more recognizable
as reality than those of the functional perspective they are, more or less,
to use Riesmann's terms ' other directed'. (Riesmann, 1969.)[4]

The Interpretative Theories

Is there yet a further perspective that we may apply to the Youth
Service? One with compelling attractions is provided by interpretative
approaches which have 'rediscovered' the individual in the analysis of
social behaviour. In the interpretative model a critical determinant of
social behaviour is seen to be the way in which individuals perceive or
construct social reality. A key exposition of the interpretative approach
is that of Berger and Luckmann (1967) which alerts us to the particular
importance of the 'social construction of reality in determining the
strength and direction of individual behaviour in social situations. The
message of the interpretative perspective is that individuals are without
power only insofar as, collectively, they perceive the social system as
'given'; that the opportunity to redefine it is open to them and, that
having taken it, they may construct a new social reality in which they
are participants rather than receivers.'

There is considerable contemporary evidence of initiatives by young
people in redefining their view of society and of themselves that suggests
something of the power of the interpretative approach and its relevance
for youth work. Perhaps the most striking manifestations spring from
the student movement in many parts of the world. Most of the advocates
of new definitions of society lean heavily on the experience of student
movements — notably Reich (1972) and Roszak (1970). Roszak in
particular cites with enthusiasm the 'achievements' of students and quotes
with obvious approval the following extract from a notice board at the
Sorbonne in 1968:

> The revolution which is beginning will call in question not only
> capitalist society but industrial society. The society of alienation must
> disappear from history. We are inventing a new and original world;
> imagination is seizing power.

Yet there are less heady and possibly more generally useful pieces of
evidence for the interpretative paradigm in the affairs of non-student

---

[4] It is arguable that if Riesmann's concept of 'other directedness' is appropriate to
the conflict perspective, so too his concept of 'traditional directedness' may be
applied with considerable relevance to the functional frame of reference.

social construct theory.

youth. The remarkable enthusiasm shown by young people within and without the Youth Service to participate in organizations and projects in which they are playing an effective and meaningful social role with important implications for the structure of society is a notable feature of recent years. Youth membership of bodies such as Child Poverty Action, Shelter and Claimants' Unions is widespread. Projects with the socially, economically, mentally and physically handicapped (old people, meths drinkers, destitutes, handicapped children, etc.) attract very great support. Anti-pollution activities, conservation programmes and consumer action campaigns appear to attract notably greater response from the young if they involve a realistic prospect of 'political' involvement, of the experience of power in decision making. The process bears a considerable similarity to the concept of *'conscientizacao'* used by Freire — the achievement of a critical consciousness among the people — the opposite of 'massification'. (Freire, 1974.)

Approaches of this kind tended to be more visible in the newer experimental areas of the service that are examined in this report. They are, however, increasingly being embraced by the longer standing bodies of the service. But their adoption following an initiative by the members or by the leaders of an established club may present obvious problems. Not only may this involve a challenge to the existing 'public' aims of the club (which in itself may have political repercussions), it may also present major problems within the role of the leader who, if he is to assist the members in their search for personal responsibility and power in the community, may himself have to act as their political advocate. If he himself remains personally untouched and secure in his 'establishment' role, then it is likely that his 'newly conscious' members will see him to be not only unhelpful but even insincere. It is, to say the least, unfortunate if the leader is telling his members to work out new ideas for society while at the same time he appears to be personally content to accept society as it is.

It is not only necessary for the leader to be responsive, he may well need to be highly perceptive as well in order to identify areas of potential 'consciousness' of his members and help them to develop these. Many clues are presented by young people — in speech, dress and behaviour. Essentially the interpretative approach requires an inner initiative from the individual rather than an imposed one from the leaders, but the inner initiative may often be aided by sympathetic reinforcement from without. To paraphrase Bernstein — if the consciousness of the leaders is to be in the minds of the members then first of all the consciousness of the members must be in the minds of the leaders. (Bernstein, 1970.) The consequences of ignoring this simple truth can be seen regularly in the Youth Service. At an early stage we witnessed a club programme on 'good grooming' presented by a Home Economics teacher to which a group of girl members came regularly. We were repeatedly astonished that the teacher seemed unable to recognize that most of the girls were, by contemporary standards, remarkably well groomed and that the teacher seemed to be presenting standards and values that were unrelated to the consciousness or perceptions of the girls. Not to our surprise the attendance began to fall off after about six weeks. A spokesman for the girls who abandoned the programme put the matter with understanding when she said, 'that teacher always makes us feel so inferior.' The belief that many of the young have little if anything to contribute, especially in the sphere of values and judgement, is possibly as widespread in the Youth Service as it is in the schools. While it remains so, the full implications of the interpretative theories may well be missed by many members of the service — who may be confused and even critical of the attention we give to them in this report.

Overall it was felt that each of the three perspectives offered valuable theoretical formulations that could provide effective guidelines to investigations of the Youth Service. Moreover it was felt that, despite the claims of some theorists, the interrelationships and compatibilities between all three allowed them to be used concurrently rather than as alternatives, as I have suggested in the introduction to a collection of research papers (Eggleston, 1974). Certainly our preliminary view of the field suggested that this was likely to be possible in our analyses, and a series of accounts of the 'youth scene' published during the life of the project confirmed our view. The 'youth roles' outlined by Milson (1972) provide an example. These range through a lengthy list that includes assenters, the deprived, desocialised and socially rejected (who may be, among others, self-educators, social deviants or 'can copes') and the experimenters (poltical or personal revolutionaries, anarchists or hippies).

The Development of the Hypotheses

How did we begin to explore the role of the Youth and Community Service in the light of these perspectives? An obvious starting point was to examine in detail the aims of the various organizations of the service. We initiated a programme of interviews with personnel at all levels of the various component bodies of the Youth and Community Service and again the response of the service was consistently helpful and supportive. However, it became clear that the result would be unlikely to be of much use. Committee members, leaders and other adults were clearly faced with very great difficulty in talking about the aims of the organization. Not infrequently they lacked the words and even occasionally felt incapable of expressing the aims of an organization that they had for many years taken as given. At best their answers were couched in the terms of the official prospectus of the organization. It became clear that the 'offical' aims of the constituent parts of the Youth and Community Service could more readily be ascertained by analysing the official reports and the various statements made on behalf of the organizations in the Year Book of the Youth Service (Youth Service Information Centre).

But even as we undertook this task we realized from our preliminary visits that the public statements of and about the service, though sincerely written and honestly presented, gave at best an incomplete picture of the aims of the organizations. In particular they failed to reveal the important 'ideological' differences between the various clubs; groups and organizations which we had noticed and which seemed in subtle ways to influence the whole multitude of activities of the various clubs and groups we saw. These ranged from the obvious differences between the religious, cadet and scouting groups to the less obvious, but equally important, differences between the activities of the mixed voluntary clubs and the mixed statutory clubs. We found a valuable guide to exploring these differences in the recruiting literature of the various organizations, designed to attract the attention of existing and potential members. The analysis of this elusive but abundant material provided us with insights that had not been possible from the purely 'adult directed' literature that was first made available to us.

The results of this study confirmed our view that the important motivating forces in the service were often not the offical statements of policy which, as we have already indicated, were not infrequently unclear even to the personnel within the organization. Rather they were the subtle and often latent ways in which the aims are interpreted within the organization. In short, we quickly realized the relevance of the interpretative proposition that the way in which the reality of the organization is perceived and acted upon is the crucial determinant of the realization of the organization's aims and of the human behaviour that takes place within the organization. As a result we became even more careful in our discussion of the values both of the organizations and of the members to emphasize the importance of the way in which they were perceived. We realized too that the same emphasis had to be put upon the ways in which the service as a whole is perceived, the perceptions of individual clubs and groups, the perceptions of activities and the perceptions of individual behaviours within the Youth Service. Every social situation is capable of being interpreted in different ways by the participants. The orienteering exercise may be seen by the leader as a challenging and demanding intellectual and physical experience; as an aesthetic experience of landscape and as an introduction to natural history by the assistant leader, while the member himself may perceive it as an escapist adventure or even a chance to 'get lost' with a partner in an unfrequented area, or as an opportunity for a coach party outing with chips, beer and all the trimmings.

It is all too easy in an approach that takes account of individual constructions of reality to find oneself undertaking an analysis of individual behaviour that, although interesting, fails to offer any generally relevant insights to the nature of the organizations under review. It can come to resemble the projection tests extensively used by psychologists in which the individual is presented with a representation of a social situation and asked to explain what is happening. Yet the message of the new approaches is missed if this analogy is accepted. The important feature of sociological approaches to constructions of reality is that these constructions are shared by large numbers of people: though individual they are regular and recurring and, if we can identify these shared perceptions, we can gain insight not only into the nature of human behaviour but also into its motivation particularly in apparently informal situations such as the Youth and Community Service provides.

At this point we felt able to establish one of the main working hypotheses of the research: that the aims as perceived by the providers of the service — adult committee members, youth officers and adult workers — would not necessarily be the same as those perceived by the members of the clubs, groups and organizations. Our hypothesis was that there would be conflicting perceptions of the service and of its activities and relationships on the part of the clients and that in consequence their response would not necessarily harmonize with that which was 'officially' anticipated. Moreover, it was hypothesized that these differences would be unacknowledged by a significant proportion of the adults in the service either because they were insensitive to the differing perceptions of members or because they found it desirable to ignore these differences even after having recognized them.

In order to explore the members' perceptions of the service different strategies were called for. With the possible exception of the members of student unions and a few other organizations, there were no official statements of members' views of the service: no publicity notices expressing their response to the specific situations in the clubs or groups or organizations. Accordingly, a detailed study of the views of members in a range of clubs and groups was undertaken. A case study of each club or group chosen was mounted and within each of these clubs and groups a sample of members was investigated in an attempt to study their perceptions of the club or group. Information was sought through direct questioning, the recording of behaviour and participation, and the exploration of members' views of other clubs and groups. Structured and unstructured interviews were undertaken. The results of this extensive study, which are reported in Chapter 6, strongly confirm our hypothesis.

We considered it important, however, to explore the broader views of society and the local community, the context in which members formed their views of both their own club or group and of other clubs and groups. Many of the statements of aims noted in the previous chapter concern, often in intimate detail, the 'development' of members' roles in society. Yet a number seem to take little or no account of the fact that the individual who joins the club or unit must have already taken many steps to establish his role in society. The members as well as the service exist in a social context. It was quite clear that if we were to achieve any meaningful measure of the needs of members and their response to the Youth Service, it would be essential to explore, in detail, the way members perceived the social system, the class and power structure and their own position within it. Here the work of Goldthorpe *et al* (1969) was of special relevance, particularly in helping us to identify the clubs for our study. This is discussed fully in Chapter 5. All that need be said here is that the Goldthorpe study drew attention to the importance of the individual's experience within his particular community or group for the formation of his beliefs and about the organization of society; and, crucially for our purpose, that these beliefs appear to be consistent with values and attitudes in other spheres of social life.

By probing beliefs and attitudes along these dimensions it was possible to build up a considerably fuller picture of the values of the same group of members whose perceptions of the club had been explored. In interpreting this evidence it was of course important to realize that the members' views of social reality, like their views of the club or group, will have been determined in part by the experience of membership.[5]

Despite the undertaking of a major exploration of values and motivations within the service one major area remained comparatively unexplored. This was the position and orientation of the leaders in the clubs and groups. Confirmation of our earlier hypothesis placed particular emphasis on their position between the conflicting perceptions of the 'official hierarchy' on the one hand and of the members on the other. Our investigation of this 'man in the middle' hypothesis through studies of their role and their perceptions of it provided further abundant evidence of the general appropriateness of a conflict model for the analysis of important aspects of the leadership role.

The study of values, motivations and perceptions within the service had led us to the view that a substantial number of members were at best only incompletely satisfied by the provisions of the service. In particular their chance to participate fully in the decision making role of the club depended greatly on their willingness to accept the ideological or value commitments of the club or group. Were there alternative forms of organization that might be explored? In order to answer this question we investigated a range of the experimental projects, most of them with strong community-involvement features, that were coming to play an increasing part in Youth and Community Service arrangements in the late

---

[5] In the last resort there are, of course, no uncontaminated sources of evidence in social science research.

60s and early 70s, many of them having little connection or administrative relationship to the long established statutory and voluntary
organizational structures of the service. In particular we undertook a case
study of a typical initiative in the field of community development by
one of the major initiating organizations in this field. The results of the
study are all discussed in full at appropriate stages in the chapters that
follow together with more detailed consideration of certain critical stages
in the investigation. A full resumé of the results is presented in the
concluding chapter. However, it will be clear already that the study is
characterized by a breadth of theoretical perspectives springing from
functionalist, conflict and interpretative approaches.

   This, we hope, will enable it to generate a contribution to our knowledge of adolescence and community that may be of relevance to the
development of social policy. It is important, however, to realize that
the research reported here cannot conveniently be labelled policy-
oriented research. Our conclusions are not recommendations; rather they
are evidence that may be of value to those who go on to make recommendations and policy decisions. Like the adults and the members of the
Youth and Community Service, the decision makers in the social services
have their own constructions of reality. But we hope that this report
will sharpen their perceptions and, in some cases at least, lead them to
restructure their awareness of the purpose and practice of the Youth and

Community Service. However, one of the features of the Youth and Community Service that emerges from our findings is that decisions are not only taken by an elite group of decision makers but also by a wide ranging group of individuals. Indeed, our evidence suggests that this group is a growing one; increasingly it is likely to include the members of the clubs, groups and organizations that consititute the service. In consequence we anticipate that the contents of this report may be of use to a large group of readers. For this reason, if no other, particular care has been taken to express the findings in a language and style that will be meaningful and helpful to such a diverse and extensive readership.

4 Ideology and values

There is great emphasis on physical fitness and the boys are kept strenuously occupied from 6.30 a.m. until lights out at 10.30 . . . There is no smoking, no drinking, no slacking and no whistling on board. The boys are given a hosing down with cold sea water on deck first thing every morning; they are required to keep up a high standard of tidiness and in the few spare moments they have to themselves they are required to keep a log to be shown to the course organizers when they leave. (Caption to cover picture, *Youth Review*, Autumn 1972.)

Over two thousand Lilliput league football tables are in super successful operation throughout Great Britain and abroad. Fitted with patented Fiddleproof coin mechanism, 2p., 2½p., or 5p. Buy Litliput the football table with a pedigree. (*Advertisement in a club magazine, 1972.*)

The Youth Service should provide education for active membership of a participative democracy. (*Albemarle Report, 1960.*)

It is perhaps inevitable that the Youth Service which they offer should be about conformity, a kindly device to contain the young until they have the 'good sense' to recognize the value of that which is. It must therefore be largely about play, like the bread and circuses of ancient Rome. It must, above all things, avoid such issues as 'politics' as 'race' as 'poverty', for as long as the young are happy with their five-a-side and their discotheques, they are nice people; not like those hairy students breathing revolution around every cloistered corner. So we devise a youth service which reflects the beer and bingo conformity of our safe society. Even when the kids are unemployed (as so many of them are now), we offer the day-time opening of the youth club so that they can play snooker or ping-pong in case they get into mischief or vent their anger at the arc lamp-post. (Ewen, 1972).

What are the beliefs and values of those who provide the Youth Service — the statutory and voluntary bodies and their officers and

51

committees? In the previous chapters we have described some of the complex patterns of organization and practice in the Service and the successive waves of policy that have influenced them — reconstruction, the 'building boom', the experimental era and, most recently, the community phase. All have to some extent indicated changes in the orientation, ideology and values of the service. Consequently it seemed important to devise strategies to examine the aims of the service more closely. We wanted to explore the depth of the apparent diversity, to see if underneath there was a gerater degree of consensus than appeared on the surface. We wanted to ascertain whether there were fundamental differences between the statutory and the voluntary sectors, differences that might be suggested by the very considerable variations in history, structure and organization. Did the unstructured nature and localized autonomy of the voluntary sector really indicate the greater adaptability or flexibility that we suspected? Were the values proclaimed by the various organizations consistent and coherent? These questions seemed important, and lead inevitably to a consideration of the very *raison d'etre* of the various organizations and the strength or weakness of their motivation. An obvious first source of this information was in the major reports on the service that have appeared in recent years and to which we have already alluded.

But we needed fuller information about the aims and ideology of the various component areas of the Youth Service. Here we began by scrutinizing the published statements that appeared in the *Year Book of the Youth Service in England and Wales,* 1970/71 issue. Originally this had been intended as a prelude to a more detailed exploration through interviews with the officers and committee members of the various organizations. Despite a considerable amount of good will on the part of these people however, it became clear that this was not likely to be a very useful strategy. As described in the previous chapter, officers and committee members found it extremely difficult to speak in general terms about the aims and objectives of their organizations; it was astonishingly difficult to structure and analyse their replies. And even the most useful replies tended to be a little more than an elaboration of the aims of the organization as indicated in the *Year Book.* Accordingly, we decided to undertake a content analysis of a sample of the details of organizations presented in the Year Book and the results of this form an important contribution to this chapter.[1] This is not to say that we found our discussions with officers and committee members of little value, as our chapter on the structure of the service has indicated. Indeed, even the task of identifying committee members was illuminating. A very high

[1] In taking this decision we were also influenced by our discovery that, in most organizations, very considerable care had been taken in compiling the information submitted to the *Year Book.*

proportion were members of the professional and executive groups — ministers of religion, bankers, business men, teachers and civil servants. (This finding was subsequently confirmed by Judy Lowe in *The Managers* (1973).) The social distribution of committee members was in fact markedly at variance with that of the members of most of the organizations we visited. Also illuminating was the preoccupation of committee members with administration and finance rather than with policy and aims. Again this was confirmed by *The Managers*. The 'elite' membership of the committees of the voluntary organizations at the local level was matched by those at the national level, as the Political and Economic Planning report (Thomas and Perry, 1975) makes clear.

But even this analysis of organizational aims seemed insufficient as many of the statements were couched in general terms that seemed to have little to do with the day-to-day aims of the organization. It was at this time that we became aware of a wide range of other literature issued by the organizations that tell us very much more about the way in which the organization saw itself. This literature was aimed not so much at other bodies but at members and potential members. We discovered that this 'recruiting literature' richly documented the 'self image' of the organization. Pictures of young people smartly on parade in the uniformed organizations; pictures of the members orienteering — striding over the fells with their feet hardly touching the ground — and with the girls always a few paces behind the boys; pictures of the scene at the club with the hard-fought table-tennis match taking place between the two club champions and an admiring throng of lesser members standing in the wings: all these convey an important and illuminating message about the orientation, values and structure of the organizations from which they emanated. Even the physical appearance of the members illustrated in the brochures is informative. The males are 'clean cut', upright and with modest hair styles. They exude healthiness and clean living. The girls who partner them are characterized by a remarkable freedom from problems of overweight, acne and defective vision and posture. Well groomed and well endowed they share with the boys an enviable soundness of limb and physique. Though it is inordinately difficult to analyse, we shall attempt to catch the flavour of at least some of these fascinating and illuminating publications later in this chapter. But first we shall examine the portrayal of the service by further quarrying from the various reports that have already served us in previous chapters. We make no apology for the repeated reference to the same reports in these early chapters; they provide some of the few clearly visible landmarks within the Service as a whole.

Aims expressed in The Reports

The board of Education Circular 1516 of 27 June, 1940 indicated that
the general aim of the service was 'to be found in indirect social and
physical training . . . The common task was to bring young people into
a normal relationship with their fellows and to develop bodily fitness . . .
The overriding purpose was to be seen in the 'building of character' . . .
Young people were to be given a happy and healthy social life in
association with their fellows, perhaps sharing in some common project,
accepting and exercising the authority which a free relationship
involved.' Yet even at the formal inception of the new Youth Service the
apparently uncontroversial statement and its aims reflected a major
ideological division. While it was agreed that a Youth Service was needed
in face of the widespread disruption of family and social life during the
war, there was on the one hand a strong lobby wishing to go the whole
way to a National Youth Service and another, successful one, that feared
that the excesses of the Nazi youth movement of Germany might recur
in Britain.

Following the 1944 Education Act, the Standing Conference of
National Voluntary Youth Organizations affirmed that the aim of
education in their kind of organization was not only good citizenship but
to 'live the good life' and to many, possibly a majority of adults in the
Youth Service, this meant 'Christian life in a Christian church'.
(National Council of Social Service, 1945.)

Overall, the emphasis in the mid 1940s was on the informal
socialization of the young often through the youth service corps, into
certain approved and non-contentious cultural values such as citizenship,
character, the good life and physical fitness; the young were also to be
helped to make satisfactory social relationships and they were to be
trained and helped in 'self-government.' It was an emphasis that
appeared to be born out of the confidence of the adult population that,
despite the pressing social problems of the period, they knew what was
right for the young and could make it available to them in established
and clearly structured organizations.

The Albemarle Report (1960), while reaffirming these aims and
values, made certain additions that reflected changes in the 1950s. These
were related to the apparently increasing affluence and independence of
the young, apparently verified by such studies as *The Adolescent
Consumer* (Abrams, 1959), which was believed to have led to a
breakdown of the 'traditional constraints of authority and poverty'.
Concern with an apparent rise in juvenile delinquency was evident
throughout the report, as was the emergence of skinheads, rockers and
similar behavioural groups.

To counteract these trends it was felt that youth needed to be offered
a challenge comparable to that which, some suggested, had been offered

by National Service, which had continued after the war until the mid 50s. Some of those who felt that National Service had made a major contribution believed that some form of organized voluntary service — overseas or at home — could provide a suitable substitute for it. The importance of commitment to the club was still strongly stressed but it was also recognized that steps would have to be taken to reach the 'unattached' — a word that came to have a central role in Youth Service thinking following the publication of an influential book with that title. (Morse, 1965.) Somewhat tentatively the *Albemarle Report* also recognized the possible role the Youth Service could play in two other spheres: economic and political. In the section entitled 'Preparation for Adult Life' it was suggested that controversial subjects might have to be broached, such as religion, politics and industrial relations. The committee recommended that youth organizations with religious affiliations should become eligible for public funds from which they had previously been excluded — a recommendation that was accepted by the government of the day. At one step both the values of the religious organizations and the diversity of religious commitment became officially recognized — and fundable — by the Youth Service. The committee did not, however, suggest any formal relation between political youth organizations and the Youth Service but felt that political organizations might provide speakers for debates in the service.

Yet though the report did conceive some extension of the service's aims and values, the main emphasis was on imaginative development of traditional objectives with the aid of increased funds and training and with new experimental projects and unattached workers to take the values of the service into areas not readily reached by traditional approaches. In the nine years between the publication of this report and *Youth and Community Work in the 70s* a considerable shift in emphasis occurred. The radical tone of the latter is at variance with that of its predecessor. One of its dominating and recurrent themes is the social and political involvement of the young:

> The primary goal of youth work is the social education of young people. We are not so much concerned today as in the past with basic education or with economic needs, or with the communication of an agreed belief or value system; but we are concerned to help young people to create their place in a changing society and it is their critical involvement with the community which is the goal. We have in mind not that [the young person] would simply be practicing democracy for *future* use in real life; but rather that he would be living and contributing directly towards a democratic way of life. Indeed, where the community is little developed, young people operating within this framework may act as a ginger group. This means that young adults will become involved in activities and discussions which are by their

nature controversial and which have indeed until now been labelled
'political' and thus not within the province of youth organizations.

Yet the report displays a welcome realization that its aims were
prescriptive rather than descriptive for almost at once it goes on to say.

> We agree with the National Union of Students when they say that
> they are concerned that however much lip-service may be paid to the
> idea of young people challenging the accepted values of the
> community, there is an underlying complacency that these values are,
> in themselves, absolute and beyond challenge.

All this is not to say that there were no organized groups of young
people who were actively involved in trying to 'contract in' to political
decision making processes. On the contrary the late 1960s had seen a
remarkable upsurge of radical fervour among the youth of Europe and
North America: *Youth and Community Work in the 70s* was written
against such a background. Yet the report still did not offer, and perhaps
could not have offered, any clear indication of the extent to which such
events were influencing the orientations and aims of the statutory and
voluntary organizations.

The Aims of Individual Organizations

The aims expressed in the reports combine a mixture of perceptive
insight, self-evident truths, a re-vamping and re-legitimizing of existing
aims and values and a fair element of stylistic elegance. But what guide
do they offer to the day-to-day working of the service? One of the major
purposes of this study was to indicate which aims are considered to be
important within the component units of the service and whether these
differ in the various sectors. To what extent are these generalized aims of
relevance to the various parts of the service? Are they prescriptive or
discriptive? Are there other orientations and beliefs to which we should
also attend?

The aims extracted from the two major reports refer to young people
'finding their place' in one or more major social systems:
1. The political system — integration with other decison making systems,
   active or passive
2. The economic system — integration within the productive system
3. The cultural system — the acceptance or 'discovery' of approved
   values and beliefs
4. The integrative system — Integration into approved social milieu

This classification strikingly resembles Parsons' typology of the functions which, he claimed, must be fulfilled by every society if it is to remain

viable (Parsons, 1965) and confirms the functional orientations that
provide much of the *raison d'etre* of the Youth Service. How could we
begin to explore the incidence of these orientations in the various
components of the Youth Service of England and Wales? Fortunately
we were able to discover a relevant approach that had been developed in
another European system.

Parsons' typology had been successfully used to analyse the aims of
the Finnish Youth Service (Aalto, 1970). To obtain some measure of
the aims, ideologies and orientations of individual units comprising our
Youth Service, we made a content analysis of the stated aims of the
organizations along the lines developed by Aalto. Table 4.1 at the end of
this chapter shows the sectors of activity relevant to these aims. The
remaining tables show the aims of the organizations in relation to this
classification. It is important to emphasise that these are aims which are
expressed in the formal and informal written statements of youth
organizations and are not necessarily related to actual practice. Certain
adaptations were necessary because of the differences between Finnish
society and our own. Such adaptations were minor and did not affect the
structure or the outcome of the analysis.

The Youth Service Year Book Sample

To explore these orientations a sample was drawn from the
organizations, voluntary and statutory, which contributed to the *Year
Book of the Youth Service in England and Wales,* 1970/71. (Youth
Service Information Centre.) According to the compilers, 'lengthy
questionnaires were despatched in December 1969 to all known
voluntary youth organizations, to all local education authorities, to
relevant training institutions and to various allied bodies. The entries
have been compiled on the basis of the responses to questionnaires and
have been in all cases approved by the agency concerned . . . It is
recognized that the amount of material submitted varies from agency to
agency and that a few agencies who were invited to submit material did
not respond.'

The choice of the *Year Book* as a sampling frame provided several
distinct practical and theoretical advantages. Because of the vast range of
Youth Service literature some selection criterion had to be used. The
Year Book presented a comprehensive collection of comparable
statements made by the units comprising the Youth Service. Secondly,
each organization was aware that the information they submitted would
be presented alongside information from other organizations. It was
logical, therefore, to suppose that contributors were likely to emphasize
the most salient features of their organizations.

This led to a further important consideration. It is possible (indeed it
has been suggested by some Youth Service personnel) that simply

because the *Year Book* is for public consumption, the statements made by youth organizations will not represent actual practice; and that the contributions are submitted in full knowledge of this discrepancy. It is however, important to stress again that 'stated' aims are not necessarily 'real' aims (Zald, 1970) and that the focus of the study was the analysis of the stated aims of youth organizations. And it is certainly arguable that the 'competitive context' of the *Year Book of the Youth Service* would have led contributors to express the underlying aims and ideologies of their branch of the service even more clearly in the hope of achieving a further and more favourable response from the public reader-ship — employers, teachers, parents and press.

The sample consisted of 73 voluntary organizations and a representative random sample from 36 local education authorities (statutory organizations), in all a total of 109 units. Training organizations and similar bodies were not included. The aims expressed in each organization's contribution were measured by means of a simple content analysis. They were classified according to the typology discussed above and recorded as being either present or absent. Table 4.2 indicates the kinds of Youth Service objectives classified under each section. The material was coded by two researchers working independently. The number of times a particular dimension was mentioned by each organization was *not* taken into account.

The first part of the analysis was concerned with the dominant values in the Youth Service taken as a whole. One of the questions originally raised was the extent to which *Youth and Community Work in the 70s* was prescriptive rather than descriptive in its recommendation that the service recognizes the economic and poltical needs of young people. Table 4.3 shows the number and percentage of organizations endorsing the different types of aim. The results clearly demonstrate the strong overall orientation the Youth Service retains towards its traditional role in the socialization and integration of the young into society, the aims, in fact set out so clearly in the *Albemarle Report*.

Substantially fewer organizations included political or economic aims in their charter. To illuminate the situation, the results were next examined according to the voluntary/statutory nature of the units. The data obtained clearly demonstrate that both sectors are aware of the development of political and economic demands, which are, however, less incorporated into organizational aims in general. Differences are also revealed between the two sectors. In both spheres, proportionately more organizations in the statutory sector than in the voluntary sector mention such aims. Of the statutory organizations 36% and 25% of the voluntary organizations include aims relating to any kind of political activity and in the economic sphere, although 23 organizations helped specifically in the transitional process, only three organizations (two voluntary and one statutory) specifically offered any sort of vocational guidance; four voluntary and three statutory gave help in finding a job while ten provided accommodation for young workers (nine voluntary and one statutory).

We have drawn attention to the importance of social control mechanisms and also to the problems of discussing them explicitly, particularly in a Youth Service context. The difficulties, ambiguities and inherent tensions in this area of Youth Service work are further discussed in later chapters. It is not surprising that only limited evidence of social control aims have been visible in this analysis. We were able to identify two kinds of areas in which the aims of the organizations seemed to be specifically concerned with the regulation and control of behaviour. These may be summarized as committing people to what is already provided and making efforts to extend the range of this commitment to others. These two types of behaviour are not necessarily distinguished in a clear cut way. Table 4.5 presents the data we obtained.

In certain situations counselling may also be defined as an instrument of social control. Cicourel and Kitsuse (1963) in a review of American practice have suggested that counselling may be not so much a means of guiding the young to express their own needs but instead, of ensuring, more effectively, that they come to comply with existing provisions and the values that influence them and determine them. Though this is a controversial and unproven view of counselling we thought it would be interesting to refer to the debate which surrounds counselling at a time when it is being strongly advocated within the Youth Service.

We found that 87 out of the total of 109 organizations in the sample play some sort of social control role. Although both statutory and voluntary sectors encouraged people to join in organized activity (53% and 73% respectively) somewhat surprisingly, however, statutory organizations included a wider range of commitment extention in their aims than did voluntary organizations (67% as opposed to 14%). This trend was also related to the emphasis on counselling (41% as opposed to 12%).

The 'Membership Literature' of the Service

So far we have only considered the formally stated aims of the organizations in the *Year Book*. How far are these employed by the statutory and voluntary bodies in their day-to-day work with members? To answer this question we can turn for illumination to the brochures and leaflets issued by the clubs and organizations to their present and prospective members. We have already noted the difficulty of analysing such material and we shall content ourselves with presenting a short series of quotations grouped together under the typological headings that we have been using throughout the chapter. The selection has been presented only to affirm the relevance of the typology items gathered during the research, a collection that will be presented and analysed more fully in a subsequent paper.

The Political System: Typical approaches by the organizations are represented by quotations from NAYC and YMCA literature.

Why not indeed! We are living in a world where people have to learn to be responsive as well as responsible; peacemakers as well as protesters; realists as well as reformers. The YMCA is based on a faith that knows there are timeless values which we desperately need to retain in a world of change. The YMCA can enable young people to be agents of char.ge, while retaining these timeless values. For those who have faith in these things there is a bright tomorrow — today! *(Young Men's Christian Association.)*

How do people come to *power?* Examine the many processes by which people in leadership — in national and local life — are appointed or achieve office — cabinet minister, bishop, chairman of a company, head of a school or university, editor of a newspaper. See what you can find out through reading, interviews and observations of the way we evolve leaders in this country and the various pathways to power. *National Association of Youth Clubs.*

The Economic System: Quotations from the literature of Shelter and NAYC are used as representative examples here.

A crime is doing something that is wrong. But not all wrong-doing is a crime. For example, it is wrong to tell a lie. But only some lies are crimes. If you tell your friends you have been twice round the world when in fact you have never been further than Blackpool or Brighton, that is a lie. It is certainly wrong, for if you tell the story well your friends might believe you. If they do believe you, you are exploiting their trust in you. But it is not a crime. It becomes a crime only when you lie with some extra reason, not just to impress them or to get out of a difficulty but in order to obtain something over and above that — something they actually possess. If you go to a friend and tell him "I'll buy your old motorbike for £25", and give him £5 as a down-payment and drive away knowing you will never be able to pay him the rest, that is a lie which is also a crime. The criminal law protects your friend, not against being lied to, but only against being lied to for the purpose of fraudulently obtaining a motorbicycle.

Question 1: If your group could take over an island, build your own homes and make your own laws, what laws would you pass?

Question 2: Being greedy is wrong, but it is not a crime. Why?
(National Association of Youth Clubs.)

The playing of Tenement is usually preceeded by some other form of
presentation, either a slide show with a hesitant talk by one of us or
a series of short acting sketches done by a few of us designed to show
firstly that the finding of any house is difficult and needs to be
planned, and secondly that it is possible for a family to get into
serious trouble through little fault of its own. *(Shelter.)*

The Cultural System: Four examples from a very large number of
references are presented as representative examples.

The worst possible weather conditions prevailed throughout the first
day and night of the walk. Some members fell by the way-side
(including the writer, and this was his third unsuccessful attempt!). By
the time the first check-point was reached, everyone, walkers and
helpers alike, were soaked to the skin. The conditions were so bad
that two hundred soldiers who were attempting the walk, and who
had all the support the army can give, were withdrawn at the half way
point.

On Blakey Ridge, one thousand three hundred feet above sea level,
the party halted in an attempt to get some rest in a coach, a tent and
a Dormobile. At 3:30 a.m., right on schedule, members of the South
Bank County Girls' Club arrived with their leaders, and a hot break-
fast of porridge, bacon, sausages and beans — all prepared during the
night by the girls — disappeared like magic. *(North Riding Association
of Youth Clubs.)*

There were 'high jinks' on Saturday night, — some damage was the
result — apparent only on Sunday morning. The matter serious, a
minority had misbehaved; but worse, the built-in, accepted
responsibility to maintain a very high standard of behaviour had
failed. *The conflict here was resolved by the delegates alone.* The
organizer brought the matter to their attention; expressed his
disappointment and the warden's annoyance; he and the consultants
left a clearly defined conflict situation for delegates to resolve. The
delegates found a working party to repair the small amount of
damage, money was collected to pay for the additional expert
attention required, and an apology mission sent to the Warden of
Otterburn Hall. *(Young Men's Christian Association, N.E. Division.)*

It is of vital importance that some definite kind of Christian worship
and observance ought to feature in the club programme from the
inception of the club; that every member should be expected to
attend it; and that sustained efforts should be made to ensure that this

is so. 'To wait until they ask for it' is to be idealistic in a wrong fashion. 'To begin as you mean to go on' is far more satisfactory. *(Methodist Association of Youth Clubs.)*

Let us turn to the Boy. Is drill an attraction? To the average youngster, Yes! *if it is efficient.* A well disciplined, well turned out Company will always attract, and such Companies have no recruiting problem. An undisciplined sloppy Company will always repel. Unfortunately, the sloppy Companies turn out most often, with disastrous results to the Movement as a whole. The small Boy loves to be ordered about. He would die rather than admit it, but he does, and the more roughly he is treated the better he likes it, but if drill is slack he soon tires. *(Boys' Brigade.)*

The Integrative System: Again four examples from an extreme range of references have been selected.

'These are the times we shall dream about and we'll call them the Good Old Days'. *(Stoke-on-Trent Scouts. Gang Show Programme 1974.)*

CELEBRATION Little worship was planned in advance — but it all happened, mushroom-like throughout the week. There was no pressure to go to worship at the Catholic Cathedral on the final evening — three miles away — but nearly everyone went. All the media, all the ways of communicating (mind, spirit and body) were in use. Jesus was central, and more explicitly so than often in the past. *(British Council of Churches' Youth Department.)*

We were able to meet the 'Gypsies' outside the club as they arrived, and to their consternation, comment on how quickly they had travelled from the other club. We went on to explain that, if possible, we wanted to make them welcome but we were understaffed and had to wait until reinforcements arrived until we could responsibly let them in. We also pointed out that a large group of local youngsters were already using the club and we didn't want them displaced.

The 'Gypsies' seemed stunned at our organization, not to repel them, but to accept them. On the first night they streamed in, boisterous, swearing, and dodging paying subs as far as possible. We managed to get a few names — mostly 'Jack Green'. Very evidently, however, they did not set out to break up the place. *(Methodist Association of Youth Clubs.)*

'I know one thing, I will never again refuse my mother's food.' *(Outward Bound Trust.)*

Overall, our exploration of the membership literature, only incompletely reported here, confirmed our impressions that the Parsons' typology was a meaningful one and that the Youth Service, despite contemporary emphasis on political and economic orientations, still remained predominantly concerned with the traditional, cultural and integrative orientations. Moreover, it is suggested that the attention given to these orientations within the service is primarily to their *socially conformist* rather than their *socially non-conformist* manifestations. A further dimension also became apparent — a recurring emphasis on their socially higher status rather than their socially lower status manifestations. At the risk of even greater arbitrariness than we displayed in our diagram at the end of Chapter 2, we have essayed a further grid in which we have attempted to indicate the possible location of a range of youth groupings within and without the Youth Service. This is shown in Figure 4. The diagram, though no more than tentative does suggest that the Youth and Community Service is almost wholly located in the top right hand sector — the high status, conformist area — an indication that can be usefully explored in subsequent chapters.[2]

We have been able to identify a number of features of the values and aims of the individual organizations within the Youth Service. Overall, they strongly confirm the picture of the official 'ideology' of the service outlined in the early part of this chapter. It is not too great an over simplification to suggest that the *Albemarle Report* remains the most convenient and certainly the most reliable guide to the 'official' ideology and values of the service. Certainly it is as yet far more sure a guide to the 'mainstream' of the service than *Youth and Community Work in the 70s.*

Again and again the emphasis of the various organizations, both statutory and voluntary is placed upon the highly traditional, conformist and high status aspects of cultural socialization and integration. Often echoing the very words of Albemarle, organizations speak of character building, leadership training and the development of self-confidence. But all of these are to be found in a context of conformity to a basic set of

---

[2] An interesting corroboration of the diagram arose by chance with the arrival of the Autumn 1973 issue of *The Glaswegian,* the magazine of the Youth and Community Service of the Glasgow Corporation Education Department. The contents not surprisingly, were certainly strongly emphasized social conformity. The final page bore a picture of 'smartly' turned out Glasgow youths, some in uniform, captioned 'On parade . . . the Youth of Glasgow. Some of the city's voluntary bodies show off their contributions in the procession of floats which marked the opening of Clyde Fair.' By the same post arrived a copy of the recently published and widely reported study by Patrick (1973) *A Glasgow Gang Observed* with its account of predominantly low status non-conformist activity. To say the least the team found it difficult to realize that both publications were describing adolescent behaviour in the same city.

Figure 4

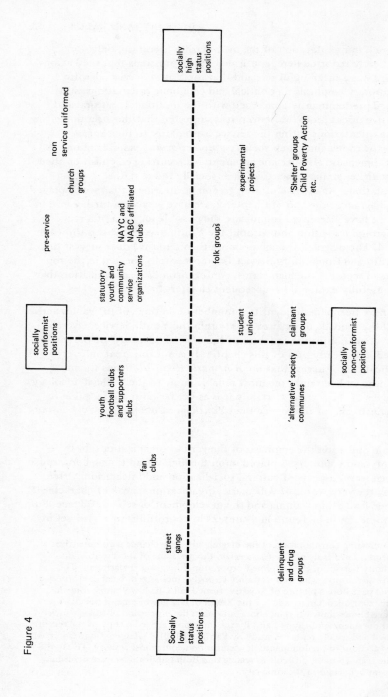

HYPOTHETICAL POSITIONS OF TYPICAL YOUTH GROUPS
WITHIN AND WITHOUT THE YOUTH SERVICE

values, attitudes and beliefs. Important in all is the concept of what is 'right' — the right kind of character building, leadership to achieve the right goals, self-confidence to confirm oneself in the right course of action. In the voluntary sector the values and beliefs are defined by the organizations' history and connections. Emphasizing, in their various ways, Christianity, militarism, public service, political involvement, scouting and the like, they are publicly proclaimed, well known and well regarded. They tend to occupy established, even establishment, positions in the value system of our society and to find themselves in compatible, even convergent positions within it. And the orientation and ideology of the statutory organizations, though less explicit, is similarly compatible and convergent.

In short, the tasks of cultural socialization and integration seen as central by most organizations are carried out in the context of safe, traditional middle ground values and for the most part are relatively unconcerned with change in the established order of society — in its occupational system, in its social system and in its belief system. In doing this the Youth and Community Service is clearly undertaking an important social control function. However, it is worth noting that while the voluntary organizations, with their more specific value orientations and ideology, often appear to be content to endeavour to reinforce the commitment of the members to them, the statutory organizations with their less specific values often appear enthusiastic to increase the range of committed young people beyond the bounds of their membership.

In the face of the evidence of the emphasis on traditional values in socialization and integration, it is hardly surprising that both political and economic socialization is less emphasized and, in particular, that the emphasis is less in the voluntary sector rather than the statutory sector. The enthusiasm of *Youth and Community Work in the 70s* for innovative work in these areas is still not greatly in evidence. It is suggested that there are two reasons for this. The first is that the specifically economic and political aspects are subsumed into the more general life values presented in cultural socialization and that these are seen to offer a kind of blanket commitment within which to accept the existing political and economic arrangements of society. Hence there may appear to be no purpose in attending to them separately or specifically. The second is that these areas may be seen to be dangerous or unwise ones by the organizations. They may, for example, give rise to a demand for participation or involvement by the young that is in conflict with the commitment to the social system held by the organizations or, as we have suggested earlier, with the positions occupied by the adult leaders or local and national committee members. The community service project, for example, may escalate from digging old people's gardens to writing challenging letters to local councillors about old people's housing and welfare. And, at the latter stage, it may be feared that the sponsors of the clubs, many of them senior local citizens, may be unwilling to continue their support if such 'deviant' behaviour is sanctioned or even tolerated by the club.

But implicit in the questions that are being raised in this overview may be an assumption that the members of the Youth Service are characterized by a pervasive radicalism and a desire to challenge. Clearly it is important to probe more deeply into the members' views of society and their places within it as a prelude to the consideration of their participation in and their response to the Youth Service. We shall undertake such a probe in detail in the next chapter.

Table 4.1   **Parsons' typology as used by adults to show the sectors of activity through which youth become part of society**

G.*	A.*
Political	**Economic**
Becoming part of the decision making system	*Becoming part of the productive system of society*
Participation in planning, opportunity for making opinions known	Schooling, vocational guidance, finding a job
Participation in political power	
L.*	I.*
Cultural	**Integration**
Joining the cultural system	*Joining the contact and communition system*
Learning and internalizing values	Friendship, family, membership in clubs and organizations
Innovation of values	
Receiving awards	
Consumption	
Rest and relaxation	
Participation in cultural and recreational occupations	

*Parsons calls these cells respectively: goal attainment (G), adaptation (A), pattern maintenance and latency (L) and integration (I).

Table 4.2 **Classification of youth service objectives**

Political	*Economic*
Participation in planning	Vocational guidance
Opportunity for making opinions known	Help in finding a job
Directing into social action by:	The teaching of occupational skills
giving social information	Transitional courses
training in social procedures	Providing accommodation for young workers
directing into political activity	
acting as an interest group for members	

Cultural Values and Beliefs	*Integration*
Innovation of new values	Social Relationships
Internationalism	
Inculcation of Traditional Values	Acquainting different kinds of people with each other
A: Character building	
Self discipline	Increasing the common identity of similar kinds of people or people with the same background, e.g.
Initiative	
Leadership	
Obedience	
Citizenship	Uniform
Self improvement	Badges
Maturity	Club loyalty
Self confidence	Publications
	Expression of similar views, e.g.
B: Religion	religion
Temperance	
Healthy way of life	Social Control
National tradition	
Patriotism	Drawing young people with organized activity
Conservative attitude towards society	
Sense of responsibility	'Extra mural' measures e.g. detached workers separate provision
Latency type activity	
	Counselling
Providing worthwhile hobbies	
Providing enjoyment and recreation, rest and relaxation.	Helping young people with their personal and social problems

Table 4.3   **Numer and percentage of organizations endorsing the different types of aim**

Type of Aim	Organizations' Endorsements	
	No.	%
Political	31	29
Economic	47	45
Cultural	105	98
Integrative	108	99

Table 4.4   **Organization structure and organization aims**

Type of Organiza-tion	Aim								Total Organiza-tions
	Political		Economic		Cultural		Integrative		
	No.	%	No.	%	No.	%	No.	%	
Statutory	13	36	21	58	36	100	36	100	36
Voluntary	18	25	26	36	69	94	72	99	73

Table 4.5   **'Social control' mechanisms used by the two sectors**

Type of Organiza-tion	Mechanism						Total Organiza-tion
	Establishing Commit-ment		Extending Commit-ment		Counselling		
	No.	%	No.	%	No.	%	
Statutory	21	53	24	67	10	41	36
Voluntary	53	73	10	14	9	12	73

5 Members' views of society

Hypothesis and method

A notable feature of the evidence reviewed in the previous chapter was the absence of any statements originating from members themselves. An essential next step was therefore to consider the views of members and their responses to those of the providers. Long before reaching youth service age, young people are subject to the socializing influences of families, peer groups, schools and neighbourhoods. Yet all too often, as we have seen, the discussion of aims and values of the youth service, particularly those concerning the member's role in society, take little account of the fact that he already has gone a considerable way towards establishing such a role in society outside the service, or even that the members as well as the club exist in a social context. If we are to achieve any meaningful indication of the needs of the members and their response to the youth service, it is essential to explore in considerable detail the beliefs, values and attitudes formulated 'outside' the service: a task undertaken in this chapter. We shall then, in the following chapter draw out the implications of these for the youth service.

In order to make sense of their social experience individuals commonly structure it in some way. People hold beliefs about the social order and particularly the class structure, and there is evidence to suggest that beliefs, the values held and attitudes to more specific items tend to be consistent. These social perspectives, it seems, are related to the social groups in which people live or with which they have contact and to the nature of this experience. But these ideas about how society operates do not necessarily accord with reality since the sum total of an individual's experience is only a small part of the whole that is possible. It could be argued that because experiences vary from person to person, each individual will have a unique social perspective. To some extent this is true. However, large categories of people do share many similar experiences which have a direct bearing on life styles and life chances, for example level and type of schooling, work and its availability, level of income and housing. Thus it is likely that recognizably similar perspectives are held by broadly similar categories of people.

In order to explore young people's views of society we took as models[1] the formulations of Goldthorpe, Lockwood, Bechhofer and Platt, (1969 pp. 118-21, 147-54), who discussed three major types of social perspective: the traditional working class perspective, the middle class perspective and the 'money' model of class seen to be held by affluent workers.

In the traditional working class perspective it is suggested that 'The basic conception of the social order is a dichotomous one: society is divided into "us" and "them". "They" are persons in positions in which they can exercise "power" and "authority" over us'. (Goldthorpe et al., 1969, p. 118) The division may be perceived by the individual to be virtually unbridgeable. Social circumstances are taken as given 'facts' of life which have to be 'put up with' and can only be altered by exceptional strokes of luck. Consistent with this, wants and expectations are relatively fixed. Concern tends to be with maintaining a certain standard of living rather than raising it. Orientation is towards the present rather than the uncertain future and consequently a premium is placed upon present enjoyment rather than planning for the future (about which it is believed that little can be done anyway). Mutual aid and group solidarity are prime values and there is restraining pressure upon individuals who try to make themselves a 'cut above the rest'. Aspiration is usually confined within the limits of working class values and life styles, for example, apprenticeship rather than professional qualifications.

From the middle class perspective 'the basic conception of the social order is a hierarchical one: society is divided into a series of levels or strata differentiated in terms of the life styles and associated prestige of their members.' (Goldthorpe et al., 1969, p. 120) The structure is seen as being open, that is, given ability and the appropriate moral qualities (hard work and determination), people can and do 'move up'. What a man achieves depends upon what he makes of himself. There is a moral obligation to assume responsibility for one's own life and to 'get on'. Wants and expectations are seen as capable of continuous enlargement and there is a firm expectation that advancement will occur both within and between generations. The dominant orientations is towards the future and moral approval is given to deferred gratification. The ethic is essentially individualistic and a prime value is set on achievement, which is taken as an indication of moral worth.

---

[1] It is emphasized here, as elsewhere in this report, that the concept of models is employed as an aid to identification and analysis. It is not suggested that in the pure form described here any of these models actually exist. Real life is far more complex than any model. But it is suggested that elements of these models form familiar components of many individual's views of society that are frequently grouped in the manner we indicate.

It is suggested that highly paid manual workers hold a 'money' view of the class structure. Money, that is 'differences in the incomes, wealth and material living standards' is seen as the primary differentiating feature of the social order. (Goldthorpe *et al.*, 1969, p.147.) Society is seen as comprising one large central class plus one or more residual or elite classes. The central class includes the vast majority of people and the manual — non-manual distinction tends to be disregarded. An ever increasing standard of living is expected but this is unrelated to status enhancement. Aspirations are held for children but these may not reach fulfilment, not because of any lack of 'seriousness of intention in their parental efforts, but rather uncertain dispositions and capacities necessary to make such support really effective.' (Goldthorpe *et al.*, 1969, p. 137.) The style of life is essentially family centred but not in the manner of the traditional working class extended family. In the case of the affluent worker, overriding importance is placed upon the conjugal family, home and family life. But in addition there is an absence of any 'solidaristic' feeling; the affluent worker is seen to be essentially isolated and inward looking.

With these perspectives in mind, five clubs were selected for intensive study. Three were considered to be directly comparable with the models: a traditional working class club (Colliery Bank), an affluent working class club (Colourview Rise) and a grammar school club (Uptown

Grammar). Two additional clubs were chosen because it was felt that the above models do not exhaust the range of social perspectives. They were a working class club in a relatively deprived area (Coronation Estate) and a rural club (Ambridge Green). Selection was based on the social milieux of the clubs for, as Lockwood observes, 'Men visualize the class structure from the point of view of their own milieux. Perceptions of the larger society will vary according to their experiences of social inequality in the smaller society in which they live out their lives.' (Lockwood, 1966, p.249.)

By confining the study to five general purpose clubs rather than a wider range of youth service institutions it was possible to restrict, at least to some extent, the differences arising from organizational, administrative and specialist interest features, thereby allowing a closer focus on the social and cultural aspects under investigation. A detailed description of each club and its facilities can be found in Appendix 1.

Club lists were used as sampling frames. However, it was found that the nature of club lists varied from club to club. Clubs tended to have one or more of a membership list, attendance book or register, a visitors' book or a guest list. The guest list in some cases was of people who attended the club regularly but paid on a nightly basis; in others, of people who 'dropped in' from time to time. However, all the clubs had lists of some sort and the membership sample was drawn from the list or combination of lists which appeared to give the most comprehensive account of attendance. When the club had 'visitors' but no list of 'regular visitors' a sample was taken from a 'good night' — one with a high attendance figure. In only one case, the girls of the boys' grammar school club, was the selection non-random. We considered it important that the major variables of age, sex, school and work be sufficiently represented and the sample was stratified accordingly.

The total number of interviews conducted was 105 out of a possible 130 (an overall response rate of 81%) and the sample and response rate for each club is presented in Table 5.1. The extent to which refusals and non-contacts biased the results cannot be fully determined as it is difficult in such cases to obtain more than minimal information. However, as the response rate was generally good, we did not feel that results would be unduly influenced. Details of the membership sample and reasons for non-response are also summarised in Table 5.1. This, with other tables giving the results of our investigation, can be found at the end of this chapter.

The enquiry fell into two distinct parts. First we examined perceptions of the class structure and secondly perceptions of the local community. Values and attitudes were then considered in relationship to the social perspectives which emerged.

In the section on the larger society we examined how society, in its fullest sense, was perceived. For example, was there any kind of awareness of a class structure and what were seen as the major differentiating criteria? If a class structure was recognized was it seen as negotiable? Was it possible to change one's relative position and what were the attitudes exhibited towards such change?

It was further assumed that respondents would be aware of two widely disparate groups in our society: the rich and the poor. Consequently we asked respondents how they thought people came to be members of these particular groups.

We also examined perceptions of the local community since, as we have noted, it is experience in this context which plays a large part in social awareness. Respondents were also asked to locate and describe their own and other families in the local community. Finally we examined the extent of personal aspiration.[2]

Because of the complexity of the relationships involved, each club is considered separately, as a unique configuration. In cases where comparison between clubs serves to illuminate a particular point this is then undertaken.

Social Perspectives

Colliery Bank

The club served a mining community on a National Coal Board housing estate: a traditional working class community with a strong emphasis on class solidarity and mutual support. In addition, the estate was socially isolated from the rest of the local community comprising a council estate and groups of private housing. Consequently we hypothesized that the social perceptions of members of this club would reflect the social isolation they experienced locally as well as demonstrating attitudes usually associated with traditional working class communities.

Perception of the Wider Society: Not unexpectedly there was no overriding consensus about the class structure. There were, however, several significant findings. Eight people, that is over one third of the sample, had no conception of any kind of class structure. For them, the question was meaningless. This was not merely a lack of understanding of the term class, as six of these respondents were also unaware of any social differences or different groups in their local community — a community in which such social awareness, where it was found, was particularly pronounced. The remaining two had only the vaguest notion of the social

[2] It should be noted that the concept of class was not introduced until perceptions of the local community had been fully explored.

divisions in the area. In one case this was of note as the boy had had personal experience of the social pressures to conform to different standards when his family had moved from the mining estate to a private housing area.[3]

Among those who had some notion of a class structure, differentation was largely seen in terms of money or occupation (the two often seen as synonymous). Teaching, typing and office jobs were seen as high class, working in a factory or a mine as low. The area in which people lived was also cited as important. Attributes of dress and speech and attitudes were expressed in such terms as 'will mix' or snooty' or 'look down on us for no reason'.

In view of the hypothesis that in a traditional working class community society is likely to be viewed in terms of a power dichotomy, it is interesting that only two respondents perceived two major classes, differentiated in terms of manual and non-manual occupations. Respondents were, however, generally very much aware of their own position at the bottom of any social order. A number saw themselves as the people on whom others 'look down' irrespective of whether or not they accepted the legitimacy of this differentiation.

Negotiating the Structure: Nine respondents thought it was possible to change one's class. Although four people felt that winning the pools was one way of negotiating the structure, only one of these felt it was the only way. Three mentioned the importance of a special skill (such as being a star footballer) and two mentioned marriage. Six respondents saw a relationship between education and type of occupation as a major way of changing one's class.

But whereas only nine respondents felt it was possible to negotiate the class structure, sixteen said they were going to 'try to get on'. Getting on was not seen as changing one's class position but being secure in a respectable job, having a skill or trade and possibly owning one's own house[4]. One could 'get on' by dint of hard work and not spending all one's time enjoying oneself. Getting on was seen as a reward for a certain type of behaviour which would bring money and promotion in its wake. Only one respondent (a girl of fourteen) felt that people should be content as they are. Thus, in sum, the perception of upward social mobility and the interpretation of getting on was set within strictly limited boundaries. The class structure for the majority was non-negotiable.

---

[3] When the father decided to keep pigeons, neighbours stopped speaking to the family.

[4] This distinction between social mobility and getting on was found throughout the enquiry.

Interesting light was shed on their attitudes when reasons for both wealth and poverty were examined. While poverty was predominantly seen as the direct result of personal failure or inadequacy, factors external to the individual played a leading role in the acquisition of wealth. Only three respondents gave such reasons as 'vicious circle' of deprivation or 'little opportunity' as having a bearing on poverty, but seventeen respondents felt improvidence was the underlying cause. This was reflected in such responses as 'drink and gamble', 'don't try', 'can't manage' and 'lazy'. In contrast to this, the reasons given for 'being well off' allowed for a greater element of chance. Although other reasons were also given, twelve respondents ascribed 'being well off' to either inheritance, winning the pools or other circumstances outside the individual's control. Ten respondents, however, did ascribe wealth to the result of hard work or abstemiousness, for example, 'don't drink', 'save', 'plan', 'have small families'.

The rationale behind such reasoning is understandable in the light of the limited opportunities in such a community. It is, however, significant that a relatively low status group holds such a derogatory opinion of the poor in our society.

Perception of the Local Community: Six of the eight members noted earlier as having no conception of any class structure similarly saw little or no variation in the local pattern of social differentiation. Any comment was confined to the immediate area of the club, for example, 'All houses round here are the same, it's a slum.' If they were aware of any difference it was between the 'good end' and the 'bad end' of the estate. (Kuper, 1953, p. 148.)

However, a vivid picture of the local community as they perceived it emerged from the responses of the majority of the members. The community was seen largely in terms of two groups of people: those who lived on the mining estate and those who lived in the adjoining areas of private housing. The council estate did not really fit into this scheme in any significant way. In the two cases where the council estate was mentioned respondents suggested that 'all estate people are likely to stick together.'

The dichotomy was expressed in several ways. Smaller families, tidy gardens, 'collar and tie' jobs were given as characteristics of people living in the private housing areas. However, these observed social differences were indicators of the major difference as perceived by the young people on the mining estate: social status. The high status of the people in the 'residential area' (as it was called locally) was felt to be self-ascribed, whereas the low status and stigma which attached itself to the mining estate was felt to be imposed upon the residents by this high status group. The following examples give an indication of how respondents expressed this: 'They look down on us', 'we have to look up to them', 'they run the estate down', 'they're snobbish and won't mix'. In sum, the relationship was seen to be one of power. It was, however, not a power relationship in the sense of one group giving orders and the other group obeying them. It was a power relationship in which one group was able to isolate another group socially and maintain the resulting relationship over a period of eighteen years. Evidence of this was reflected in such statements as 'we would mix if they would.' This structure had important implications for the estate people's self-conception and for their general aspirations. There was also evidence that local youth clubs were one of the mechanisms by which the social barriers within the community were maintained. (Allatt, 1973.)

Position of Family in the Local Community: Four of the twenty respondents described their families as respectable (that is, 'don't drink', 'clean', 'always go to work'). Twelve of the twenty saw them as helpful and friendly (as opposed to snobbish). Only one person said that his family was 'not like the rest on the estate' because his family 'had higher aims'. This respondent had a brother and a sister at Colleges of Education. Families who differed from the norms of the community were seen to fall into two categories. They were either improvident and neglectful of house and family, noisy and given to fighting, or they were 'stuck up' and 'kept themselves to themselves'.

General Aspirations: The most striking feature here was that of the twenty respondents, seventeen expressed a wish to move off the estate. This was also the hope of the parents for the child and gives some indication of the strength of the label attached to the estate. Eight members hoped for a better life than their parents' while a further eight were satisfied with their parents' standard of living and way of life, and had no desire to improve upon this. When asked what was important to them personally, seven expressed a clear concern with their present or future job. This ranged from getting O-levels to keeping or finding a job. In six cases parental aspirations for their children were limited to 'being happy'. It was interesting that several respondents made a distinction between training and education. They were prepared to undertake the former for a specific job (usually skilled manual work) but not the latter.
As in their perception of the wider society and local community, horizons were circumscribed. It would seem that this was, at least in part, affected by their special position in the local community. It could be argued that the stigma of the estate provided an incentive to raise their asperations, since moving off the estate almost amounted to an obsession; on the other hand it did not help those who stood no chance of ever owning their own home. While several respondents were not discontented with their position as low income 'ordinary' people, they did object to the low assessment accorded them by others. The social boundaries in the community severely circumscribed the opportunity for contact with different social groups and the possibility of extending experience. Such a finding is salutory in view of the youth service's expressed aim of extending the individual, both personally and socially, in just such an area as this.

Coronation Estate

The club served a deprived urban area: a council estate in an 'educational priority area' with a general atmosphere of poverty and neglect. Statistics privately available to us revealed that this particular estate had the lowest educational and occupational status in the borough and townspeople saw it as the most undesirable area in which to live. Thus in some ways, but by no means all, the situation approximated that of Colliery Bank. Consequently the focus of our interest was the extent to which the social perceptions and attitudes of the members of this club differed from the members of the club in the traditional working class community.

Perception of the Wider Society: Fifteen of the twenty respondents from this club had some notion, however limited, of a social structure in which groups of people stood in relationship to each other. Of these, eight gave money as the major differentiating feature and four gave occupation. Whatever the terminology used, respondents saw themselves in the category of the respectable, skilled and hard working. Taken in conjunction with the other data obtained, members placed themselves firmly in the ranks of the 'respectable' working class. It is interesting to note the amount of diffentiation which was perceived at the lower end of the status scale, in the category which is commonly recognized as working class. Again there was a clear awareness of a group which could be called 'the undeserving poor'.

These children of manual workers however, did not see themselves as members of a large powerless group but as being at some position with appropriate power in a hierarchical structure.

Negotiating the Structure: Thirteen respondents thought it was possible to move from one class to another: eight by saving and working hard, the remaining five by inheriting money, winning the pools or using personal influence. All respondents said they would try to 'get on', that it was a good thing — even relating it to instinct or the survival of the fittest. However, the methods were largely limited to such means as apprenticeship, hard work, saving or postponing the start of a family. Once again, getting on and social mobility were not synonymous. One could 'get on' and still remain in the same broad section of society and, indeed, this was often seen as desirable.

Reasons for wealth and poverty followed the same pattern as those supplied by members of the club on the mining estate. Thirteen respondents attributed wealth to non-personal factors, while nine gave 'hard work' and prudence and five 'a good job' as the major reasons. In contrast only five respondents mentioned any factors external to the individual as having any influence on poverty.

Perception of the Local Community: The key to understanding the
attitudes and perceptions of the members of this club was not solely
identifying where they lived, but also relating this to the manner in
which they described their own family. As mentioned above, the locality
in which the club was situated had a bad reputation. However, despite
the fact that the club's catchment area was small, membership was not
confined to the low status estate, although this did, in fact, detract from
the club's wider appeal. What appears to have happened is that members
were either from the 'respectable' families of the low status estate or
from the higher status council estate nearby.

Evidence of this appears in first, their perception of the local community and secondly the location of their own family within it. Again,
horizons were limited. The majority of the respondents could only
describe the immediate vicinity. However, they were fully conscious of
the respectable element in the low status estate as well as the relative
respectability of the council estate. This must now be related to the
desciptions of their families.

Position of Family in the Local Community: The importance of this
self-definition is shown by comparing the responses of this club with
those of the previous club on two variables: whereas the majority of the
members of Colliery Bank described themselves as friendly, the majority
of the members of Coronation Estate described themselves as respectable.

Differences between the clubs were also apparent in the manner in
which they described other families. Whereas the members of Colliery
Bank saw virtually no desirable traits in other families, members of
Coronation Estate club were less conscious of undesirable traits and
they also emphasised different traits. Personal traits included such
aspects of behaviour as 'nosey' and 'gossipy' while negative social traits
subsumed neglect of children, avoidance of work, etc. It was the latter
that the Coronation Estate members were most aware of. Respondents of
this club also recognized positive social traits, for example 'respectable',
'hardworking', whereas no positive traits were acknowledged by Colliery
Bank respondents.

General Aspirations: Although 'getting on' was important to all
respondents, aspirations were largely limited to having 'a decent standard
of living', 'owning a house', having 'a decent home' or being 'respectable'.
Eight respondents felt that happiness was very important. Advancement
at work was largely seen in terms of apprenticeship. Twelve respondents
wished to be better off than their parents, but in financial or personal
terms rather than social. This was indicated in such responses as 'a better
house', 'not to have to scrape' 'more money but content to live in the
same area as my parents'. Only one respondent said, 'my father was
content to stay as he was but I'm not.' (It was striking that nine respond-

ents hoped not to live in a council house.) Parental aspiration was limited in a similar manner. Within these limits all felt confident that hard work and determination would achieve such ends.

The analysis so far seems to suggest that while there were certain similarities in, for example, aspirations, there were also substantial differences in both the social perspectives and social awareness between the members of two apparently similar clubs

Colourview Rise

The club served a private housing estate on the outskirts of a prosperous Midland city. The impression was one of well kept detached and semi-detached housing. Residents tended to be either non-manual workers or 'affluent' manual workers from the local automobile plant. This led to the hypothesis that, for the members of this club, the perceived .differentiating feature of any class structure is money.

Perception of the Wider Society: Two thirds of the respondents from this club (fourteen out of twentyone) gave such items as money, standard of living and possessions rather than inheritance as the basis of the class structure. In contrast to Coronation Estate, noticeably less differentiation was perceived at the lower end of the status scale. Indeed, these respondents held a much simpler view of the class structure although several respondents were aware of the many graduations and of the difficulties in generalization. In three cases manual workers were clearly seen as part of the middle class. Social indicators cited as measures of income were housing, use of leisure, and speech. Unlike the previous two clubs, all respondents were aware of the term class although two refused to discuss it because they did not 'believe in a class system'.

Negotiating the Structure: Fourteen respondents felt that it was possible to change one's class. It is worth reproducing the comments of those who said it was not possible as they indicated an awareness of subtle aspects of social mobility:

'It is not possible to move because basically you always belong to the family in which you originate.' (This girl assessed herself as 'working class' although her father had recently become the owner and supervisor of a launderette).

'You can't quite change. Those on the perimeter may have money but they are not quite upper class because of the general attitudes.' (This boy perceived two classes, the 'Secondary Class' forming the larger part of society.)

'It is not possible to move because when people get to know you they can put you in a class and can gather your background. So they won't think of you as higher because your husband starts to earn more money.'

'Movement is possible but you're not always "accepted" by people in a higher class.'

Respondents saw this movement as possible through occupation and education (seventeen), by their own effort (eight) or by inheritance or personal contacts; five did not know. Eight people gave money or increased standard of living as a reason and nine felt that it was worth attempting for its own sake, or for personal development or a sense of achievement. All felt that hard work and education would bring this reward. The emphasis on education again differentiates this club from the two previous clubs.

All respondents felt that those who tried to get on were to be admired. The prevailing sentiment was that it was morally wrong to be too satisfied: one should always strive to improve oneself and one's condition. 'Getting on' was seen both as a testing of oneself and as being the basic purpose in life. Through this life would also become more enjoyable because of the rewards of money and prestige. However, one should not attempt to change one's class, even though, according to earlier statements, this was possible.

In comparison with the previous two clubs, there was a marked difference in attitude to the poor. While personal endeavour (eleven) and circumstances outside the individual's control (seventeen) were seen as contributory factors to being wealthy, a greater number of these respondents also gave external circumstances as a reason for poverty (personal failure: eighteen, external circumstances: thirteen). Circumstances beyond the individual's control included, for example, no ability, only low paid jobs available, and illness. It seemed that an increase in personal security tended to be related, in some cases at least, to a more sympathetic appreciation of the position of others in society.

Perception of the Local Community: It was striking that no general consensus emerged in their perception of the local community. All respondents were able to give a range of three to five areas which made up the local community but although the ranking of these areas was broadly similar, perceptions of them differed. While most agreed on the composition of the area of lowest status (poor, elderly, coloured and un-skilled) the description of the higher status areas showed least consensus.

The following comments on the high status area in which the club was situated illustrate this:

'Think they're better than anyone else, mainly office workers'
'Car assembly workers, but seem to have a lot of money'
'Two parts: well-to-do and working class'
'Many council houses'
'Not too many factory workers'
'More upper class'
'Mixture of jobs, mixture of statuses'
'Look down on others without reason'
'More money, managers of companies and shops'
'An old working class part and a new estate of expensive houses'

A second high status zone in the catchment area was described in a similarly conflicting way.

There are probably many complex reasons for this lack of consensus. Only two are offered here. First, both high status areas contained predominantly private housing. They had, however, working class housing either within or on their boundaries. Consequently respondents might have been assessing the area from different bases. Alternatively, the fact that well paid manual workers were moving into expensive housing in a formerly select, high status area, could lead to confusion and difficulty in making any assessment.

Family Position in the Local Community: None of these respondents placed themselves in the lowest status area in this community. Eight people described themselves as from a high status area or described their family as middle class families. Others described themselves as 'ordinary' but living in the high status area.

Descriptions of the respondent's own family showed a shift in emphasis when compared with the previous clubs. Whereas the emphasis in Colliery Bank had been on friendliness and in Coronation Estate on respectability, here the emphasis was on standard of living. Eight described themselves as comfortably off, one as having not much money, six as ordinary or average and four as sociable.

Eleven respondents also used the criterion of money when comparing other families with their own. The following examples indicate the tone of the responses:

'Some are worse off and some are better'
'They think they're superior because they have money and goods'
'They flash their money around'

One respondent described others as materialistic, three as unsociable, the remaining either did not know about others or said they were the same. It is interesting that no moral disapproval of those who did not work or were improvident was shown by respondents from this club.

General Aspirations: Thirteen respondents definitely wanted to be better off than their parents. They wanted a better education, a better job and financial security. However, a further six said that although they wished to be better off than their parents this was not necessarily in terms of income but in terms of job, for example, 'Similar to parents, who have their own house and a reasonable income, but I would like a better job than my father.' (Father was a track line worker in motor industry.) A similar phenomenon was noted in the Goldthorpe study (Goldthorpe *et al.,* 1969, p. 148).

Interestingly, these respondents were less sure of achieving this. Seven did not know, two felt life was unpredictable, five felt that determination and hard work were the key, three felt that life was already going that way and one that the aspirations were so moderate they were likely to be achieved. Of those who felt qualifications were necessary, two aspired to university and five to apprenticeships. It would seem that, despite a belief in the importance of education and desire for a better job than their parents, for the majority actual achievement was likely to be circumscribed.

The examination of the perceptions, attitudes and aspirations of members of this club confirmed the pattern often observed in other studies of affluent workers. It is of interest that this pattern was as applicable to the adolescent age group as it was to the adults in the other studies. The difference in attitude and breadth of horizon, compared with those prevailing in the working class clubs whose members were financially less secure, was significant. It is, however, important to point out that the members of this club did not live in close proximity to the 'undeserving poor' as did members of the earlier clubs; neither was their own status threatened by them.

Uptown Grammar

The club held its meetings in the boy's grammar school near the centre of the same Midlands borough as Coronation Estate. Membership was restricted to the fourth year and upwards of the boys' and the parallel girls' grammar schools. Because of the selective nature of the school, the club catchment area was wide. Consequently the immediate neighbourhood of the club did not have the same significance as in the previous cases. However, the fact that the schools and club were selective meant that it was possible to test the hypothesis that members of this club would hold a middle class view of society and the attitudes commonly associated with such a view.

Perception of the Wider Society: All respondents were able to define the term class in some way. Sixteen respondents gave money as the major differentiating feature. This is marginally higher than the responses from Colourview Rise. Of the remainder, three gave occupation and two social attributes such as dress and speech. In terms of the actual class structure, eight respondents saw the three conventional classes, upper, middle and lower. The division between lower or working and middle was that between manual and non-manual occupations. As measured by father's occupation, these respondents accurately located themselves in this structure. The people in the lowest class were seen by these respondents as those 'not having enough money', who 'might have factory or office jobs but did not want promotion', who 'had dirty jobs', and who 'just manage to scrape a living'.

The remaining respondents fell into two groups — those who saw a more and those who saw a less differentiated structure. The five respondents who perceived a less differentiated structure combined the middle and working classes and called this combined group either working class or middle class. Flanking this group they saw an elite and a lower or bottom class, the poor and unskilled. Respondents who saw an increased number of strata differentiated them along the whole range of the scale. Although able to give specific categories, several respondents were aware of 'a gradual blending' between the strata. Unlike the other respondents, they had been introduced to the concept of class at school and this might account for the increased ability both to define and to describe the phenomenon.

Negotiating the Structure: All respondents from this club felt that it was possible to change one's class. Only one thought that this was possible by winning money; the vast majority tended to mention the relationship between hard work, ability, education, better jobs and promotion. Several respondents made perceptive observations on the difficulty of being accepted by a higher class:

> 'Social contacts are important as well as determination and hard work.'

> 'It's easier if you are born in the middle class because you are in touch with the upper class socially and gradually begin to think as they do.'

Getting on was overwhelmingly approved (by seventeen respondents) although one observed that if there were no such thing as class one would not feel the need to try, an indication of an awareness of a relationship between 'getting on' and changes in social status. The fundamental reasons given for attempting to get on were that it was both natural and sensible to attempt to better oneself as this led to an increase in income, an interesting job and increased independence. Three respondents, however, tempered this attitude towards advancement:

> 'Wanted to live comfortably but not to be an executive and the job to dominate life'

> 'Not for economic gain but want to be a better person'

> 'The job must be interesting, it's not *just* the money that matters.'

Once more, examination of the reasons adduced for wealth or poverty threw interesting light upon attitudes, especially when considered in conjunction with those found in other clubs. Practically all respondents saw two avenues to wealth: hard work (seventeen), birth or inheritance (eighteen). Three respondents felt that winning the pools was one way and one respondent felt that the rich had only achieved their position at the expense of others. 'Personal endeavour' was stressed more here than in any of the other clubs. This finding is not unexpected in view of the special composition of this particular group.

    When the reasons given for poverty were examined this group showed a similar response to the members of Colourview Rise, the affluent

working class club. Twelve respondents mentioned personal failure such
as 'don't worry or try', or 'content as they are', while eleven mentioned
circumstances beyond the individual's control, for example, 'unlucky',
'no ability'. Four mentions were made of poor jobs because of the poor
qualifications. Thus this group was even less censorious of the poor than
the respondents from the affluent workers' club.

Perception of the Local Community: As selective nature of the school
meant that the club had a wide catchment area, there was no local
community as such and consequently no interplay between the
immediate neighbourhood and the club. This also meant that respondents
tended to see the community in more global terms and described the
major areas of the town rather than the area round the club.

The community was seen as a series of council estates and private
housing areas which all respondents were able to range in a status
hierarchy. There was quite a degree of consensus on the ranked position
of each area. In addition, areas were described in less emotive terms than
in the descriptions made by respondents of Coronation Estate, the club
in the same borough. Six people described a particular area as shabby;
eight used the terms dirty, rough, etc. and two said that a particular
area was 'coloured' and therefore undesirable.

Position of the Family in the Local Community: When asked to place
themselves, members of this club made one of three responses. Some
said they lived in a middle class area, were average middle class or lived
in 'a private snob area'. A second group said they lived in a low status
area but that they were different from the rest of the people living there,
For example, 'a detached house in a council house area' (father a
butcher), or 'we live on a huge housing estate of factory workers but we
are the sort of people you would find in [a high status area] ' (father a
doctor). Nine middle class respondents (as measured by father's
occupation) made such qualified statements. A third group of working
class respondents (four) gave some indication of their respectability or
difference from the rest:

'We are ordinary working class like the people where we live. We live
in a council house but have luxuries others don't have such as a car,
a caravan, and colour TV.

'We fit between the snobbish and the rough areas — in a well looked
after council house.'

When respondents were asked if other families differed from their own
and if so how, the predominant tone was one of neutrality. Approximately one third made comparisons in terms of money and a further

third thought other families were similar to their own. In a way this is surprising as these respondents were able to differentiate between social groups both in the wider social structure as well as the local one.

General Aspirations: When achievement and material benefits are combined, fourteen respondents gave either one or both of these as important to them. When parental and personal aspiration is examined, seventeen respondents mentioned college, university or some sort of qualification which would provide entry to a profession. The remaining three respondents were children of manual workers, one of whom wanted a trade like his father. The other two had no specific ambitions.

Respondents also felt that their assessment was realistic although they realized it was possible that plans could go wrong, for example, failing GCE. Overall, the dominating ethos was one of realistic assessment of life chances and knowledge of, or ability to conrol, the means by which this could be achieved. It will be seen later that this latter characteristic was evident in attitudes and behaviour of members in situations within the club.

Ambridge Green

Unlike the previous clubs, which were urban, this club was located in a rural setting. Ambridge Green served a scattered rural area characterized by valley and moorland farming, quarrying and a very limited range of agriculturally-based light industry. Our main interest here was whether or not there was any major difference in perception and attitudes of rural and urban club members.

Perception of the Wider Society: The majority of the respondents from this club had some conception of the social structure of the wider society. Two respondents, however, said that they did not believe in class or that there was no such thing, although it might be possible to categorize people according to others' opinions.

Ten respondents gave occupation as the major dimension along which individuals were classified. Many suggested a combination of money and occupation. The way in which group boundaries were perceived revealed interesting differences. Eight respondents saw society in terms of three classes: the central class, called variously, working, ordinary or middle, contained the body of people who had to work for a living. At the bottom of this structure there was a class of poor or unemployed and at the top the rich and the landed gentry. This view of the class structure is interesting in the light of the Goldthorpe-Lockwood studies of affluent workers who showed a tendency to perceive a similar structure. (Goldthorpe *et al* . 1967.)

A further group held a more differentiated view of the structure, this differentiation appearing in the middle range. Three respondents perceived two classes only. All respondents except these placed themselves near the centre of any spectrum. Taking their terminology into account, their self-ascribed position was realistic when compared with their father's occupation and their own where relevant.

Negotiating the Structure: Eighteen respondents felt that it was possible to change one's position in the class structure, two thought it impossible and two did not know. It is interesting that in this rural club hard work and marriage were suggested more frequently than any other method as means of negotiating the class structure.

While all respondents felt that it was laudable to try to get on, five said they were not going to try. However, of those who said they were content as they were, one was the daughter of a managing director. Another who said she had no intention of doing anything with the sole intention of raising her status was the daughter of a primary school head. One respondent said that he did not know whether or not he would try to get on. He would have 'liked to earn a bit more money' but expected that he would be a farmer all his life.

Of those who were going to try, three were considering some form of higher education or professional study. One intended eventually to run his own farm. The remaining respondents aspired to apprenticeships and advancement in a particular trade. Getting on was perceived as 'natural' and 'gave some purpose to life'. Once more these aims were seen to be achievable by hard work and determination.

The members of this club were more akin to the poor working class clubs in their beliefs about the reasons for poverty. While fifteen respondents mentioned personal failure (dirty, lazy, improvident) only six ascribed it to circumstances outside the individual's control (bad luck). Unemployment was also mentioned by two respondents. Again, reasons given for being 'well off' contained a greater element of chance. Sixteen respondents suggested inheritance or luck or both (inheritance: fourteen mentions, luck: four mentions). But thirteen respondents felt that hard work and prudence were also a means of achieving wealth.

Perception of the Local Community: Members of this club had a totally different perception of the neighbourhood than those of any other club. In fact as many as twelve respondents could only describe it in terms of its scenery or as a pleasant place in which to live. Two people described the nearby small towns in terms of their facilities. Four people saw the community as 'close knit', while only three people gave any slight indication of being aware of social differences.

This is possibly related to the perception of occupation as the major differentiating feature of the class structure. Those who, when talking about class, indicated an awareness of social status referred to it in a manner which suggested that they had met such social differentiation in places where strangers came into contact with each other — shops and pubs. A shop assistant said, 'You get all types of people coming in here. The upper class has more money and they look down on you.' Another member saw people as falling into two categories, 'Daddy's car' and 'farmer'. This finding would suggest either that the rural respondents have a more limited awareness of social differences or that, for them, the subject should have been approached in a different way.

Family Position in the Local Community: The responses to the questions on family seemed difficult if not impossible to categorize until we realized that these reflected the lack of any real sense of location in a social structure, the corollary of the descriptions of the community discussed above. When describing his or her own family, seven members said they were friendly, kind, or happy-go-lucky. This was the largest category. Moreover, when people attempted to describe other families, the responses were even more diverse, including 'same as mine', 'everybody is different' and 'got on better as a family'. These were interesting findings and in direct contrast with those from the urban clubs.

General Aspirations: A similar phenomenon was observed when general aspirations were examined. Friendship and happiness appear to be the two most important aspects of existence for several members of this club. It is difficult to make any comment on the other values and aspirations which are indicated in the tables, but it is interesting to note that no one suggested being better off than their parents and that while five showed an interest in money, this was qualified with such additional statements as 'not poor, but living within your means' and 'not too much but enough'. All felt that the aims were within their reach, which indeed, as they were so limited, was probably true.

In sum, of the five clubs studied, the rural club was unique. There was consensus neither in aspiration nor in perception of any social structure. Indeed, it would seem that sensitivity to social differences in terms of the class structure was markedly limited. Further, when attitudes and behaviour within the club were examined, the same phenomenon was apparent: the members of the rural club were characterized by their heterogeneity.

In the next chapter we go on to consider attitudes and behaviour in all the clubs we have examined here. Here we have undertaken the essential prelude to this task by building up a 'social profile' of the members — their beliefs, attitudes and values and above all their own role and situation in society. Arguably such information should preface any formulation of aims in any club or organization, certainly it must precede any consideration of the needs of members and of their response to what is provided. Any experienced youth worker will be aware of the value of this information in his day to day duties; it is of at least equal importance in research. Its utilization will be apparent in the following chapter.

Table 5.1 **Details of the sample**

Club	Sampling Frame	Sex Ratio		Sample	Responses	Total Responses	% Response Rate	
Colliery; Bank	50	59%B 41%G	16B 11G	27	13B 7G	20	74%	B: 3 in army G: 2 left district; 1 mentally retarded 1 unknown either at club or given address
Coronation Estate	54	62%B 38%G	16B* 10G	26	12B 8G	20	76.9%	B: 1 refusal; 1 left district; 2 left home untraceable G: 1 refusal; 1 left district
Ambridge Green	53	46%B 54%G	13B 12G	25	12B 11G	23	92%	B: 1 untraceable G: 1 refusal
Uptown Grammar	400**	60%B 40%G	13B 13G	26	10B 11G	21 21	80.7% 80	B: 2 left, no response when contacted; 1 refusal G: 2 no response when contacted
Colourview Rise	71***	57%B 43%G	17B 9G	26	13B 8G	21	80.7%	B: 1 refusal, 3 left district G: 1 refusal
Totals				130		105	81%	

*Coronation Estate: The sample was drawn from the members' list and the visitors' list. Of the 16 boys in the sample 10 were members and 6 were visitors. Of the 8 girls in the sample, 2 were on the visitors' list All non-responses were from the members' list.

**Uptown Grammar: The final sample was taken from one evening's attendance of 219

***Colourview Rise: This total was a combination of membership list (50) and guest list (21). They were only differentiated at the time the sample was drawn in order to ensure a representative sample.

Table 5.2   **The class structure as perceived by nine members of Colliery Bank Club**

High (teaching & typing) *Low (factory workers)	Top (Collar & tie) *Lower (labourer)	Lots of money Enough *Not enough	Stuck up Some mix *Mix	
High Middle (better jobs) *Working (us)	Gentry Bit richer Not so poor *Poor *Poor	Monarchy and titled Money *No money	Rich *Comfortable Poor	High *Medium Bottom

*Respondents self-ascribed position

Table 5.3 **The class structure as perceived by 15 members of Coronation Estate Club**

Higher (most money)	Rich	Higher	Higher	Gentry	Inherit	Upper (owners)
Middle	Manager Skilled worker	Middle (new council houses look after possessions)	Middle (take life as it comes)	Middle	Chauffeur driven	*Middle (nice council houses)
				*Working		Working (respectable)
*Working	*Unskilled workers who look after their houses	Lower (old council houses — some look after possessions)	*Lower (unskilled	Scroungers	More responsible jobs	Lower (on Benefit or factory workers)
					*Higher standard of living	Higher (private house)
					Bottom (2) Upper Middle	* Lower (slum)
Upper (good possessions)	Upper (bank manager)	Upper	Top (brag)	(Upper)		
Middle *(averge)	*Middle (workers with trades)	† Lower	Middle (work don't brag)	*Middle (normal)	*Working	
Lower (don't care)			Bottom (don't work)			

*Respondents' self ascribed class position

Figures in parenthesis above a model indicate the number of respondents who perceived the structure in this way

The line indicates the manual — non-manual distinction

† The respondent said there were two classes only. When asked to place himself, he saw himself as *between* them.

Table 5.4 **Respondents' description of their own families**

Club	Friendly	Respectable	Other	Total
Colliery Bank	12	4	4	20
Coronation Estate	3	13	4	20
TOTAL	15	17	8	40

Table 5.5 **Respondents' descriptions of other families**

| Club | Traits | | | | | | Total |
	Negative Personal Traits	Negative Social Traits	Positive Social Traits	"Stuck Up"	"Better Off"	Other	
Colliery Bank	8	6	0	3	1	2	20
Coronation Estate	0	10	6	0	3	1	20
TOTAL	8	16	6	3	4	3	40

Table 5.6 **The class structure as perceived by 18 members of Colourview Rise Club**

(3)		(3)	(2)		(2)
Upper Middle (well off) *Working	Higher Pretence ―― *Working Labouring	Upper *Middle (white collar) ―― Lower	Upper ―― *Middle Lower	Upper Middle ―― *Working Lower Working	Upper *Upper Middle ―― Middle (comfortable) but have to save for consumer durables Lower (dole)
Upper Middle)combined Working)	(2) Upper Middle (majority) ―― *(comfortable) Unskilled (lower)	Upper large *Secondary	Middle *Working		Upper *Middle Upper Middle Middle Lower Lower

*Respondents' self ascribed class position

Figures in parentheses above a model indicate the number of respondents who perceived the structure in this way.

The line indicates the manual — non-manual distinction.

Table 5.7 **What respondents from the Coronation Estate Club thought was important**

Response	No. times mentioned
Happiness	7
Standard of Living	7
Friends and Family	12
Education and Job	5

Table 5.8 The class structure as perceived by 21 members of Uptown Grammar Club

(9)
Upper
*Middle
—
Lower

Upper
*Upper middle
Lower middle
Working

Aristocracy
Upper middle
Lower middle
—
*Working
Bottom

Rich
Upper middle
*Middle
—
Working
Poor

Higher
Middle
(look down on council)
—
*Working
Slum

Rich
Nearly rich
*Quite well off
Poor

Upper
*Working (work)
Bottom (out of work)
(Father office job)

Upper
*Working
Lower

Upper
Middle
—
*Upper lower
Lower

Upper
Middle
—
Working
(Illness in council house)

Top
*Middle
(vast group)
Bottom

Upper
Middle
*Lower middle
Working

Top (rich)
*Middle
Working
(drink and bingo)
(Father foreman)

*Respondents self-ascribed class position
Figures in parenthesis above each model indicate the number of respondents who perceive the structure in this way
The line indicates the manual — non-manual distinction.

Table 5.9   **Comparison with other families by members of the Uptown Grammar School Club**

Response	No.
Others are the same	6
Others are better or worse off	5
Worse off	1
Better off	1
Unhappy	1
Different life style	4
Neglect children	2
Total	20

Table 5.10   **What members of the Uptown Grammar School Club considered important**

Response	No. times mentioned
Enjoyment	5
Achievement	8
Material benefits	7
Family and friendships	10
Happiness	2

Table 5.11 **The class structure as perceived by 19 members of Ambridge Green Club**

	(2)					
A. High Working (Factory Worker teachers) Unemployed	Upper Middle *(ordinary working people can afford to buy house not rent) Lower (unemployed)	Higher *Working Tramps	Better Off (money and jobs) *Middle Ordinary jobs Lower (unemployed)	Rich *Middle Ordinary working jobs Poor	Higher (well off) *Middle (between) Poor	Upper (more money directors look down again) *Middle Have to work for a living Lower poor jobs not much money
B. Upper (look down) *Working *Lower	Upper (landed gentry) *Ordinary (get on if possible) Working (not interested in getting on)	'Daddy s car type' *Farmers				
C. Rich Business *Working Unemployed	Upper *Middle/ Working	Money Top (pen pushers) *Average (everybody else trained) Lower (poor and don't work)	High salary Middle *Working	Upper (intelligent) Middle (little difference in intelligence but politically split)	Very rich *Middle (good jobs, save) Working Poor	Royal Family Upper (don't work) Professional (special jobs) Working (factory jobs) *(mixed)

Additional C column:

Very wealthy
*Slightly above average
Average
Poor

*Respondents' self ascribed class position
A,B,C. are the three types of structure perceived
Figures in parenthesis above a model indicate the number of respondents who perceive the structure in this way.

Table 5.12 **Means of negotiating the class structure as seen by members of the Ambridge Green Club**

Method	No. of respondents
Marriage	7
Hard work	7
Education	4
Better job	2
Inherit	1
Win the pools	1
Total	22

Table 5.13 **Description of respondents' own family by members of the Ambridge Green Club**

Response	No.
Friendly	7
Honest/hardworking	3
Average	3
Independent	1
Middle class	2
Working class	1
Poor	1
Total	18

Table 5.14   **Description of other people's families by members of the Ambridge Green Club**

Response	No.
Same as mine	3
Richer or Poorer	2
Envious	1
Too concerned with money	1
Unfriendly	1
Dissatisfied	1
Everybody is different	2
Hardworker	1
Stand-offish	1
Old fashioned	1
Get on better as a family	1
Total	15

Table 5.15 **What members of the Ambridge Green club considered important**

Item	No. of times Mentioned
Happiness	3
Interesting job	3
Interesting people	4
Honest people	1
Family	2
Friends	9
Marriage	1
Independence	1
Education	1
Not to be rich	1
Success	1
Snow at Christmas	1
Security	1
A bit of money	1

Table 5.16 **General Aspirations of members of the Ambridge Green Club**

Item	No. of times Mentioned
To be happy	3
Interesting job	4
Higher education	4
Married	5
Money, but not too rich	5
To be my own boss	2

6 Membership and participation

Membership and Participation

Earlier chapters have made it clear that with regard to both organization and objectives it has not been possible to present a tidy, consensus view of the Youth Service as a unitary organization. In the last chapter the analysis focused on the members themselves, rather than the organizations and providing bodies, and there was evidence of a diversity of social perspectives and attitudes even between groups which superficially appeared to be of a broadly similar kind.

In this chapter we explore behaviour and attitudes within the clubs themselves — those of both members and leaders — and here again find ourselves having to examine a situation which is characterized by diversity. No two clubs or organizations are alike, leaders vary widely in styles and may even see the development of their idiosyncracies as an important feature of their professional image.

The Bone and Ross Survey (1972) has mapped out in a most useful way a number of the areas of diversity to be found in the clubs, societies and the other groups that comprise the Youth Service. It has drawn attention to the disparity of success of various parts of the service in attracting adolescents from differing social backgrounds. It has suggested important differences between the degree of involvement of boys and girls and between older and younger adolescents. It has indicated the incidence of overlapping memberships and the variation in the 'holding power' of different activities in different areas of the service.

In our preliminary visits to clubs, societies and groups there were striking differences in what we found. One interesting difference which turned out to be symptomatic, was in the role of the committee. As we have seen the members' committee plays a central part in the official ideology of most of the providing bodies. It is here that an important part of the socialization into the values of the club is believed to take place, an arena in which democratic values can be both experienced and expressed. Adult workers within the clubs are regularly urged to institute committees and are called upon to demonstrate that they work. Yet in many of the units we visited, even those where participation of members in the all round life of the group was of a very high level, it was often the case that the committee was viewed with indifference, even apathy and, despite the repeated efforts of the leader, it played only a marginal part in the making of decisions. Real decision making was effectively taking place on the floor of the club where the leader, well tuned to the often incompletely articulated views of the members that reached him in the coffee-bar, in the games room and indeed in almost every part of the premises, would be responding quickly and almost intuitively to the messages he received.

It seemed that in many clubs there were at least two models of committee activity. On the one hand there was the 'official' view of the committee as a kind of round table in which each committee member was expected to present a contribution that he had achieved by careful thought and full consultation with his constituents in advance of the meeting. The other view that appeared to be commonly in the minds of many of the members seemed to be much more akin to a forum wherein the committee was seen as a vehicle for a leader to present his case, usually to be endorsed or, very occasionally, to be refuted.

There were a thousand other variations in practice. Within this kaleidoscope of activities it was clear that important social processes were taking place that it was essential to investigate. There was, above all else, the way in which members responded to the organization and the values it stood for. Even at a preliminary examination it was evident that these responses varied greatly. Some members were evidently deeply involved and committed; others appeared to be tolerant but possibly uncommitted; still others were ill at ease, even restive, yet clearly enjoying their participation in the activity or interest programme being offered. We also wanted to ask questions about what could be called the life cycle of membership of the various organizations. In most it was possible to see that there were recognized initiation procedures, rules for the achievement and recognition of full membership status and, equally important, routes that led to departure from the life of the group. All of these questions led us to want to consider the culture of the unit, its pattern of life, its territorial implications, its recruitment area and the message it transmitted about itself to its community. We wished to explore the central roles of the leaders and other adults in the working of the club and to learn something of their background, training and experience.

Not only were such questions interesting, the answers to them were necessary in order to achieve the objectives of our research. At this stage we reached a precisely similar conclusion to that which Bone and Ross (1972, p. 207) subsequently reported: 'Psychological theories and list of needs, whatever their theoretical status, are of little practical value in considering the effectiveness of services in meeting needs.' Like Bone

and Ross we accepted the argument of Goldthorpe *et al*. (1970 p.178):
'What is in fact of major interest is the variation in the ways in which
groups differently located in the social structure actually experience
and attempt to meet the needs which at a different level of analysis
may be attributed to them all.' The tables at the end of the chapter
present the data we obtained.

Membership patterns

It will be recalled that the clubs were selected according to differences
in the type of community setting or, in the case of Uptown Grammar,
because of special characteristics of the members. These differences were
taken as indicative of differences of location in the social structure and
proved fruitful in the analysis of the social perspectives of members.

It was, however, necessary to examine the clubs in more objective
terms. In the first place it was important to have a more objective
measure of club type. Secondly, it was a means of establishing the
relative social status of each club. Consequently two other social
variables were examined: the occupational status of the member's father
and the member's intended or actual age of leaving school. We then
considered the alternative clubs available.

Social status of members

The occupation of the head of the household is frequently used as an
indicator of social status. Our data showed that there were marked
differences in this respect between the clubs. Over three quarters of the
sample of the Uptown Grammar club had fathers in non-manual
occupations and of these 38% (six out of sixteen) were in professional,
managerial or higher grade non-manual jobs.[1] In contrast, the Coronation
Estate and Colliery Bank clubs were predominantly attended by young
people from homes where the father was a manual worker — the majority
semi-skilled. Broadly speaking, the higher the status of the club, the
higher was the occupational grade of members' fathers.

But the father's occupational status, although often closely related to
a child's, is not necessarily the sole determinant of a young person's
future social status. To gain some measure of the prospective social status
of the sample, members were asked when they had left school or
intended to leave. Their replies suggest that the Ambridge Green club is
heterogeneous in social composition since approximately two thirds of
the members indicate they will leave (or have left) school at fifteen while

---

[1] Using the scale from Hall and Jones (1950).

one third of the members will stay in full-time education until they are eighteen or over.

The data also indicate an interesting situation in the Colourview Rise club. While only 14% of the sample intend leaving school at the earliest opportunity and 29% intend staying in full-time education until they are 18 or over, over half the sample intend to have one extra year of education, that is they have educational aspirations but these are circumscribed. The educational aspiration of the members of the other clubs follows the expected pattern in that it appears to be related to the occupational status of members' fathers.

In conclusion then, the rank ordering of the clubs by social status follows approximately the same pattern when measured in terms of fathers' occupation and duration of education. This ranking provided further insight into the behaviour and attitudes in the members of the clubs.

Alternative Clubs

The stated aims of the Youth Service, when analysed, indicated an emphasis on the pursuit of worthwhile activities. This was especially true of the statutory sector. There is, however, considerable evidence of a relationship between the social status of an individual and the degree and kind of formal leisure time pursuits. This relationship has been demonstrated in the case of adults and of young people. (MacDonald *et al.*, 1949; Goldhammer, 1942; and Bottomore, 1954, p. 368). In broad terms, the middle class join more clubs, which are in addition more likely to be activity centred, than do members of the working class. The work of Goldthorpe also suggests that the affluent worker might display instrumental attitudes towards, for example, trade unionism, and see the union more as a service organisation than as a central interest in their lives. (Goldthorpe *et al.*, 1969, p. 170.) It was emphasized here that the children of these workers would display an instrumental attitude towards youth club facilities. Yet although in the present study social status was an important consideration, the type of club was the major focus. We therefore hypothesized that the degree of activity was related not only to social status but also to type of club.

The clubs were examined first for the extent to which their members belonged to other clubs and organizations and, secondly, as regards the type of other clubs and organizations attended. It was important as a prelude to establish the availability of other facilities in the area. The major part of the sample (86%) considered other clubs and organizations to be available. Such opportunity was not perceived significantly differently by the members of the different clubs.

The sample was then examined to establish the extent of membership of the other clubs and organizations. As was hypothesized, the results revealed a marked difference between clubs at the social status extremes. There is also, however, a notable difference between different types of working class club, Colliery Bank recording much lower multiple membership than Coronation Estate and Colourview Rise.

There are other points of interest. First, 50% of all respondents went along to other clubs or organizations. Secondly, although the middle class club (Uptown Grammar) and the club in the 'educational priority area' (Coronation Estate) are in the same borough, there was a marked difference in the average number of clubs attended (2.48 and 1.9 respectively). An examination of the raw data indicates that these differences are not merely due to the activities of one or two individuals. The difference remains evident when the data are grouped to show the percentage of members attending other clubs.

These scores might be explained by the greater opportunity for other activities provided by the school to which the middle class club was attached, or to differences in income and spending power. However, consideration of income and spending money suggests that there are no great variations between the clubs. If anything, the members of the middle class club have perhaps the lowest personal income.

A wide range of other organizations and clubs had been named by the respondents. These were classified according to whether or not they were social clubs for young people, social clubs for adults or uniformed and interest groups. It was hypothesised that differences between the clubs would be reflected most clearly in membership of interest and uniformed groups. Though the data are crude the pattern that emerges lends support to the hypothesis that the middle class club members show a predominance of interest type activities while members of the remaining clubs have a much lower score. Two interesting observations can be made. There is more activity in adult or commercial clubs among members of the 'affluent' club than in the others. Secondly, only one respondent (from the middle class club) was a member of a uniformed organization.

At this age young people are commonly supposed to be 'widening their horizons', trying different clubs and interests, meeting new people. As a measure of this, respondents were asked what clubs or organizations they had 'tried' and left. Of the total sample 63% had tried other clubs and organizations at some stage and subsequently left. The most striking figure is that for the Colourview Rise club. All except one member had tried other clubs and left them. The Colliery Bank club produced the lowest score. The data here are limited but they suggest that members of middle class clubs tend to leave clubs of a social nature, while members of working class clubs, especially in the 'affluent' workers' area tend to leave interest clubs and uniformed organizations.

It appears that the degree of participation varies according to the social status of the club. This was especially marked in the case of

Uptown Grammar and Colliery Bank, whose members had both tried and
joined fewer clubs. Again, when the type of organization joined is considered, the higher the status of the club the more likely are members to
join interest groups. Colourview Rise club is of particular interest because
of its memberships' high participation in adult social and commercial
clubs and low membership of other youth clubs. In the present case,
the actual opportunity to join interest and activity groups is no doubt
related to membership of a high status school, and this very fact is of
considerable interest not only when the aims of the Youth Service are
taken into account but, more importantly, when it is considered in
conjunction with the particular social group at which much of the
service is directed: the group whose members do not continue in
full-time education beyond the statutory leaving age.

Club Territories

So far we have indicated a number of differences in the characteristics
of the clubs and their members in their different social locations. Before
we proceed further, however, it is important to explore the extent to
which club membership comes from the area in which the club is
situated. Not only can knowledge of each club's catchment area provide
a further measure of social homogeneity or heterogeneity but it can also,
by implication, measure the breadth of narrowness of the experiences
possible within each club. The way 'territory' is defined is also an
important determinant of the culture of the club. A number of writers
have drawn attention to the increasing loyalty and adherence to clubs
and groups whose boundaries are tightly and exclusively drawn,
particularly if this is associated with a competitive 'border dispute'
with similar groups outside the frontier. (Patrick, 1973.)

As would be expected, the rural club drew from a fairly wide area.
Furthermore, 90% of the respondents in the Uptown Grammar Club
came from distances of over half a mile due, no doubt, to the fact that
this was a club attached to a selective grammar school. It is of interest,
however, that the two clubs of lowest social status drew their members
from an extremely small radius; indeed the respondents in the traditional
working class club all lived within a quarter of a mile of the club. Even
the 'affluent workers' club, Colourview Rise, drew 67% of its sample
members from within half a mile of the club.

Exactly how tightly drawn these boundaries are is problematic. A
related study, however, throws some light on the situation. (Allatt, 1973.)
The Colliery Bank area in which the traditional working class club was
situated was part of a large community made up of several housing areas
of varying status. In the area of highest status there was a second youth
club, not part of our study. It was found that the two clubs had tightly
drawn boundaries which were related to the status of the area in which

each was situated. Secondly, the perception of these boundaries increased with age. Twelve year old children were more aware of them than eight year olds; high status parents were still more acutely aware of them. Thirdly, lower social status adults who rejected the low status club tended, if they sought alternative Youth Service and similar facilities, to look outside the community rather than look to the high status club, whilst high status adults increasingly gave preference to the high status club within their community. In sum, the clubs both reinforced and perpetuated the social status and social interaction patterns of the adult community — a finding which lends support to those of Elias and Scotson (1965, p. 129) and which underlines the importance of an intimate knowledge of a community before such decisions as for example, location of clubs are taken.

Forms of Participation

It will be recalled that the clubs selected were predominantly social clubs. We hypothesized, however, that the differences in their social contexts would be related to differences in activity and expectations within the clubs. In an attempt to explore this relationship the following areas were examined: committee participation, self-originating groups within the club and loyalty to the club.

The Club Committee

Democratic representation is a strongly held tenet of Youth Service philosophy. Our examination of the structure of the service has demonstrated the extent to which this is an inherent part of the organization; the presence of a member's committee is seen to be an important aspect of social education.

The kind of committee procedure envisaged by many of the youth organizations is that described at the beginning of this chapter — the round table in which each member is expected to present a contribution that he has achieved by careful thought and full consultation. Committee membership of this kind is widely considered to be a 'middle class' activity (Bottomore, 1954). Although the extent to which this may be true for young people is not known, it has been observed that many youth leaders find club committees difficult to maintain. In clubs of mixed social class, the committee is often dominated by young people with middle class parents, while leaders of other clubs have wished for a larger middle class membership to vitalise or even form a committee.

As far as our data permitted, two relationships were examined: the relationship between social class and committee membership and the relationship between different types of clubs and committee membership. Respondents were first asked whether or not their club had a committee. (All clubs in fact had a committee though in the case of Colliery Bank this was an adult committee with member representation.) Of the total sample, 87% said their club had a committee. Of the 13% which reported no committee, the majority were in the Colliery Bank and Coronation Estate clubs. Respondents were then asked if they were either on the committee or would like to be on it. Of the 94 who responded, 34% were either on the committee or wished to be on it. The majority (66%) had no desire to be on a committee. The reasons most often given for not wanting to be on the committee were 'don't want the responsibility' or 'not interested'.

When the clubs are examined individually, however, the results are not as would be expected from earlier findings. In the traditional working class club the percentage of members wishing to be on the committee is higher than would be expected and indeed this club showed the highest percentage of all the clubs. However, apart from this the other clubs follow the hypothesized ranking order with Uptown Grammar next, and Coronation Estate scoring the lowest percentage.

The data were then examined for any relationship between the social status of the individual and committee membership within the clubs. Overall, 30% of the children of manual workers and 40% of the children of non-manual workers showed interest in the club committee. However, when the position within the club was examined, it appeared that in the predominantly middle class club, Uptown Grammar, no children of manual workers were either on the committee or wished to be on it. This was also reflected, to some extent, in Colourview Rise. When the attitudes of the members of the traditional working class club (Colliery Bank) and the club in the culturally deprived area (Coronation Estate) are considered together the picture is strikingly different. Though their social composition is similar, 50% in the traditional working class area as opposed to 21% in the deprived area would like to be on the committee. The latter follows the expected pattern, the former is markedly different. It is difficult to suggest reasons for this but the local significance of the branch committee of the National Union of Mineworkers, particularly at the time of the survey when a major national strike was taking place, may have some importance.

The results of the section may be summarized as follows: over two thirds of the total sample showed no interest in the club committee. In middle class clubs no working class members showed interest in being a committee member. In rural clubs few middle class members were interested in being a committee member. There were observed differences between the working class clubs. The club in the deprived area followed the expected pattern but the traditional working class club showed a high interest in committee membership. Again it will be noted that, though clear trends emerge, they are overlaid with a diversity

that has always characterized the working of all parts of the Youth
Service.

Self-Originating Groups

Youth leaders themselves often expect to frame the programme for the
young, and to coax them into support of activities already decided. If
they find that this does not work, they may then allow members to
enjoy the purely social activities of the club without strings attached.
This too can lead to dusty boredom. The middle way, to encourage
groups of friends to work out their own programme within the shelter
of the club, can help to create the new spirit needed. *(Albemarle,
1960.)*

Ought not the club to be thought of . . . as the centre within which
small groups can find their own enthusiasms and from which they can
be encouraged and aided to develop into self-programming groups?
(Albemarle, 1960.)

Although in many branches of the service the maintenance of
representative members' committees proved difficult it was often
acknowledged that self-programming groups frequently emerged. Such
groups, however, tended to be interested in short term projects
originating from their own interests and ideas. On completion of the
project, while possibly remaining as a friendship group, the group as an
organized group ceased to exist. Meanwhile another group with another
project emerged in some other part of the friendship network. The social
structure of the club could be conceived as a network with different
'nodes' of the net coming into prominence at different points in time,
the whole a series of undulating, crosscutting ties.

Because of the lack of continuity of involvement of any one particular
group, certain leaders tended either to overlook these self-originating
groups or considered them to be of less significance than long standing
groups (if such existed) which were involved in recognized activities or
committee membership. It would seem, however, that the presence of
such short term self-originating groups could be an important aspect of
club life. With these considerations in mind two questions were asked:
did members ever organize things 'off their own bat' and, if yes, how
successful were these activities?

In the first place the results gave some measure of the awareness on
the part of the members of what was happening within their club. It is
interesting to note that in no case was there unanimity on the presence
or absence of the kind of group activity under consideration. The clubs
which showed most consensus were those of Uptown Grammar (71%).
Ambridge Green (83%) and Colliery Bank (85%). Significantly there was

greatest awareness of initiative in the middle class club. (It should be mentioned here that respondents were not asking how many times such activities had taken place since our preliminary enquiries showed they found this extremely difficult to estimate.) The two clubs in which there was least consensus on the presence or absence of self-originating groups were those with the greatest number of 'visitors', that is where people were allowed to drop in: Colourview Rise and Coronation Estate. In these two clubs roughly half thought there were such groups and half denied their existence. This aspect of a club, that is the ratio of 'visitors' to regular members, appears to have important consequences for the social structure of the club. Awareness of the kind of activity taking place in the club, is one indicator of the extent of the club's communication channels and their corollary, the social structure.

The data was next examined to gain some estimate of the success rate of self-organizing activity. Because of the low numbers involved caution must be used in interpreting these results. They are, however, suggestive in several ways. With one exception, whatever the type of club in which self-originating groups emerged the majority of respondents in that club thought the groups were usually successful. The exception was the Colliery Bank club. In this club few people were aware of any such groups and apparently such activity as there was usually failed in the estimation of the respondent. Once more it is interesting to note that whereas the responses in the Coronation Estate club and Colourview Rise club were more consistent in their responses.

This lends further support to the suggestion that within these particular clubs there was greater involvement on the part of those attending them, with consequent differences in communication patterns and social structure. The importance of the relationship between channels of communication and social structure has been noted in other studies (Elias and Scotson, 1965, p.89).

When the size of each club is considered, the largest club (Uptown Grammar) was one of the clubs which displayed a high degree of consensus. We therefore considered it legitimate in this case to discount the influence of size as such. It should, however, also be pointed out that because this was a school club members had more opportunity for contact and consequent dispersion of information about the club during non-club time. It should also be stressed that although the perceived success rate was highest for this middle class club (87%) there was not a great difference (with the one exception already noted) between this and the other clubs, the lowest being 75%.

Our findings may be summarized as follows: in some clubs there was greater awareness of the presence or absence of such groups which suggested differences in structure and communication patterns related to the 'open' or 'closed' nature of the clubs. Yet it would seem that the cohesiveness of a club is not necessarily related to the existence of self-organizing groups. Three important points emerge from the analysis. First, the middle class club (Uptown Grammar) appeared to be more oriented towards this kind of activity. Secondly, if such groups emerged in any club there was a tendency for them to be successful. Finally, it is of interest to note that the apparent absence of such groups was most pronounced in the traditional working class club and the rural club.

Loyalty

The content analysis presented in an earlier chapter drew attention to the importance of club loyalty and commitment as an objective of the Youth Service. Following the work of Goldthorpe and Lockwood (1968, pp. 118-21, 149-56), we hypothesized that respondents would display different attitudes towards the club depending upon the social context of the particular club. The following hypotheses were also constructed as a means of exploring this area:

1. Members of the working class clubs (especially the Colliery Bank 'traditional' working class area club) would show loyalty to friends rather than the club.

2. Members of the Uptown Grammar and Ambridge Green clubs would show loyalty and a sense of responsibility towards their club.

3. Members of the Colourview Rise club would show an instrumental attitude — that is they would tend to use the club and its facilities as an end in itself rather than as part of a commitment to the club.

As a measure of their loyalty, respondents were asked how they would react, first if a friend were barred for serious misdemeanour and, secondly, if banned for a reason the respondent considered unfair.

In response to the first question, 'Would you leave the club or stay if a friend was banned for a serious misbehaviour?' the overwhelming majority of the 91 who responded said they would stay (90%). This appeared to be unrelated to the type of club or status of the club. The reasons given for this were of two kinds which, for the purpose of this study, have been labelled as responsible or instrumental. The responsibility category included such items as 'it would encourage him if I gave him support'. The instrumental type of answer is epitomized by the response 'It's no concern of mine.' The usual reason for leaving was that the respondent was committed to the friend but this, in fact, applied to very few respondents.

However, when the reasons for staying were examined, certain differences between the clubs emerged. Broadly, the three clubs of the highest social status tended to give a more 'responsible' reply, while the two clubs with the lowest social status tended to give an instrumental response.

Within this analysis a further distinction emerged: proportionately more members of the rural club adopted a responsible attitude than those in any of the others. This is an interesting finding when considered with the content analysis of Chapter 4. This was a voluntary club and the analysis indicated the marked emphasis on club loyalty in voluntary organizations. It is of further interest when the social perspectives and attitudes of members of this club are taken into account.

In contrast to this the hypothesized solidarity of Colliery Bank, the traditional working class club, was not evidenced. Proportionately more members of this club demonstrated an instrumental attitude than the members of Colourview Rise, the 'affluent workers' club. In fact the members of Colourview Rise showed a marginally more responsible attitude than Uptown Grammar. This was unexpected.

Respondents were then asked what their reaction would be to a friend being banned for a reason they considered unfair. Although with a smaller percentage, the majority of respondents (59%) said they would stay. In this case, however, with the exception of the middle class club which showed an overwhelming tendency to stay, the situation within the clubs is more ambivalent.

To explore the situation further, two additional questions were introduced: If the banning were considered unfair would the respondent make some kind of protest and, if so, what form would this protest take. The responses were illuminating. Of all respondents 61% felt they would make some form of protest at what they considered to be unfair treatment. However, although the figures are small, the data suggest certain differences between the clubs in the form the protest would take.

Only six out of a total of 64 respondents said they would leave the club permanently, four of these, however, were members of the rural club. The rural club in fact is notable in that the full range of possible attitudes appears to be more represented here than in the other clubs. In Ambridge Green 40% would leave in support of their friends; 33% would stay and query the decision; and 27% would stay because they felt the matter was no concern of theirs. The lack of social awareness and the diversity of responses which was revealed in the analysis of the previous chapter would seem to be related to the situation found here. When the other clubs are examined, the Uptown Grammar club clearly stands out as one where members articulate their friends' case while remaining within the club. Interestingly, in terms of actual numbers and percentage of those in the club who make this sort of protest, the 'affluent' club. Colourview Rise, ranks next. The figures from the club in the 'educational priority area', Coronation Estate, are too small to allow any real comparison but the numbers likely to take each kind of action in the traditional working class area club, Colliery Bank, suggest that there is a certain ambivalence between the two modes. Members here are more inclined to leave than are members of the club in the deprived urban area. This suggests that there is a particular kind of solidarity within the traditional working class club, although its effectiveness for the reinstatement of a friend is open to question. Again the responses of the clubs can be related to their social perspectives. While members of the middle class and affluent worker clubs attempt to alter the situation, members of the traditional working class club tend merely to respond to it.

In sum, few (10%) of those responding would have supported their friends against the club in cases of serious misbehaviour. Reasons for this lack of support, however, varied between clubs. The rural club, Ambridge Green, was the highest on 'responsibility' and lowest on 'instrumental' attitudes. Among the other clubs there was a tendency towards a 'responsible' attitude amongst the higher status clubs (Uptown Grammar and Colourview Rise) and a tendency towards an 'instrumental' attitude on the part of the two lower status working class clubs (Coronation Estate and Colliery Bank).

If treatment of a friend were considered unfair, respondents indicated they were more likely to leave temporarily or make some form of protest while remaining with the club. Again differences emerged between clubs. Members most likely to protest belong to Uptown Grammar, Colourview Rise and Colliery Bank clubs. When examined according to the way protest was made, the two former clubs contained the highest proportion of members who would express the case to leaders through a members' committee. This was especially true of the middle class club. Thus the traditional working class club was less 'solidaristic' than hypothesized and the affluent working class club less instrumental. The rural club showed a sense of responsibility, concern about friends and a low tendency to express grievances with authority. In all cases any loyalty was to friends rather than the abstraction of the club.

To sum up the evidence that has been presented in this chapter so far, important differences emerged in the character of membership and participation in the five clubs under scrutiny. There differences are related to the social context of each club — to the social status of the community from which most of its members are drawn. Membership of other organizations was related in both type and extent to social status and type of club. The lower the status of the club, the narrower the experience in formal leisure time pursuits. Members of the 'affluent' club were exceptional in their attendance of adult social organizations.

There was evidence that clubs had both social and geographical boundaries. These, in turn, set boundaries on the type and extent of social intercourse experienced within the clubs. The youth clubs appeared to reinforce and perpetuate the social status patterns of the adult community.

Over two-thirds of the sample showed no interest in formal committee membership. With the exception of the traditional working class club, any such interest was largely related to the social status of the club. Within the middle class club no one from a working class home showed interest in committee membership.

Although they appeared predominantly in high status clubs, where self-originating groups emerged they had a likelihood of success. The degree of consensus on whether or not they existed suggests that clubs differ in the density of their social structure and communication pattern. This is probably related to the 'closed' or 'open' nature of the clubs. Clubs which encourage 'visitors' are not likely to be as cohesive. This factor differentiated the middle class club, the rural club and the traditional working class club ('closed groups') from the 'affluent' and 'deprived' working class clubs ('open groups'). It should be noted that the closed or open nature of a club is not necessarily intentional. It may be the unintended consequence of a club's geographical position or social attributes.

Club members did not condone serious misbehaviour but the reasons for this varied between clubs. The three clubs of highest status tended to demonstrate a 'responsible' attitude while the two clubs of lowest status showed an attitude of non-involvement. If a friend was considered unjustly treated, behaviour differed according to the type of club. Some form of protest was most likely to be made by the middle class, affluent and traditional working class clubs. However, once again, the form the protest took differed, members of the two higher status clubs tending to stay and present the case. Where members felt 'a sense of loyalty' this appeared to be to friends rather than the club.

Profiles of the Members

Even though this chapter has reported on part of our 'micro' study it has still not contained specific details of individual members of the clubs. The reasons for this are clearly evident. Any survey that attempts to offer an analysis of the results of a sample population of over 100 people can only utilize the evidence of general characteristics that emerge. Only in this way can the data remain representative and allows the results obtained from the sample to be extended back to the whole large population from which it was drawn. To discuss in detail any individual responses from the enquiry would not only be statistically unsound it would also invoke, in part, a breach of the confidentiality we guaranteed to members of the clubs.

Yet, notwithstanding these limitations, the perceptive reader will have already begun to build up a composite picture of the members of the clubs and to see several 'typical' club members emerging. It may be helpful to facilitate this process and suggest several models of membership and response. It is important to emphasize that in doing this we shall in no way be describing any individual members. The models are in fact 'ideal types' — to which are attributed a range of personal characteristics that in whole or in part tend to be found in individual members. In real life no such members actually exist. Like the service itself, members are too individualistic, too disparate, too idiosyncratic to exist in pure and simple categories. But we will commence by constructing two such models — the *committed* member and *non-committed* member.

Sybil, the *committed* member has been sighted in a number of the tables. She is likely to have been a member for two years or longer and to attend the club at least once a week. Not only will she be aware of the committee, she will probably be a member or at least willing to serve on it. She may or may not be a member of a self-programming group but it is quite possible that she has played a part in one — even that she was caught up in the club by such a group initially and stayed on when the group had achieved its short term goals. She is likely to display considerable loyalty to the club and what it stands for, standing up for it even against her friends if the occasion arises. Even though the club may, in her view, have been in error she will attempt to put matters right inside the club. Overall, her attitude will be one of identification with the club; the facilities and opportunities provided by the club will be, for her, a means to involvement rather than an end in themselves. She is more likely to be a middle class girl in a middle class club but this is by no means essential.

Kevin, one of the far more numerous *non-committed* members, may share many of Sybil's characteristics though he is less likely to have been a member of the club for so long or to attend so regularly. But his attitude to the committee is different. He may claim no knowledge of it, he is unlikely to be a member of it or to have any desire to join it. What the club stands for, its values and purposes, are not of particular interest to him. This is not to say he is hostile to them — he may be prepared to go along with them without protest and join in prayers or club duties or, in a cadet corps, participate in parades and inspections and take at least sufficient care in the wearing of his uniform. But he accepts such things — or at least allows them to happen — as part of the price he pays for the chance to participate in the activity or interest programme or the social opportunities the club affords. He would prefer not to be put to the test of a choice of loyalty between the club and his friends and would probably find an 'out'. But if the issue was forced upon him he would be as likely to leave, at least for a time, as to stay. Overall his attitude to the club is instrumental, but once a member he would not relinquish the advantages lightly. He is more likely (but by no means essentially) to be a working class member of a working class club.

But in certain circumstances Kevin can turn into Terry, the *alienated* member. We know less about him because he has left or is in the process of leaving during every survey, and his picture, because it is painted by those who remember him and his participation, is incomplete. But eventually he is the member on whom the club's values have begun to bear heavily — entailing a compliance that he is no longer willing to make, a boredom he is no longer prepared to suffer, or an incursion on his freedom that is no longer tolerable despite the instrumental advantages offered in return. At a certain point he rejects the implicit contract of membership either passively through non-attendance or actively through disruptive behaviour or vandalism or more subtle forms of 'aggro' directed at the leader and the committee members.

Having identified three 'ideal types' of member from behind the statistical tables it is important to remember not only that they are not to be found in pure form in real life but also that there are elements of all three — and much more — in every member. No member is devoid of instrumental attitudes to his club or organization, otherwise he could hold no more than a very abstract commitment to it. No member is totally lacking in commitment and this is especially noticeable if his unit is 'threatened' by outsiders with a conflicting commitment. And, of course, one of the central but unspoken beliefs of the service is that, in the end, every member must and should experience some form of disengagement from the Youth Service as he reaches more mature years and takes on different roles in adult society.

Table 6.1   **Occupation of father**

| Club | Occupation of Father | | | | | |
| | Non-Manual | | Manual | | Total | |
	No.	%	No.	%	No.	%
Uptown Grammar	16	76	5	24	21	100
Ambridge Green	13	57	10	43	23	100
Colourview Rise	9	43	12	57	21	100
Coronation Estate	3	15	17	85	20	100
Colliery Bank	1	5	19	95	20	100
Total	42	40	63	60	105	100

Table 6.2   **Father's occupational grade**

| Club | Occupational Grade | | | | | | | | |
	Professional	Managerial/ Executive	Non-Manual Higher Grade	Non-Manual Lower Grade	Non-Manual Routine	Skilled Manual	Semi-Skilled Manual	Routine Manual	Total
Uptown Grammar	3	2	1	5	5	5	0	0	21
Ambridge Green	1	3	1	0	2	7	9	0	23
Colourview Rise	0	0	5	3	1	9	2	1	21
Coronation Estate	0	0	0	3	0	4	8	5	20
Colliery Bank	0	0	0	1	0	3	16	0	20
Total	4	5	7	12	8	28	35	6	105

Table 6.3 **Age of leaving school or intended leaving**

Club	Age 15		16		17		18 or over		Don't know		Total	
	No.	%	No.	%	No.	%	No.	%	No.	%	No.	%
Uptown Grammar	0	0	1	5	6	28	10	48	4	19	21	100
Ambridge Green	14	61	1	4.5	1	4.5	7	30	0	0	23	100
Colourview Rise	3	14	11	52	0	0	6	29	1	5	21	100
Coronation Estate	14	70	6	30	0	0	0	0	0	0	20	100
Colliery Bank	14	70	5	25	0	0	1	5	0	0	20	100
Total	45	43	24	23	7	6	24	23	5	5	105	100

Table 6.4 **Club members who considered other clubs, organizations and groups to be available in the area**

Club	Facilities Other facilities considered available		No other facilities considered available		Total	
	No	%	No.	%	No.	%
Uptown Grammar	20	95	1	5	21	100
Ambridge Green	21	91	2	9	23	100
Colourview Rise	16	76	5	24	21	100
Coronation Estate	17	85	3	15	20	100
Colliery Bank	16	80	4	20	20	100
Total	90	86	15	14	105	100

Table 6.5 **Number of clubs attended including the present club**

Club	Clubs attended						No. Respondents
	1	2	3	4	5	6	
Uptown Grammar	8	3	5	2	3	0	21
Ambridge Green	8	8	5	0	0	2	23
Colourview Rise	12	2	5	1	1	0	21
Coronation Estate	9	6	4	1	0	0	20
Colliery Bank	16	2	2	0	0	0	20

Table 6.6 **Incidence of multiple membership**

Club	Membership This club only		Other clubs and organizations		No respondents	
	No.	%	No.	%	No.	%
Uptown Grammar	8	38	13	62	21	100
Ambridge Green	8	35	15	65	23	100
Colourview Rise	12	57	9	43	21	100
Coronation Estate	9	45	11	55	20	100
Colliery Bank	16	80	4	20	20	100
Total	53	50	52	50	105	100

Table 6.7 **Standardized club scores from table 6.5**

Club	Raw Score	Standard score (Average)	x 10
Uptown Grammar	52	2.48	25
Ambridge Green	51	2.22	22
Colourview Rise	40	1.9	19
Coronation Estate	37	1.9	19
Colliery Bank	26	1.3	13

Table 6.8 **Income of members in full-time employment**

Club	Income Over £14.50		£9.50-£14.50		£6.50-£9.50		Under £6.50		No Response		Total	
	No.	%	No.	%	No.	%	No.	%	No.	%	No.	%
Uptown Grammar	0	0	0	0	1	100	0	0	0	0	1	100
Ambridge Green	4	27	4	27	5	33	1	7	1	7	15	100
Colourview Rise	1	14	2	29	4	57	0	0	0	0	7	100
Coronation Estate	3	19	7	44	5	31	0	0	1	6	16	100
Colliery Bank	5	50	2	20	2	20	1	10	0	0	10	100

Table 6.9 **Spending money**

| Club | Spending Money | | | | | | Total | |
| | £2 and over | | £1.00-1.99 | | Under £1.00 | | | |
	No.	%	No.	%	No.	%	No.	%
Uptown Grammar	3	15	7	35	10	50	20	100
Ambridge Green	1	13	2	25	5	62	8	100
Colourview Rise	4	29	7	50	3	21	14	100
Coronation Estate	2	50	1	25	1	25	4	100
Colliery Bank	3	30	3	30	4	40	10	100

N.B. Percentage totals do not always sum to 100 due to rounding.

Table 6.10 Range of clubs attended other than present club

Club	L.A. Youth Club	School Youth Club	Church Youth Club	Uniformed	Young Interest	Adult Interest	School Interest	Sports	Adult Social	Works Club	Young Social (Commercial)	No. of members Responding
Uptown Grammar	5	0	3	1	0	2	7	2	0	0	2	13
Ambridge Green	9	2	1	0	1	1	1	1	0	1	1	15
Colourview Rise	1	0	0	0	0	0	1	4	2	5	1	9
Coronation Estate	6	2	0	0	0	0	0	2	3	1	0	11
Colliery Bank	3	1	0	0	0	0	0	0	3	0	0	7

Table 6.11 **Classified analysis of clubs attended**

Club	Youth Club	Uniformed/ Interest	Adult Social or Commercial
Uptown Grammar	8	12	2
Ambridge Green	12	4	2
Colourview Rise	1	5	8
Coronation Estate	8	2	4
Colliery Bank	4	0	3

Table 6.12 **Respondents who had tried other clubs at some stage but subsequently left**

Club	Joining Attempts				Total	
	Tried and Left		*Never Tried			
	No.	%	No.	%	No.	%
Uptown Grammar	12	57	9	43	21	100
Ambridge Green	13	57	10	43	23	100
Colourview Rise	20	95	1	5	21	100
Coronation Estate	13	65	7	35	20	100
Colliery Bank	8	40	12	60	20	100
Total	66	63	39	37	105	100

*This does not mean no other clubs are attended

Table 6.13 **The distance members lived from the club**

| Club | Distance from Club | | | | | | Total | |
| | Within ¼ mile | | ¼ to ½ mile | | Further | | | |
	No.	%	No.	%	No.	%	No.	%
Uptown Grammar	0	0	2	10	19	90	21	100
Ambridge Green	1	4	10	43	12	52	23	100
Colourview Rise	1	10	12	57	7	33	21	100
Coronation Estate	9	45	11	55	0	0	20	100
Colliery Bank	20	100	0	0	0	0	20	100

Table 6.14 Attendance at the club

Club	Attendance															
	More than twice a week		About twice a week		About once a week		Less than once a week but at least once a month		Less than once a month		No Response		Total	
	No.	%	No.	%	No.	%	No.	%	No.	%	No.	%	No.	%
Uptown Grammar	0	0	0	0	17	81	4	19	0	0	0	0	21	100
Ambridge Green	0	0	0	0	16	70	3	13	3	13	1	4	23	100
Colourview Rise	3	14	7	33	3	14	5	24	3	14	0	0	21	100
Coronation Estate	3	15	3	15	7	35	6	30	1	5	0	0	20	100
Colliery Bank	6	30	3	15	2	10	4	20	5	25	0	0	20	100

Table 6.15 Length of membership

Club	Length of Membership															Total	
	4 weeks or less		Up to 6 months		Up to 1 year		Up to 2 years		Up to 4 years		4 years or more		No response			Total	
	No.	%	No.	%	No.	%	No.	%	No.	%	No.	%	No.	%	No.	%
Uptown Grammar	0	0	4	19	5	24	7	33	5	24	0	0	0	0	21	100
Ambridge Green	0	0	0	0	1	4	11	48	6	26	4	17	1	4	23	100
Colourview Rise	0	0	0	0	14	67	7	33	0	0	0	0	0	0	21	100
Coronation Estate	1	5	1	5	0	0	9	45	9	45	0	0	0	0	20	100
Colliery Bank	0	0	0	0	2	10	8	40	3	15	7	35	0	0	20	100

N.B. Totals do not sum to 100% due to rounding

Table 6.16   **Awareness of the club committee**

| | Awareness | | | | | |
| | Aware | | Not Aware | | Total | |
	No.	%	No.	%	No.	%
Uptown Grammar	21	100	0	0	21	100
Ambridge Green	21	91	2	9	23	100
Colourview Rise	20	95	1	5	21	100
Coronation Estate	15	75	5	25	20	100
Colliery Bank	14	10	6	30	20	100
Total	91	87	14	13	105	100

Table 6.17   **Committee membership of respondents**

| Club | Committee membership | | | | | | Total Responding | |
| | Committee member | | Would like to be committee member | | Would not like to be committee member | | | |
	No.	%	No.	%	No.	%	No.	%
Uptown Grammar	6	29	2	10	13	62	21	100
Ambridge Green	3	14	3	14	15	71	21	100
Colourview Rise	4	20	2	10	14	70	20	100
Coronation Estate	1	7	2	13	12	80	15	100
Colliery Bank	4	24	5	29	8	47	17	100
Total	18	19	14	15	62	66	94	100

Table 6.18   **Relative interest in committee membership**

Club	%
Colliery Bank (Traditional Working Class)	53
Uptown Grammar (Middle Class)	38
Colourview Rise (Affluent Worker)	30
Ambridge Green (Rural)	29
Coronation Estate (Socially Deprived)	20

Table 6.19   **The relationship between fathers' occupation and members' committee membership**

Club	Committee membership								Total Responding	
	Manual Occupation				Non-Manual Occupation					
	On committee or wish to be		Not on committee or don't know if would like to be		On committee or wish to be		Not on committee or don't know if would like to be			
	No.	%	No.	%	No.	%	No.	%	No.	%
Uptown Grammar	0	0	6	100	8	53	7	47	21	100
Ambridge Green	3	43	4	57	3	41	11	79	21	100
Colourview Rise	2	18	9	82	4	44	5	56	20	100
Coronation Estate	3	21	11	79	0	0	1	100	15	100
Colliery Bank	8	50	8	50	1	100	0	0	17	100
Total	16	30	38	70	16	40	24	60	94	100

Table 6.20 **The presence of self-originating groups**

Club	Members Organize		Members do not organize		Total	
	No.	%	No.	%	No.	%
Uptown Grammar	15	71	6	29	21	100
Ambridge Green	4	17	19	83	23	100
Colourview Rise	11	52	10	48	21	100
Coronation Estate	9	45	11	55	20	100
Colliery Bank	3	15	17	85	20	100
Total	42	40	63	60	105	100

Table 6.21 **The success rate of self-originating groups**

| Club | Success Rate | | | | Total | |
	Usually Successful		Usually Successful			
	No.	%	No.	%	No.	%
Uptown Grammar	13	87	2	13	15	100
Ambridge Green	3	75	1	25	4	100
Colourview Rise	8	77	3	27	11	100
Coronation Estate	7	78	2	22	9	100
Colliery Bank	0	0	3	100	3	100
Total	31		11		42	100

Table 6.22   **Reaction if friend banned for serious misbehaviour**

Club	Leave		Stay		Total	
	No.	%	No.	%	No.	%
Uptown Grammar	2	11	16	89	18	100
Ambridge Green	3	14	18	86	21	100
Colourview Rise	1	6	17	94	18	100
Coronation Estate	1	5	18	95	19	100
Colliery Bank	2	13	13	87	15	100
Total	9	10	82	90	91	100

Table 6.23   **Reason for staying if friend is banned**

Club	Attitude Responsible		Instrumental		Other		Total	
	No.	%	No.	%	No.	%	No.	%
Uptown Grammar	8	44	7	39	3	17	18	100
Ambridge Green	13	62	3	14	5	31	21	100
Colourview Rise	9	50	8	44	1	6	18	100
Coronation Estate	7	37	10	53	2	10	19	100
Colliery Bank	4	27	9	60	3	20	15	100
Total	41	45	37	41	14	15	91	100

Table 6.24   **Members' reaction to unfair banning**

Club	Reaction						Total Responding	
	Leave if only for a short period		Stay		Other			
	No.	%	No.	%	No.	%	No.	%
Uptown Grammar	1	5	16	84	2	11	19	100
Ambridge Green	7	35	9	45	4	20	20	100
Colourview Rise	6	30	12	60	2	10	20	100
Coronation Estate	3	20	7	47	5	33	15	100
Colliery Bank	6	38	9	56	1	6	16	100
Total	23	26	53	59	14	10	90	100

Table 6.25   **Respondents who would have protested at unfair banning**

Club	Protest				Total	
	Protest		No Protest			
	No.	%	No.	%	No.	%
Uptown Grammar	15	71	6	29	21	100
Ambridge Green	11	48	12	52	23	100
Colourview Rise	16	76	5	24	21	100
Coronation Estate	9	45	11	55	20	100
Colliery Bank	13	65	7	35	20	100
Total	64	61	41	39	105	100

Table 6.26   **The form the protest would have taken**

Club	Form of Protest							
	Leave		Stay and present case		No concern of mine		Total Responding	
	No.	%	No.*	%	No.	%	No.	%
Uptown Grammar	1(1)	6	14	87	1	6	16	100
Ambridge Green	6(4)	40	5	33	4	27	15	100
Colourview Rise	5(0)	29	11	65	1	6	17	100
Coronation Estate	3(0)	30	6	60	1	10	10	100
Colliery Bank	6(1)	40	7	47	2	13	15	100
Total	21(6)	29	43	59	9	12	73	100

*The figures in brackets in Table 6.26 represent those of the leavers who would have left permanently. The remainder are those who would have left for a short time as a protest.

7 Adult leadership

The Self-concept of Leadership

If the role of the member in the club is complex and difficult to analyse, then the role of the leader is possibly beyond the bounds of human comprehension. We have already noticed in previous chapters that he exercises a focal and 'absorbing' role between the demands of the organization and the demands of the members. He stands at the personal frontiers of both sides in a characteristically exposed and vulnerable 'man in the middle' position much like that of the foreman in industry or the receptionist at the airline desk. It is interesting at this stage to report a number of the conflicts expressed by leaders in interviews, training sessions and in general conversations.

There may be a *norm conflict* between the behavioural and personal norms approved by the providing organization and the norms acceptable to the adolescent community. These latter range from the length of hair, through the bare midriff down to the style of footwear, where the stiletto heels of the early 60s give way to the cripple boots of the early 70s. But they are only the symbols of confrontation — there will always be current and usually emotive vehicles wherein the members can challenge the organization in the person of the leader, and the organization can challenge the members — also in the person of the leader. A broader view of the same conflict is, of course, the conflict between the norms of the adult population and those of adolescents. However genuine or spurious the concept of the 'generation gap' may be believed to be, there are always situations where, for the participant, it is real and uncomfortable. It is at precisely these times — the discussion of vandalism or some other alleged adolescent abuse — that the leader is placed in a classic 'man in the middle' role. Does he condemn the adolescent — even if only by implication — and endeavour to 'cure' him, or does he condemn society and try to cure it?

There may be conflict between *directive and non-directive* approaches. He may see himself as a directive figure with clear educational and 'positivistic' goals, capable of filling the roles of custodian, defining the rules of the club; moralist, representing the moral authority of society and religion; and therapist, licensed to delve into and change the personal feelings and values of the members (Dearling, 1973). Alternatively he may adopt predominantly non-directive, flexible and open structures, non-active leadership that is permissive and facilitating, becoming a kind of background figure to a scene in which the major decisions are being taken by the members of the organization.

It is possible to obscure the differences between directive and nondirective approaches however. During the study we encountered a number of leaders who appeared to be exercising a kind of 'repressive tolerance'. These were leaders who were committed to directive approaches but who felt that an overly directive approach would be unacceptable to the present 'style' of their organization and unworkable in their clubs. So a tolerant easy going style was developed underneath which there was an unchanged firmness of conviction about what the members should and could do — the 'iron hand in the velvet glove'. This situation, in which members have little part in decision making — power still being exercised by the leader — is, of course, the antithesis of non-directive leadership.

There may be conflict between the *instrumental* and the *expressive* roles of the leader. There may be considerable attractions to the leader in having a 'tightly run' club — programmes and activities taking place all the time: no member need stand around looking bored because there is 'always something interesting to do' — and well attended committee meetings. Yet such a regime may be at the cost of the leader's expressive role, for his opportunities to be pastoral, guiding and caring may more readily occur when members are just standing around. They may even be at their best when arrangements break down and he finds himself immersed in 'rescue operations' along with the members.

There may be conflict between his *career orientation and his institutional orientation.* The career interest of a leader may be best served by a fairly rapid succession of appointments to a range of clubs in ascending order of size and status, followed by a move to administration, possibly taking him outside clubs altogether.[1] Or he may find it professionally advantageous to return to the schoolteaching from which he may have come or for which he may be qualified by his

[1] The recurring problems of the professional identity of the youth workers may be seen most clearly in the ambivalence of their attitudes to the teaching profession. A symptomatic news item appeared in *The Teacher,* the journal of the National Union of Teachers, 5, April, 1974: *'Youth leaders put out feelers to technicians.* Over 700 youth leaders who enjoy all the privileges of NUT membership for about 75 pence a head a year have decided to approach another union. The Community and Youth Service Association voted last Saturday, at its annual general meeting in Canterbury, to 'explore the possibility of affiliation or amalgamation with the Association of Scientific, Technical and Managerial Staffs.'

training. Yet the interests of the members may best be served by an extended stay on the part of the leader — long enough for him to have won the confidence of a generation of adolescents and their families and to have acquired an extended knowledge of the resources and needs of the community. The conflict is, of course, similar to the conflict between 'cosmopolitan' and 'local' orientations developed by Gouldner (1957-8).

There may be conflicts between his *specialist and his generalist* roles — between the roles he is 'licensed' to undertake by the terms of his appointment and training and those that appear to be needed in his day-to-day work. Most leaders experience many occasions when they feel called upon to act as careers officers, social workers, guidance counsellors, psychiatrists, psychologists, and teachers. At what stage does he refer the issue to the appropriate professional worker? To what extent does he endeavour to acquire skills himself in these and other areas? To what extent does he try to carry these requirements in a lay 'common sense' role and deny their specialist implications? The answers are not easy and may change with each changing situation.

There may be conflict between the needs of the members as a group and those of individuals — between *universal and specific* roles. To what extent can the disturbed, aggressive anti-social member be accommodated in the club? How great a price should the other members pay for his 'therapy' — in inconvenience, annoyance and withdrawal of the leader's attention? To what extent should the interest of a small minority in, say, skin diving, be allowed to draw off finance and facilities from the majority?

It is possible to extend the list almost indefinitely — the experience of any established leader would yield many further examples. And to this list of role conflicts could be added far more that spring from structural problems — for instance where the youth leader is also a teacher — where half the time it is 'please, sir', 'yes sir' and later on it's 'Jim, can I?' (Clerens, 1966.) Underlying all is the fundamental dimension of authority.[2] How does the leader obtain the authority to exercise his role in relation to the members, to parents, to the remainder of the local community, to other professional workers, to his assistants and part-time colleagues? And how does this authority come to be seen to be legitimate so that he may exercise it with confidence and without major challenge?

One answer to the problem of achieving legitimation that has attracted considerable attention in the Youth Service has been seen to lie in the development of professional training schemes. It is beyond the scope of this report to consider this complex issue. The debate has been

---

[2] When we speak of the authority of the leader and its legitimation we refer, of course, to the capacity of the leader to make decisions within the range of possibilities open to him and even to be able to extend this range. We do not use the term to indicate the development of authoritarian behaviour by the leader.

well rehearsed in the *Albemarle Report* (1960) and the documents
that have followed it. The history of the ensuing training schemes for the
statutory and the voluntary sectors, including the National College,
Youth Wings in Colleges of Education, and the Bessey schemes has been
noted, albeit briefly, in Chapter 2 of this report.

The extensive and diverse range of current schemes are listed regularly
in the Training Bulletin inset in *Youth in Society* (Youth Service Information Centre). They range from mountain rescue programmes through
to Tavistock-type seminars. They display one central feature – the
almost unbelievably wide range of competences a leader is called upon to
possess; a range to which our list of role conflicts has drawn attention.
Not only must he have a range of management, teaching, guidance and
interpersonal skills – he also needs the ability to 'do something', usually
through some form of physical as well as intellectual and personal
prowess that can be directly recognized and appreciated by members
The problems of establishing appropriate training courses are legendary
and account, in part, for the rapidity of changes in training provision.
But another and more fundamental problem is that courses of training –
both initial and in-service, tend to provide the leader with only small
components of many things. The ensuing lack of completeness and depth
in many, if not all, aspects of his professional work leads to a shortfall of
the very authority and legitimation the leader needs to handle his
conflicts – one of the very goals that training courses are established to
bring about.

One development in training which is believed to offer prospects
of alleviating both the conflicts and the problems to which they give rise
is an increase in professional supervision along the lines used in social
work training, wherein an experienced professional worker undertakes
responsibility to discuss and comment upon the work of a trainee or
junior member of a profession – usually through the retrospective,
intensive consideration of the junior's sessions with clients.[3]
Matthews (1960) has valuably discussed the technique in a specifically
Youth and Community Service context. Swannell and Muir (1973)
present the case for further developments of supervision in the Youth
and Community Service in an article that is of particular interest since it
illuminates many of the problems of leadership in the service to which
we have referred:[4]

The full-time community and youth worker, particularly in his first
appointment, quickly moves from the freedom of college routine to

[3] The technique is also capable of application to teacher training, see Caspari and
Eggleston (1965).

[4] The article formed a commentary on *Structures for Supervision* (Youth Service
Information Centre, 1972).

the isolation of working alone or with limited support. He soon misses what he had taken for granted during his period of training: the constant support from a tutor and the opportunity to discuss in depth particular situations with fellow students. He starts to have to face alone the cumulative difficulties of working with groups of young people, adults wishing to help in some way, members of advisory or management committees and youth service staff.

And while the social worker or teacher moves to a team position in the new agency or school where a structure is already established, and a supervisor is often available as part of the team, the full-time youth worker usually moves to a post where his objectives are loosely defined, where he or she might be the only full-time worker, where the immediate superior might be in the county town several miles away, and where the executive or advisory committee, although professional in their own field, have limited knowledge of youth service procedure.

It may be that yet a further part of the answer to the problems of training would be to institute a clearer labelling system for the many components of training available within the service. Perhaps in a manner similar to the driving licence that indicated the category of vehicle the licencee

is permitted to drive, the leader might have a clear indication of the many skills and capacities he is able to offer. But meanwhile, despite some notable exceptions, mainly in organizations where the range of leadership skills is more clearly delimited, the service has failed in general to solve the problems of the authority of the leader — an authority that is diminished by the conflicts that we have reviewed, by his generally low salary structure and also by the uncertainties of the role, status and financial support of the service itself, to which attention has been drawn in previous chapters.

The Members' View of the Leader

How is the authority of the leader seen by the members? We sought information on this topic in the five clubs investigated. We commenced with a fundamental question — is an adult necessary? — and then went on to ask members what they considered to be the most important part of the leader's job. The tables at the end of the chapter give the data obtained.

We found that 96 respondents (91%) considered an adult club leader necessary. The Colourview Rise club and the Colliery Bank club felt this least, but the numbers concerned were small. This tendency, however, is interesting when taken together with the data on leader attributes which members considered important.

When respondents were asked what they considered the most important aspect of a leader's job, the following classifications were used: the managerial/administrative — that is looking after the club and equipment; the provider of activities or 'resource person'; the counselling role; and the authoritarian role.

Overall the most important part of a leader's job was perceived as that of counsellor: being a helpful adult. The second most important was the control function, closely followed by the leader as resource person and manager. This ordering still held when respondents endorsed more than one activity. When the clubs were examined individually, however, a clear difference emerged in the emphasis given to each particular role. This will now be considered.

The Leader as Counsellor: The three clubs which gave the counselling role priority were the club in the priority area (Coronation Estate 50%), the middle class club (Uptown Grammar 42%) and the rural club (Ambridge Green 59%). The other clubs gave this aspect of the leader's role low priority.

The difference between the two predominantly working class clubs (50% and 16%) is of especial interest since the area in which the traditional working class club was located was recognized by the leader, local people and the local authority as an area with many social problems. It is suggested that in this long established, traditional working class area, the task of offering advice and guidance to the young is firmly held by the family groups, augmented later by the working group; the club leader is not normally regarded as an appropriate source of guidance.

The Leader as Authority Figure: Along with the managerial role, the control function was given first priority by 32% of the traditional working class club (Colliery Bank). However, this function was also considered most important by 28% of the rural and 32% of the middle class clubs. When multiple endorsements were considered, these rose to 38% and 44% respectively. This aspect of the leader's role was given lowest priority by members of the 'affluent' club (Colourview Rise) and the 'educational priority area' club (Coronation Estate) with 15% and 19% respectively.

The Leader as a Manager: The differences between the working class clubs are further confirmed with the consideration of this function. For 35% of the members of the 'affluent' club and 32% of the members of the traditional working class club the role of the youth leader as a person who looks after the club and equipment was given pre-eminence. It had low priority for the middle class (14%), the rural club (20%) and the 'educational priority area' working class club (25%).

The Leader as Resource Person: This role, interestingly, was given considerably higher priority by members of the 'affluent' club (35% more than any other club). That only 28% of the total sample endorsed this is of interest taken in conjunction with the activity orientation of much youth service provision.

In order to make some assessment of a club's orientation the two most heavily endorsed items were selected for each club. The rural and middle class area clubs saw the leader as a helpful adult who also demonstrated authority and paternalism. The deprived working class area club (55%) saw the leader as a counsellor with a much more subordinate role as resource person (25%). The traditional working class club saw the leader in a somewhat remote role as manager and authority figure. This suggests that members of this club tend to categorize the leader as one of 'them' — those in authority — despite the fact that he also lived on the estate. The members of the affluent area club displayed a more instrumental attitude than members of any of the other clubs. They strongly rejected the 'counsellor' and 'control' aspects of the leader's role and indicated as desirable the kind of requirements that could be expected at a good sports centre: well managed and well provided with opportunity for activities.

Because of the nature of the case study method, these results are necessarily tentative. They do support, however, wide differences in attitude and expectations even in clubs which are superficially very similar.

To explore any further differences between the clubs, respondents were asked for their opinion of qualities necessary in a leader. Overall, 41% of the respondents mentioned qualities such as the ability to inspire respect, control, organize, administer, initiate and decide — in other words traditional leadership qualities summed up as 'he can show who's boss if need be'. Overall, 46% stressed the importance of a leader possessing relating qualities such as the ability to understand and get on with youth, tolerance, the ability to accept criticism, tact, considerateness, sociability and so fourth — summed up as 'the sort of bloke who you can talk to and who understands you'. 51% overall, stressed the importance of personal qualities such as extroversion, cheerfulness in adversity, 'sportiness', and additional values such as patience, dedication, trustworthiness, hard working and so on. Percentages for the individual clubs are given in table 7.4.

Although this was a very simple measure, it suggests that young people have an extremely traditional view of youth leaders. Aalto (1970, pp. 7,24) made a similar finding in this study of Finnish youth. Young people had more traditional expectations of the Youth Service than had youth workers. In the present study, young people's image of the ideal youth worker was parallel to the Youth Service's image of the ideal citizen. No mention was made of any innovative or radical qualities; both images are bland and harmless.

Profiles of Leadership

In the same way as we 'created' ideal type models of members in Chapter 6 we may now attempt to draw models of leadership. But the cautions expressed in the previous chapter must be reiterated with equal strength here — the models we draw could never, in their pure form exist in any known sector of the service. The infinite complexities of reality preclude this.

The *administrative* leader is efficient, highly organized, able, by consulation of his timetable, attendance records and diary, to produce detailed and accurate responses and reports to any questioner. He is likely to have an extensive programme of activities and interest groups. Resources in his club are likely to be good because he is alert to the strategies whereby funds may be obtained from his organization or local authority and because his control and maintenance is effective in preventing equipment from 'walking' or from damage through carelessness and misuse. His club will have a committee with regular meetings, agenda and minutes. It will be a committee that tends to endorse the leader's controlling and initiating activities, for young people unwilling to respond to this type of leadership tend not to join, let alone reach the committee. His regime may well be one of 'repressive tolerance' of the initiatives and values of members — where, under an apparently liberal, tolerant regime, the leader remains responsible for the key decisions of the club or organization. Essentially he is a leader who is respected by the providing body, he may even be regarded by some of the lay representatives as 'the kind of leader we really need.' He may be found in all kinds of clubs and groups — but in some his relationships with members may take a form different than in others.

The first form is where his administrative style is *positively endorsed* by members; where it is seen as the proper way to run an organization and style not only to be respected but even adopted in appropriate circumstances, by the members. Such a positive endorsement is more likely to occur in predominantly middle class clubs and organizations whose members may well see this as the normal and desirable model of attitudes. For such members the regime would not be definable as 'repressive'.

The second form is one of *negative endorsement* where the members accept the style of the leader for the advantages it brings — in the preservation of the club and the provision of facilities. They may well match 'repressive tolerance' by the leader with 'conscious toleration' of his repression. Negative endorsement is far more likely to occur in a predominantly working class club where the members define the leader as 'one of them' not 'one of us' but nonetheless as useful, even essential, if they are to have the activities or facilities they desire. Whichever kind of endorsement occurs, it is likely to provide an important experience of social learning for the members and to influence relationships both with other adults and with 'the system' as a whole.

In contrast to the administrative leader, however endorsed, the *permissive leader* is essentially non-directive. His aim is to ensure that members make critical decisions — both for the club and as individuals themselves. He sees it as his role to put them in a position where they may do this and to give them the necessary information and support to decide, and the resources and facilities to implement their decisions. A major part of his role is just to 'be around' to respond to the needs of his members when the members need him to do so. Above all he is a counsellor, consultant, adviser and advocate for his members. Like the club itself the leader's personal time is predominantly unstructured and flexible. This is not to say that there is no authority in such a club or group. In the case of transgressions of the norms of the club, however, such a leader would tend to emphasize the authority of the club itself — bringing the judgments of members to bear on the transgressor and inviting him to explain why he did what he did in response. But such an event could lead to a 'redefinition of the situation' and the establishment of new norms. Again the situation is one in which effective power is with the present membership who are exercising authority and who are not 'on the receiving end' of the authority of others — either of the leader, or of the organization, the local authority or past members as expressed by the leader. This is not to say that the views of the leader and those he represents are ignored — the evidence may be quite to the contrary[5].

In the realities of life of the Youth Service it is probably even more difficult to be wholly an administrative or a permissive leader than it is to be a morally neutral teacher in a school. An adult in a club, group or other organization must share the qualities of both. A convenient example is in the area of innovation. Our evidence suggests that few members of the clubs wish to take an active role in innovative radical approaches. A majority are distinctly conservatively and traditionally oriented. Yet clubs and groups in which 'nothing changes' are almost certain to die or disintegrate. But if 'innovative renewal' is to come in many clubs it may only arise through the leader. Such innovation however is only likely to succeed if it is fully and actively endorsed by the members. The paradox not only illuminates the problem inherent in the leader's role but also, once again, the unresolved ambivalence in the aims and practices of the service as a whole.

There is, also, a third kind of leader who has hardly been sighted in the clubs other than standing well in the background. He is the adult with special adult skills brought in to make an appropriate specialist contribution. Commonly he is a craftsman, a karati or sub-aqua specialist, a musician or an artist. Less frequently he may be a tradesman who can advise on decoration and home maintenance in a community development project or a naturalist who can give an intellectual component to outdoor pursuits. Lacking all recognized 'professional Youth Service' qualifications[6] he may nonetheless be viewed as a leader because he exercises real leadership in his activity. Perhaps he can be best labelled an *ephemeral leader*. But in the conventional club or group his time is a limited one. If he is successful and wishes to stay, he is usually placed under strong pressure to become 'professional' — to take recognized training courses and thereby to fit into the more professional roles we have just described. If he does not, he is likely to find either that his activity is not of continuing relevance to the club or that one of the

---

[5] A close resemblance to the permissive leader can be found in the 'morally neutral teacher' envisaged by the Schools Council/Nuffield Humanities Project (1970). But the morally neutral teacher is also a model for, like the leader, no teacher is ever without his own views on what is right or wrong and can never totally eliminate these from a situation in which he is involved.

[6] He is, of course, likely to be well 'qualified' in his specialist activity and be seen to be so by the members.

'professional' leaders has attended a course that will give him the skills
to supplant the ephemeral leader. If, notwithstanding, he remains, he will
usually be obliged to stay in a marginal role and be denied the status or
title of 'leader'. In short, ways will be found to translate, eliminate or
minimize such persons for they represent an unacceptable lay intrusion
into the professional model of the Youth Service.

Yet the situation in the experimental areas of the service to which
attention is now about to be given suggests a very different state of
affairs. These new and de-structured areas may well be giving rise to a de-
structured and de-professionalized concept of leadership in which the
pattern may be one of succession of resourceful adults each making a
series of short specialist contributions. The model of the ephemeral
leader may become the dominant one and his 'non-professionalism'
instead of being a disadvantage may be seen as being highly
advantageous.

Moreover, his orientations may change from 'safe' traditionalism to a
more adventurous radicalism. While the changed nature of the new
experimental and community approaches may be a primary reason for
such inversion, the ambiguities and uncertainties in the leader's role may
have also facilitated the change. But above all, we shall look to the
growing incidence of 'client participation' that dominates the new
approaches to find the most fundamental explanation of this changed
concept of leadership. In doing so we shall find further evidence not only
on leadership but also on the roles and orientations of the young.

Table 7.1 **Respondents who saw the necessity for an adult leader**

| Club | View of Leader | | | | Total | |
| | Necessary | | Unnecessary | | | |
	No.	%	No.	%	No.	%
Uptown Grammar	20	95	1	5	21	100
Ambridge Green	22	96	1	4	23	100
Colourview Rise	17	81	4	19	21	100
Coronation Estate	20	100	0	0	20	100
Colliery Bank	17	85	3	15	20	100
Total	96	91	9	9	105	100

Table 7.2 **The tasks of the leader as seen by club members**

| Club | Leader's task | | | | | | | | No. of Respondents | |
| | Administrative/ Managerial | | Resource Person | | Counsellor | | Control | | | |
	No.	%	No.	%	No.	%	No.	%	No.	%
Uptown Grammar	3	14	4	19	10	48	8	38	21	100
Ambridge Green	6	26	7	30	10	43	10	44	23	100
Colourview Rise	8	38	8	38	3	14	3	14	21	100
Coronation Estate	5	25	6	30	11	55	5	25	20	100
Colliery Bank	7	35	4	20	4	20	7	35	20	100
Total	29	28	29	28	38	36	33	31	105	100

Table 7.3 **The most important tasks of the leader as seen by members**

| Club | Most important tasks of the leader | | | | | | | | Total | |
| | Administrative/ Managerial | | Resource Person | | Counsellor | | Control | | | |
	No.	%	No.	%	No.	%	No.	%	No.	%
Uptown Grammar	2	11	3	116	8	42	6	32	19	100
Ambridge Green	2	11	4	22	7	39	5	28	18	100
Colourview Rise	7	35	7	35	3	15	3	15	20	100
Coronation Estate	2	13	3	19	8	50	3	19	16	100
Colliery Bank	6	32	4	21	3	16	6	32	19	100
Total	19	21	21	23	29	32	23	25	92	100

146 ADOLESCENCE AND COMMUNITY

Table 7.4 **Leadership qualities postulated by members**

Club	Leader Qualities							
	Traditional		Inter-personal relating		Personal		No Responding	
	No.	%	No.	%	No.	%	No.	%
Uptown Grammar	11	52	9	42	11	52	21	100
Ambridge Green	8	35	8	35	9	39	23	100
Colourview Rise	15	71	17	81	11	52	21	100
Coronation Estate	4	20	6	30	11	55	20	100
Colliery Bank	5	25	8	40	12	60	20	100
Total	43	41	48	46	54	51	105	100

N.B. It was possible for members to give more than one response, consequently totals do not sum to 100%.

8 Spheres of experimental activity

Non-Institutionalized Youth Work

Development

Traditionally, the mainstream of youth work has been largely based on the social and physical aspects of the club or organization — in short it has taken an institutionalized form. This has had important consequences because a building plays an important part in defining an institution for both participants and non-participants. In the first place, bricks and mortar provide tangible evidence that the group of young people are indeed a club and have to be taken seriously as such; and secondly, the physical outward structure symbolizes the internal structure of relationships that constitute 'club behaviour'. It is well known that the architecture of a building is not only used to symbolize the status of those who will use it but that it also, at least in part, determines their behaviour. Thus social relationships in an 'open plan' office, school and club are likely to be different from those where space is compartmentalized and 'privatized'. And the very existence of a club functioning within a building is likely to suggest to a visitor to a club (young or old) the likelihood of discipline (whether self-discipline or imposed by same external authority), respect for people and property, co-operation between participants and so forth.

Within the last decade, however, forms of youth work have evolved that have violated these expectations. They are neither club based, nor do they, apparently, conform to the expected patterns of social relationships. Using Milson's terminology (1971) it is these 'non-institutionalized' forms of youth work which we now examine, in particular work with the unattached and community development projects, both of which are usually conceived as dealing with the socially inadequate and the underprivileged sections of the community.

The de-institutionalization process can be seen to have occured in several phases. The first wave followed the *Albemarle Report*'s (1960) concern with unclubbables. Ewen (1974) has noted the interesting

147

implication of this concern: the conventional wisdom of the Youth Service that it was abnormal not to be clubbable which led the service to provide 'club' situations (coffee bars and teen canteens) 'assumed to be a milieu closer to that of the unclubbables' cultural expectations, something like the transport cafe.'

Approaches of this kind which dominated development work in the 1960s were in general overtaken by events later in the decade. On the one hand the increasing sophistication of many young people associated with a far greater range of acceptable commercial provision led to a rapid withdrawl of support for the generally 'primitive' youth service provisions. On the other hand the new approaches led many of the established youth clubs themselves to become informal social centres rather than places where programmed activity took place. A number of these clubs, with new 'Albemarle' buildings came to match their commercial competitors; in short the 'developmental' became 'mainstream', appealing to a wider range of clients with the consequence that the 'unclubbable' population was by definition, reduced.

In the late 1960s, particularly following the influential work of Goetschius and Tash (1967) and of Morse (1965) and the considerable concern with the social problems of the young that we have noted in Chapter 2, experimental projects increasingly emphasized the attempt, not to 'club' young people who had problems, but rather to help them to achieve identity, self-respect and, to use a phrase we have used on a number of previous occasions, 'to contract in to the decision making' in their environment.

While projects at the time were often sponsored by bodies that were concerned to eliminate vandalism, delinquency, drug taking, or some other social vice attributed to the young, it is clear that most of them have become providers of personal social service — often to a very limited number of young people — within which the detached workers have often developed radical views of society that are markedly at variance with those of the sponsoring bodies or of the mainstream Youth Service.

In the 1970s these approaches, with the support of the publication *Youth and Community Work in the 70s,* have spread out to a widespread involvement in community action as it has become clear that the objects of work with 'problem youths' cannot be achieved without matching intervention in the community in which they live and which must share responsibility for the problems. Hence the emphasis on counselling and other individual social work techniques has come to be replaced by community social work and the promotion of community action and self help. It is clear that the developments of the late 1960s and early 1970s have presented a challenge to the traditional values of the Youth Service that did not exist in the events of the early 1960s. While our evidence suggests that as yet there is no indication that mainstream values have changed, it is certainly noticeable that almost all the voluntary and statutory bodies are now involved in forms of community action project involving strategies and approaches of a radicalism that would have been undreamed of ten years previously.

Yet the emphasis on development work with its multi disciplinary community involved approaches, often more linked with the practice of the social services rather than the education services, is still small. At the time of writing rather less than 10% of all professional youth workers are engaged in these sectors, the vast majority hold 'mainstream' appointments, mainly within the education service. (This is not of course to say that they are not influenced by the new approaches.)

There are, however, interesting signs that this approach is becoming recognized by Government ministries outside the Department of Education and Science, the 'guardians and overseers' of the Youth Service. The Home Office and Department of Health and Social Services are increasingly prepared to finance community self help programmes in urban stress areas and 'intermediate' programmes for young people at risk.[1]

Still more recently there has been evidence of a wider range of agencies beyond the normal youth service area inviting the young to participate in community projects. SCANUS, the student community action group of the National Union of Students, has involved not only students but also other young people in an active range of community action projects, emphasizing the participative role in decision making in the 'contracting in to the political system' envisaged by *Youth and Community Work in the 70s*. A number of other, predominantly adult, associations also appear to be achieving considerable success in attracting participation by young people — notably Shelter, and Child Poverty Action (see for example Lister, 1974). Often organizations of this kind appear to offer a more effective opportunity to the young to 'count for something' than specifically youth organizations. On a more local level there are the 'official' projects such as Community Industry and a range of spontaneous independent groups such as Claimants Unions to the near 'underground' All London Squatters Federation; all with considerable emphasis on 'direct' community action.

One of the notable features of the de-institutionalized approaches has been the increased burden placed upon the professional worker. We have already alluded to this in the previous chapter but in the context of the present section it is useful to notice the particular pressures that are placed upon the worker as a 'community action social worker'.

1. The relative lack of the traditional institutional support that has defined and supported the exercise of the role of the 'mainstream' worker.

---

[1] Details of Department of Health and Social Services linked intermediate programmes are listed by Johnstone (1974).

2. The wide range of professional, administrative and 'personal' skills that he is called upon to use — skills that are unlikely to be developed fully in any training course.

3. The conflict that is likely to arise between the needs of his clients to change the social system to enable them to play a part within it, and his own established position as a professional worker within the existing social system. The conflict is exacerbated by the need — and frequently the desire — for the worker to identify fully with the clients and the demands of his employing body and often his mainstream colleagues that he identify with their values. [2]

The problems of credibility, identity and conscience to which these conflicts give rise have emerged clearly in our discussions with workers in contemporary projects. Certainly they have led to a rapid turnover of workers, many remaining in a post for little more than one or two years and many visibly suffering from emotional and stress problems.

Much of the new work we have noted takes the form of 'experimental projects' and it is by examining 'non-institutional' youth work within the framework of 'the experiment' that we hope to shed light on some of the distinctive features of such approaches.

The YSIC folder on 'Experiments and Development Projects in Work with Young People' (Sept. 1971) contained particulars of more than 200 such schemes (though not all, of course, were concurrent). Some 67 of the schemes were concerned with the provision of community services by young people, 37 were coffee bar projects, 32 provided counselling centres, 30 catered for 'special activity' groups (ranging from art to motor-cycling) and eight were drug addiction centres. The NYB review *Developmental Work with Young People* published in 1974 (Gardner, 1974) lists some 900 projects that exist or have existed since 1960 ranging from Coffee Bars through Arts Projects, Play Schemes, Sex Education, Street Theatre, Accommodation and Community Newspaper Projects. Detailed information on most of the projects is not readily available. The YSIC/NYB publications provide a source of numerical

---

[2] As an example of the magnitude of the conflict the following quotation from the *Squatters Handbook,* well used in many community action projects, is illuminating: 'In London and other cities there are always many thousands of houses standing empty. The logic of the system says they should just go to waste. Common sense says that the system is wrong and these houses should be used. Squatting means taking control over our living conditions — saying to councils and landlords, thank you very much, but piss off, we can look after our own affairs. It means learning what makes houses work and how to fix them up, spreading skills instead of always employing someone else to do things for us, and refusing to be passive consumers like the bosses want us to be. It means finding the space to do what we've always dreamed of — becoming part of a many-sided movement of people taking control over their own lives.' *(All London Squatters Federation 1974.)*

reference, but the information given either in these, or in the 'further
notes' available from NYB, is usually sketchy. There were however, at
the time this part of our work was begun, lengthier reports on several
individual projects which are listed in the bibliography.

Aims and Methods

Almost all the projects concern themselves with young people who are
clearly regarded as being in some way socially disadvantaged. Their dates
of origin, however, show that many predate *Youth and Community
Work in the 70s* whose definition, therefore, of the priority to be given
not 'to buildings, organization or membership', but to 'young people
who have left school' and 'whose social environment is inadequate' can
be seen to follow an existing trend, rather than to initiate a new one.

Indeed in view of this wide range of provision, there is a remarkable
unanimity about the expressed aims of those projects, almost all of
which are focussed on the 'late (social) developer'. Typical examples are
'to foster a sense of belonging, and through this to help (young people)
to become adjusted to accept the society in which they live' (Rocker
Club, Sydenham); 'to modify anti-social methods and behaviour'
(Action Research, Manchester); 'to make a long term evangelistic contact
with some of the unattached young people in the area, providing a
setting within which they could be helped to explore the nature of
authority' (Hideaway Club, Manchester); to help those with 'personal
or environmental inadequacies who may be involved with drug taking —
have left home or have agressive attitudes to society' (Heanor Project);
'wanting to influence and modify others' behaviour' (Brighton Archways
Venture).[2]

Aims, however, when expressed with this breadth might allow an
enormous variety of methods. Superficially the experimental schemes
would seem to involve such variety — motorcycle clubs, coffee bars,
provision of overnight accommodation, weekend camping schemes,
acting groups. Looked at more closely, however, they are almost all seen
to have as a major methodology the establishment of contact by the
workers with selected target groups of young people. One Liverpool
project actually calls itself 'Contact' and describes its voluntary workers
as providing 'first aid, in the nature of a listening ear, interesting
conversation, and just being there.' Similarly, the Basildon Play Leadership Extension Scheme gives as its *raison d'être* 'contact and group
work'. The Brighton Archways Venture, whose ostensible purpose was to
provide overnight accommodation for young people who would

---

[2] 'At all ages a higher proportion of boys than girls went to groups so that in all,
72% of boys currently went to a club (that is were 'attached') but only 58% of
girls.' (Bone and Ross, 1972.)

otherwise sleep rough in Brighton, openly states: 'The development of personal relationships was the reason for the existence of the facilities,' and in its summary of work the YSIC folder supports this: 'Supplying overnight accommodation provided an opportunity for ten hours working and talking with young people.' The Oval House (Drama and Arts) Club is equally clear about its purposes: 'while activities abound in the club the work is about relationships.' The Bournmouth Wheelhouse Club shows that it aims at a similar effect with the claim: 'The interest of the customers in cars and motorbikes provides one of the main means of working with young people.'

This contact of workers with young people is often held to provide an 'enabling' or 'facilitating' influence. Thus Goetschius and Tash (1967), describing an early project in London with unattached youth, give the purpose of the enterprise as being 'to contact and work with those unattached young people who showed signs of not being able to cope on their own with problems of growing up', and describe the situation they created as 'an enabling relationship, the purposes of which were to pass on information, to pass on simple social skills, to show acceptance and to give recognition and support.' In similar terms the Brighton Archways Venture suggests: 'The worker's role is to enable the young person to see his position and choices open to him more clearly,' and a report of an MAYC weekend in the country (MAYC, 1970) sets out the functions of its workers as *enabling* (young people) to feel part of the weekend, and *facilitating* some recognition of others' worth,' and claims that the workers were, in fact, 'not seen to be part of the "establishment", but as enablers and facilitators.' The Liverpool Contact project suggests that 'the worker who is communicating with an individual or group, and contributes by way of ideas, suggestions, information, is enabling this individual or group to make its own decisions and solve its own problems.'

The importance attached to contact as such, regardless of the attendant circumstances or of the nature of the development of relationships established, is so great that one can legitimately view the majority of experimental projects as attempts to provide the advantages presumed to be inherent in personal relations for a group (of young people) who are thought to have been 'put off' by the impersonality of the youth service as an institution. They are, in effect, attempts to assist young people, usually 'to help themselves' in variously defined ways through the mediation of a new relationship with an adult who might well be seen in a new category that could be labelled 'the professional friend'. One might compare the category with the more official, though more transitory, 'friend of the accused' in courts-martial, or, even more appositely, with the new category of 'counsellors' in schools. Indeed an account of a Bristol experimental youth course for school leavers (reported in *Girls in Two Cities*, 1967) concludes: 'A counsellor should be attached to each course from the beginning, with no particular respons-ibility in the running of the course *save that of building up a friendly relationship* with the members.' (our italics). Similarly Barbara Ward (*Youth Review,* Spring 1970) describes her work ('mostly just standing by while the young person worked towards his or her solutions') in terms which recall strongly the rationale of 'counselling'.

This attempt to make 'the personal friend' part of the institution can be seen in the stress put by almost every experiment on the personality of the particular youth workers involved. Two reports include a quite specific description of the types of people needed for the work; neither of them make reference to training, both stress that qualification is in terms of personality: 'capacity for feeling, ability to organize under stress, honesty about ignorance and failure, clarity of perception, and willingness to act in uncertainty' ('Brighton Archways Venture'); 'what signs are there in the applicant of recognition of legitimate differences in systems and values and standards between individuals, groups, institutions within the community?" (Goetschius and Tash, 1967). And the second of these is quite clear about its preference for 'naturals' over trained professionals, at least in terms of pre-service training. The editor of another report MAYC, 1970 acknowledges a similar belief when he describes himself as 'technically unqualified'. Much in-service training, too, supports this view, since it tends to be seen as 'senstivity training'. In a number of experimental projects the workers met for a 'one-day group sensitivity course'.

Many reports show the importance attached to the personality of the workers by giving an initial, extremely personal, description of the worker in terms of family background, personal credo and motivation to youth work or by introducing descriptions of the worker's leisure activities into the middle of a report (Hartley, 1971,). Furthermore, importance is frequently attached to the principle that the experimental youth worker should himself be young (YVFF Stoke, Brighton Archways Venture), that the service should be provided 'by young people' (BIT). And, indeed, one worker with the Brighton Archways Venture explains his failure to make useful contacts with young people in coffee bars in the town as being caused by the fact that, at 29, he is too old to gain acceptance. As one worker himself expressed it, 'If you ever wanted anything would they offer you something that fell off the back of a lorry? Are you one of "them" or one of "us"? The question of acceptance is vitally important for any social worker.' The journalist's comment is even more pertinent, 'Actually (he) at 25, fresh from a Birmingham college course on community work, is *indistinguishable from many of those he works with.*' (our italics).

Clearly, questions of personality and age are very important if the job is that of being accepted as a friend, since personality and age are two of the more important criteria for friendship choices. Such factors will be even more important where work is to be undertaken in coffee bars which, in general, have a clientele of a very restricted age-range.

The *nature* of much experimental provision is also a clear indication of the trend towards the provision of 'professional friends', since coffee bars, detached work, and counselling services (which together constitute a large part of experimental provision) can expect to provide just that — and, in the latter cases, only that.[3] Since 1967 Brent Consultation Centre has provided a counselling service for young people where no prior appointment has been necessary on the part of the client.[4]

Work with Immigrant Youth

A multi-racial approach to youth work with young immigrants was strongly emphasized in the Hunt Report *Immigrants and the Youth Service* (Youth Service Development Council, 1967). The report gave expression to the fears of potential racial conflict that were widespread at the time; the Youth Service was seen to have an important role in the integration of racial groups, particularly during their leisure hours. Such integration, that is the social mixing of white and coloured youths in the same club or organization, rather than the provision of separate clubs, was seen to be essential to the development of racial harmony within the community at large. Thus, when considering how the Youth Service might best provide facilities, the Report made clear recommendations that segregated clubs should not be tolerated (except possibly in the case of Asian girls) and that every effort should be made to attract immigrant young people into the ordinary clubs, possibly by the the use of specially appointed field workers in areas of high immigrant populations, for whom grants might be claimed under the terms of Section III of the Local Government Act 1966. These recommendations were endorsed by DES Circular 8/67.

For a number of workers 'unclubbable' immigrants represented 'a problem' because their separate groupings were seen as a potential threat to the prevailing integrative' solutions'. Some evidence submitted to the Select Committee on Race Relations and Immigration expressed such fear: 'It is most important for the future of race relations that such coloured groups should be given active support and encouragement by

---

[3] It should, however, be said that there are informal counselling services of a more structured nature. See for example the account of the Brent Consultation Centre in *Education*, 1973, 20 April, Vol. 141, No. 16 p. 461 (anon).

[4] The development of counselling techniques in non-institutionalized youth service activities received a parallel stimulus from the publication of the report *The Unattached* — a report of a three year project carried out by the National Association of Youth Clubs (Morse, 1965).

the Youth Service or they will be driven underground and be driven into an attitude of opposition to authority.' (Home office, 1969). Others, however and often those who are most closely associated with coloured young people, see a different 'problem'. They see a group of young people anxious to establish a corporate identity which is not the same as that of the host community and feel strongly that facilities should be provided where these young people may establish their own way of life. These convictions are of varying strengths, ranging from the refreshingly undoctrinaire attitude of a Methodist minister, in the evidence to the Select Committee on Race Relations and Immigration, whose club evenings are segregated just because young people of different origins choose to come on different evenings; through the more precise recommendation of the authors of a YMCA survey in Brixton (Youth Service Development Council, 1967): 'We think it more important to get the young people together than to worry over much at this stage about making them nicely 50% white and 50% coloured; to the more generalized position expressed in the NAYC evidence to the Select Committee on Race Relations and Immigration: 'It is essential that coloured school-leavers should have some sense of identity.' This implicit rejection of the youth club as an instrument for the inculcation of conformity to the larger group is made explicit in a suggestion by John (1970), that clubs themselves could deliberately set out to foster discontent with the existing social order: 'My contention is that the best social work for institutions like the churches and the Youth Service agencies with black and white youths in such localities of social decay is not to provide facilities for sport and dancing to soul music, but to sow the seeds of discontent, or at least to fertilize them.' The suggested approach is almost a classic example of the conflict perspective discussed in Chapter 3.

A further complication arises from the fact that young immigrants are clearly not shielded from another, indigenous, form of conflict, the intergenerational conflict which has become endemic in Western European and American society. For young immigrants this intergenerational conflict may even be more than usually pressing. *Youth and Development in the Caribbean* (Commonwealth Secretariat, 1970) points out: 'In the Caribbean there has traditionally been a deep-seated reverence for seniority in society, measured in terms of years.' Conversely young people who currently receive part of their education in England are likely to expect that degree of independence which has grown with 'the rise of the teenager as a self-conscious generational grouping in the community.' (Hall, 1967). An enquiry by the Manchester Youth Development Trust (1967) showed that coloured immigrants were quite unused to the idea of a separate youth culture. Thus if the young coloured immigrant attempts any kind of rapprochement with British society he may suffer not only inter-racial conflict but also a form of intergenrational conflict which may be much more pronounced for him than for his British counterpart.

If indeed the Youth and Community Service is to provide a remedial service for the socially disadvantaged it should certainly be seeking to serve the coloured immigrant community. Yet the very movement which has made the Youth Service ready to cater for an unorganized and even disaffected group within the youth culture, has been accompanied by a move away from just those 'authoritarian' attitudes which might have lessened the culture shock for coloured adolescents and could certainly have made the service more appealing to coloured parents.

Before going on to a more detailed discussion of those types of Youth Service provision which have had some success with immigrants it may be useful to consider why the Youth Service, on the limited evidence available, appears to have been less successful in promoting integration than have the schools where there has undoubtedly been a measure of success. The difference may exist because of differences in the school and club situations and because of differences in the age ranges concerned. A major difference in situation is that school, up to the age of sixteen, is compulsory and that within the schools pupils have no choice of class — the proximity this enforces almost certainly helps to engender integration (however superficial it may be), although 'there is no basis for assuming that friendship patterns in multi-racial schools will develop across ethnic group lines.' (Bolton and Laishley, 1972). Moreover, since schools are compulsory they are not challenged by commercial alternatives as are clubs. Schools, therefore, keep pupils and to some extent integrate them at compulsory ages.

Certainly there are signs that the desire for segregation, especially at this age, is not all one sided. The Manchester Youth Development Trust (1967) suggests that the sudden breakdown in friendships between black and white children at school leaving age is 'probably less the result of discrimination than the choice of the coloured child and his parents.' However, since they also claim[5] 'that West Indians, unlike Asians, wish to be absorbed into English society' the acceptance of segregation might alternatively be interpreted as a desire to avoid being rejected.

In Spring 1969, a NAYO sub-committee on the contribution which the Youth Service might make to the social and educational development of young immigrants, concluded that 'in the experience of the committee attempts which had been made to develop multi-racial youth groups had failed' (McGill, 1969); a view confirmed by much but not all of the

[5] A claim supported by Evans, (1971) who reports 65% of the Pakistanis interviewed objected to any form of integration which would abolish racial identity (p.14) 41% West Indians, 33% Indians and 12% Pakistanis favoured intermarriage (p.13) It should, however, be pointed out that the report also suggests that there is perhaps more social association between young immigrants and whites than earlier reports have indicated (p.22).

evidence available to the research team. They felt that the only types of clubs which could claim success in integration were:

1. Clubs for children under 11.

2. Single-sex uniformed groups.

3. Single activity clubs.

Of these the first category could hardly claim to fall within Youth Service work proper. The second is reported by other areas as having some degree of success, the reasons suggested being that such organizations are often international and, therefore, known to immigrants in their own countries and that the authority structure they usually provide and the levelling effect of uniform removes status differences. But this is not true for all areas: such groups are not always more successful than non-uniformed clubs. In particular, the third group, single activity clubs, may well draw a mixed clientele too, though the committee claimed that this did not lead to further integration.

The NAYSO sub-committee were not hopeful of securing rapid integration and were ready to support single-race clubs, since they felt that these were what young immigrants wanted, but with the support of the Youth Service officers with special responsibility for immigrants, who could hope to promote integration by inter-club activities such as residential weekends and special events. Certainly the information available suggests that single-race clubs had been most successful in getting the immigrants into the Youth Service.

An analysis of our information shows that successful provision, whether single or multi-racial, is fostered by a limited number of factors. The most important of these is that there should be a Youth Service which is ready and able to reach immigrants at the local and individual level. The importance of individual approaches, once it has been decided to take action, can be seen in the differing success on the one hand of one authority which sent out official letters of enquiry as to the needs of young immigrants and obtained virtually no response and, on the other, of the Youth Service officer who rang up all schools in her area and got the young immigrants to do their own survey thereby obtaining a highly articulate, even vociferous, response. Almost all flourishing schemes seem to depend on this initial personal approach, though the methods vary — for example talks to local school leavers, cooperation with Colleges of Further Education, the issuing of leaflets in the native languages of immigrant groups, approaches to the adult leaders of immigrant communities via Sikh temples or immigrant organizations generally, or by employing a detached worker who makes it his business to get to know the young people themselves in their spontaneously chosen meeting places.

Once this initial personal approach had been made, continuing success appears to have depended on maintaining sympathetic understanding and again the methods have been diverse and not mutually exclusive. Contact with young people themselves and their parents has helped the Youth Service to avoid the estrangement which may come from using a word like 'club', which has other connotations for particular immigrant groups. There is some evidence however that immigrant parents distrust the whole idea of those youth organizations which are not seen as having direct educational purpose and from which they are themselves excluded. The fact that Asians do not wish their adolescent girls to mix with men is acknowledged, but it may be that less rigid and specific community norms of immigrant groups are also upset by provision for a separate youth group, particularly when that provision is unstructured or even 'permissive'. A survey by the Manchester Youth Development Trust found that leisure patterns of young immigrants of both West Indian and Asian origins were closer to those of their families than they were to those of indigenous young people. Evidence to the Select Committee on Race Relations and Immigration suggests that there is a need for community provision for immigrant adults. Sheffield's experience with an Asian club suggests that Asian adults (who have a club of their own next to the youth club) expect to influence the youth club very directly.

One method often recommended for securing contact is to use youth workers who are themselves members of the immigrant community. Here bodies report varying success in recruiting volunteers — some suggest no difficulty, others appear to find it impossible: one local authority service reports twelve immigrants who have taken Bessey courses, only three of these actually helping with youth work subsequently. There is a further hazard, reported by one authority, that in the as yet unsettled communities the position of youth leader may well be used as one way of angling for personal control in the immigrant community to the detriment of the intended youth work.

If club membership declines (other than on a seasonal basis) it seems to be unusually difficult to get immigrant members to return even when personal visits are made to former members. One important factor, therefore, seems to be to keep up membership by offering a club programme which is attractive to immigrants. Here the importance of the Community Relations Commission's policy of support to spontaneously arising groups can be seen, since such groups may often have already determined their own needs (even if these be merely ones of association) and the simple provision of a meeting place can make for an easy start. The importance of providing the kind of club that immigrants want can be seen in one experience reported where immigrants joined a club in order to be able to register themselves in a youth football league, and thereupon established for themselves an atmosphere of 'unstructured association'; when a new leader imposed a supervised structure of activities on the club, its membership declined despite the young people's desire to remain in the football league. This is not to suggest that activities in themselves are not attractive, indeed, clubs are more successful in attracting immigrants to specific activities which, again, provide a built-in structure rather than presenting the behavioural uncertainties of the 'chat and sit' clubs.

To summarize, then, numerical success in attracting immigrants into the Youth Service has come largely in areas where provision is single-race, predominantly male, flexible enough to cater for activities or social meetings and founded on a close knowledge of the locality and the individuals concerned and geared to their needs. Multi-racial provision appears to have been much less successful and even where success is ·claimed there appears to be considerable fluctuation in the participation of immigrant club members. Hartley (1969) suggests that groups of either immigrant or indigenous youths tend to dominate and the non-dominant groups tend to withdraw in waves and then to return and dominate, a pattern in some ways reminiscent of the theories of 'circulating elite' groups propounded by Pareto and other social theorists. Methods intended to avoid rejection or withdrawal may, on closer examination, turn out to be covert methods of providing single-race provision — often in a variety of clubs under one name, perhaps with immigrant and indigenous young people meeting on separate nights or for separate purposes. But there are examples of apparently successful multi-racial provision. The Bristol Youth Service seems to be one such area. Equally, clubs held on school premises at times of day when young people appear to feel that they need them (say for two hours after school before parents come home) often attract more young people than conventional evening clubs, though here again one perceptive report points out that a large group of young people will play around the school in the play-ground but not join any after school club and any approach by youth workers from the school to join them on their chosen ground leads to their dispersal.

Other methods, for example to introduce immigrants gradually to clubs and to discuss their introduction with existing club members, may help to retain both white and coloured members but many leaders acknowledge that, whatever methods they use, their club tends to become either overwhelmingly immigrant or to remain completely indigenous. Moreover, when it is possible to analyse numbers in apparently integrated clubs it often turns out that the members are predominantly male immigrants with a sprinkling of rather young and disadvantaged white girls. Only in areas where coloured immigrants are so thinly dispersed as not to be seen as a threat to existing groups did we find there had been any approach to 'proportionate representation' of integration in youth clubs. But neither present housing allocation policies, nor the incidence of suitable employment, nor often the wishes of the immigrants (particularly Asian immigrants) themselves, in general foster such dispersion.[6]

Of current practices the one which seems to have been most conducive to integration (admittedly of a temporary kind) has come where Youth Service officers have acknowledged the existence of a racial division among their clubs and set out to encourage those clubs (or groups) which are largely immigrant to participate with indigenous groups in inter-club activities, such as games leagues, arts festivals, Councils of Youth and residential courses. Inter-club participation can lead also to situations such as the one in Sheffield where, for example, a young immigrant has been Chairman of the Sheffield Association of Youth Clubs. Another form of successful and unforced, if rather uneven, contact comes from the use of language courses (often residential) where indigenous people, with expert guidance and coaching, tutor young immigrants, often on a one-to-one basis.

One point occurs repeatedly in oral or written reports. The Youth Service is no more than a part of the community in which it finds itself and its nature is largely determined thereby. Youth Service workers in areas, often the more difficult ones, where other community services, particularly housing, police and education, are working towards integration, tend to find this part of their task easier. In this aspect of their work, as in the other experimental areas, the alignment of the Youth Service workers with social work approaches, rather than with specifically educational ones, is notable. Some Youth Service workers go further and make positive efforts to provide a form of liaison between immigrant young people and the community, particularly the police, and this is of especial importance in areas where the existence of single-race clubs could give rise to aggressive alignments (as it appears to have done in the case of the Metro Club in Notting Hill (*Guardian*, 1971)).

The Evaluation of Experimental Projects

The problem of evaluation is the recurring theme of every discussion of experimental projects, most notably those with young immigrants. Where objectives are, of necessity, flexible and have often to be formulated during the process of a project, it is clear that any conventional 'hard' evaluation by reference to predetermined 'objective' criteria is impossible. Most evaluations are probably no more than signs of intuitive assent such as that of a Director of Education who reported to us, 'The

---

[6] Although Evans (1972) found that 'most of the young immigrants questioned said that if they should want to move to another neighbourhood, they would think of it being mixed white and coloured'; he suggests that 'it is possible that to move to a more "mixed" area is seen as a corollary of social and economic advancement rather than of value in itself.'

worker eventually made contact with a group of young men organizing the discotheque. He was able to assess their needs early in the relationship and worked with them both inside and outside the setting at quite a depth.' Unlike the report of the Wincroft Project where considerable detail is given (Smith, Farrant and Marchant, 1972) evaluation in terms of value for money is even more rarely attempted. Details of costing are scarcely ever given in reports, and even when they are given they often omit relevant facts. The report 'Contact', for example, appears to give a costing of '£47 for working expenses for a twelve week period for nine workers' but omits to say how large was the 'subsidy for two training weekends' mentioned, and gives no account of the cost of employing the Detached Worker Team and the Project Director, some part of whose ongoing salaries must surely be accountable to the project. How, then, is one to compare this with the £15,000 over three years which had to cater for the total running costs (salaries of workers, rents, supervision, expenses of printing a report etc. etc.) of the Brighton Archways Venture? And how is one to compare either with the cost of running a conventional club, which may be using multi-purpose premises and employing part-time youth workers?

In so far as experimental projects are open-ended and exploratory, rather than attempts to test a particular and limited hypothesis, they will necessarily experience the problems which such a lack of definition creates. Some, though not all, of the problems which have arisen for experimental projects are of this unavoidable kind. Where particular methods of work necessarily involve difficulties and disadvantages it becomes a matter of subjective judgement whether the advantages outweigh the disadvantages. It may, therefore, be helpful to analyse some of the difficulties of evaluation which have arisen for a representative group of experimental projects.

In an attempt to make greater progress on the question of evaluation we moved from more traditional approaches to the concept of illuminative evaluation[7] a strategy that endeavours to seek the fullest information on the consequences of an activity as a whole — its rationale, milieu, operation and problems; not just its results and to make them available for use by those concerned with the activity during its progress, helping them to illuminate their problems. In consequence our search for information ranged widely and was undertaken in close cooperation with participants in experimental projects, notably with the YVFF workers in Stoke-on-Trent.

There are three problems on which we focussed such evaluation. The first and perhaps central, problem of most projects is how to reach a target population (which is in any case very loosely defined) without

[7] A term used extensively by Parlett & Hamilton (1972).

risking the principle of voluntary association on which the Youth Service is based. The difficulties inherent in this situation are displayed in the repeated confusion in which workers find themselves when they are forced to intrude upon groups and individuals in order to bring them as they hope, in the long run, to a position of independence. The clients of a 'Consultation Centre' were voluntary. 'Young people get to know about the Centre . . . through notices displayed in schools, youth clubs, doctors waiting rooms and libraries and through advertisements in the local papers' (anon. 1973b). It is, however, not without significance, that the types of problem dealt with were of a personal nature (worries, depression, loneliness, failure) rather than potential deliquency. A second problem arises by reason of the fact that the 'independence' which projects can offer to groups is never complete, since it is almost always the workers and/or their committees who have to accept ultimate responsibility, even when the worker is not attached to Youth Service premises. A third difficulty arises from the newness of the concept of 'professional friend' which, it has been suggested, most experimental workers embody, since it leads to important confusions in role definition for both the worker and his client.

These three problems, which may be inherent in trying to establish a project, may lead to a lack of frankness on the part of the workers concerned. A phamphlet, 'Making Contact with Unreached Youth', (Farrant and Marchant, 1970) openly directs itself to instruction in how a worker may gain acceptance in a particular group. The behaviours recommended to the worker in this pamphlet (the engineering of incidents such as dropping coins or spilling drinks, the ready offer of lights, or cigarettes, or lifts) are, at the least, disingenuous, since they largely involve a categorical imitation of the gestures of friendship without one vital factor of friendship — voluntariness of association. Many young people may be disillusioned if and when they realise that this relationship is not one of 'friendship' as they would define it. Thus in the Brighton Archways Venture one girl is reported as accusing the worker of talking to her 'solely because he was paid to do it'. She often put this in terms of, 'I'm your business'. Indeed, this loss of voluntariness of association seems characteristic, more especially in view of the repeated claim of experimental projects that they are less directive than conventional ones. The overwhelming impression left by many projects is that a group of young people who have deliberately opted out of the youth service are being brought into its sphere without their knowledge or consent. The projects claim to be 'enabling' but young people befriended by strangers in coffee bars, or by men behind the counter, or by youth workers not known to be such in holiday camps, are arguably being denied even the right to opt out. Thus Goetschius and Tash (1967) report: 'Frequently a worker planned the "casual meetings." The situation can be seen in an extreme in the Brighton Archways Venture where the chairman of the project reports, 'We are running a day hospital for the mentally disturbed', yet it is quite clear that the 'patients' in the hospital were in a sense involuntary since they did not think themselves to be in a 'hospital for the mentally disturbed'.

A lack of frankness may lead to disillusion if it is discovered. Goetschius and Tash (1967) report that one of their workers, anxious not to have a particular group on the premises at one time, avoids a show of authority himself by getting his committee to write him a letter saying that such numbers are not permitted since they lead to overcrowding, though this was not, in fact, the reason for 'wanting them out'. Almost always, despite the show of independence given to the target groups, the workers retain vital authoritarian rights — in particular, the right to exclude those they do not want in. It is not then surprising that the young people, told they are independent, are disillusioned by the reality. 'They did not seem to understand that they were being treated responsibly as adults', complained one worker at a residential camp, apparent recognition that 'responsible adults' would not expect to have numbers of 'enablers' and 'facilitators' dotted around such a camp. As our report on YVFF in Stoke-on-Trent shows, YVFF offer a similar show of independence to people using their premises who are encouraged to make rules for its use, apparently independently; but it is the YVFF workers who seemed to retain the ultimate sanction of exclusion.

Perhaps the most keenly felt conflict is that between the desire for frankness on the one hand, and the difficulty in describing an entirely new role in terms comprehensible (or acceptable) to the target population on the other. The worker on the Soho Project *(Youth Review,* 1970) described how people came to regard her as part of the 'welfare', but most workers (and this includes the Soho worker) do not wish to be so classified. Moore (1971) describes the dilemma: 'Many young people who are thought to need the services of detached workers have had contact with statutory social workers, probation officers, Family Service caseworkers and others throughout most of their lives and may view this "special social worker" as an extension of the prying and controlling which they associate with social workers.' Yet it is obviously difficult for the workers to put over any other concept if they are to be frank. 'I see my role as dealing with individuals and making sure they are happy,' comes surely very near to the social worker roles listed above.

Moreover, the role of 'professional friend' involves a further difficulty of interpretation. Friends might expect to accept anyone as potential members of a friendship group, but youth workers obviously have to be selective in their proffered 'friendships' if they are to reach only their target groups of young people. The corollary of the difficulty in reaching the target group, then, is the difficulty in keeping out non-members of the group who are reached adventitiously by a project which gives an unsubstantiated appearance of welcoming all. 'We wished to present an open and accepting welcome without operating barriers based on traditional criteria of social acceptability, membership, entrance fees or early closing . . . Some of these people we did not wish to have on our premises but without the conventional barriers the task of rejecting the undesired had to be done by personal approach.' (Brighton Archways Venture, 1968) Similarly YVFF, Stoke-on-Trent found that numbers of young children attracted to their project put off the adolescents and felt obliged, therefore, to exclude the children. Two ways are used of dealing with the difficulty. A project may decide on lines of demarcation, implicitly or explicitly agreed by the workers, and then use whatever method it sees fit to keep to them — but rarely telling the surrounding group what these lines of demarcation are. (Brighton Archways Venture, 1968). Alternatively, it may allow even its own very tentatively drawn lines of demarcation to be overstepped by those who are not conscious of these lines. This second method has the advantage of offering extremely flexible responses to any demand which makes itself known (Cox, 1970.) and YVFF, Stoke-on-Trent gives help to any kind of community enterprise that the workers feel can profit by such help, but, of course, the policy of not keeping the work within an accepted division may lead to clashes with the committee, and/or to difficulty in transforming the 'experiment' into ongoing work.

A further important difficulty arising from the role of 'professional friend' and its natural confusion in the minds of the clientele with the role of friend lies in the delimited and impermanent nature of the professional relationship, as compared with the unbounded and permanent nature of friendship proper. The limitations put upon 'professional friendship' are not always obvious to clients (or even to workers), and the questions that such limitations bring up have often, therefore, to be dealt with in a piecemeal way with no traditional points of reference. Should a worker, for example, be ready to lend money to clients in need, as he might well to a friend proper? (Goetschius and Tash, 1967.) If so does the money come from private or project resources? What are the limits of loyalty to someone professionally befriended? Do they extend to the condoning of legal offences? (Cox, 1970.) Such problems are likely to be all the more frequent for workers whose economic and social situation is almost certainly very different from that of their clients. Moreover, undefined limits mean that workers often undertake far more responsibilities than they can comfortably carry. The need for time off may go unrecognized until a worker feels himself dangerously near breaking point. (Brighton Archways Venture, 1968; Bath and Wells, 1970.)

Lack of permanence of workers in this quasi-friendship position repeatedly raises problems for experimental projects. 'Contact is an individual thing,' insists one report, 'it depends on the person whether they can make contact.' Goetschius and Tash (1967) are even clearer about this: 'We needed to give *ourselves* in a definite and limited way, ourselves as persons in a relationship, to be used in terms of young people's needs;' One very obvious consequence of this is that, when particular workers leave, a project tends to collapse. 'Others succeeded him but membership declined,' sums up many of the projects.

Lack of prior definition of aims, methods, and systems of evaluation naturally often lead to disagreements between workers and committees. The workers, on the one hand, may feel that only the man on the shop floor can sense what is required in the exploratory situation of an experimental project. The committee, on the other, may feel that they are nominally responsible for a project and should, in fact, be in control. Committees, like those of YVFF or Avenues Unlimited, (Cox, 1970) which allow a good deal of latitude to their workers, avoid clashes but forfeit some of their day-to-day responsibility. Clashes are likely to be especially bitter where there may have been a lack of frankness (either conscious or unconscious) on the part of a pressure group trying to get a project going. Thus the group trying to start the Brighton Archways Venture 'sought out those people who would look convincing and responsible to the Department'[8] and then were aggrieved when the committee attempted direction: 'If you trust your workers you must give

---

[8] Department of Education and Science

them money and an entirely free hand.' (Brighton Archways Venture, 1968). Disagreements with committees are likely to be aggravated by the disenchantment of the local public, if a project is working with a section of society which is felt by the public to be anti-social. Any sympathetic treatment of such young people is apt to be considered a form of alliance against society. Dave's Cave, Bradford was closed down because its image was alienating parents from the general youth service. The London Teen Canteen came to be regarded by the police as a trouble spot.

The definition of how flexible is 'flexible' also leads to the possibility of disputes between committees and workers. Goetschius and Tash (1967) record their committee's lack of sympathy with the workers' giving, or lending, money to clients. Brighton Archways Venture's use of grant money to provide legal aid for a client led to delay in payment of the DES grant.

Yet illuminative evaluation can mean that comparisons between the success of different experiments or between experimental and traditional work are often impossible. Thus, the Brighton Archways Venture and BIT appear to be attempting to provide a service for a similar clientele; how can one compare the value of the work of the one group, which describes how a worker tears up the papers carried by an annoyed client who has just smashed a hardboard painting and concludes, 'This helped to establish in Robbie's mind that the Archway was for several people, of whom he was only one,' with the value of another which describes its work in terms of '44 phone calls a week from September 1968 to August 1969, of which 1,457 were for urgent help'.

Clearly it is difficult to make any general statement about the overall success or failure of experimental projects. The newness of the concepts involved, the intrinsic difficulties in evaluation, the specific and non-transferable nature of the particular solutions projects often set out to offer, the pressures of time and the *ad hoc* decisions of people actually working on projects, all make appraisal difficult.

There are two general points to be made however. One is that what-soever response the Youth Service might make to the needs of special categories of young people in need, it must be based upon an intimate knowledge of the particular community or group concerned and the total political and social context in which it exists. And for any real evaluation to be made of the needs of the community or group to be served, penetrating questions must be asked and answered by the young people themselves. Immigrant youths and deprived youths are but categories of young people with problems to whom the new approaches are directed. Indeed, it is arguable that it might be more meaningful to categorize them under their other problems — of unemployment, poverty, poor housing and general 'powerlessness' in the community. Defined in this way, the need for specific designation could disappear. There is evidence that the new multi-problem, multi-disciplinary approaches within the

Youth Service are taking such a view; the relative lack of evidence on immigrant provision may be because, in the most relevant areas of Youth Service provision, the term is no longer seen to be of use.

The second general point is that while conventional 'objective' evaluation is of little assistance, illuminative evaluation of the kind employed can be of considerable use. In an attempt to develop this instrument more fully and to use it more fully in the way it is intended to be used, we undertook with the workers concerned a detailed study of one experimental project — YVFF work in Stoke-on-Trent. This study also serves the purpose of describing and giving the 'feel' of such a project in a manner that has not been possible in the general accounts offered in this chapter.

9 The YVFF in Stoke-on-Trent: a case study

The Aims of the YVFF

Our decision to mount a case study of an experimental project quickly led us to consider an aspect of the work of YVFF, one of the more visible, supported and radical of the new organizations. One of their projects was conveniently situated at Stoke-on-Trent as a result of the favourable response of the Stoke-on-Trent LEA to DES Circular 6/68. The response of YVFF both nationally and locally was enthusiastic and this chapter has been written in close collaboration with their workers. Parts of this chapter have been used, with permission, in YVF documents.

The Young Volunteer Force Foundation was set up in December 1967 under a Trust Deed issued by the Chairman of the Trustees, Douglas Houghton, a Labour Member of Parliament, and approved by the Secretary of State for Education. In keeping with its non- (or all) party nature, its first vice-chairmen were Selwyn Lloyd, a Conservative member of parliament, and Jo Grimond, a Liberal member of parliament. The objects of the Foundation as given in the Trust Deed has a strong 'Peace Corps' flavour. They are:

> To educate young people of either sex by teaching them, in particular, the need for and the manner of rendering service to the community and in particular the aged and the disabled;
>
> to render service, including the making of payments, to the community, and in particular the aged and the disabled, with a view to the improvement of their conditions of life, when they are in need of service by reasons of age, infirmity, disablement or social or economic circumstances affecting them.

In April 1968 a joint circular was sent to all LEAs, County Councils, Borough Councils etc. by the Department of Education and Science, the Ministry of Health, the Home Office and the Ministry of Housing and

168

Local Government. In this circular the aim of the Foundation is described as 'the establishment of an *advisory and consultancy* service' whose purpose is to make 'more effective the contacts between volunteers on the one hand and the community on the other.' The circular stresses that the YVF will only operate by invitation in any local authority area, and that it has 'no intention of duplicating or of supplanting the considerable work already done by existing voluntary agencies. The unit is to have a 'full-time staff of *young people* chosen for their experience in or aptitude for community service', though this is 'in no way to be taken to imply the exclusion of older people who would like to participate', and it is to carry out its advisory function in two ways. 'First, on invitation it will send small teams of its staff into an area for a period, to help in the setting up of machinery for stimulating and sustaining the interest of young people in community service, whether as members of youth service or other voluntary organisations or as individuals, preparing them for this, bringing them into contact with local and hospital authorities and other bodies concerned and convincing these, where necessary, of the value of the voluntary contribution which young people can make. Second, it will provide a consultancy and information service, based not only on its own experience in field work but on a study of what has been, and is being done in various parts of the country by other agencies.'

The circular also insists that, though the Foundation will be partly financed by Government grant (£1,000,000, from the DES available over three years in the first instance), 'it will depend for additional income on voluntary sources, and its independence of goverment control has also been ensured by the terms of the Trust Deed.'

In an early publication of YVF, *This Service is Alive* (Steen, 1968) the Director, Anthony Steen, makes his own declaration of intention. He stresses the fact that YVF will itself be an organization of young people, 'high calibre young staff, flexible enough to adjust to local needs' (he himself was 29 at the time) who will by their very youth avoid 'the paternalism of the educationists' which has so far served 'to inflame the situation'. He sees the recommendations of the Bessey Committee as being faulty in two ways: first, their recommendation that the energies of the young should be channelled into community service would merely mean that the young were providing a palliative for the superficial ills of society, when what is needed is a reorganization of society; secondly, their suggestion that this voluntary service should be 'under the scrutiny of local dignitaries, with control in the hands of middle-aged people already ensnared in the 'system' would mean that young people would once more 'start at a social disadvantage just because they are young.' He is glad, therefore, that 'the Government abandoned Bessey in favour of something entirely new which was to be run by young people themselves on their own terms and with independence guaranteed.' The 'newness' of the project, as seen by Steen, consists first in the fact that young people's involvement will be, at least partially, self-directed ('The field teams help volunteers to identify the local problems, decide priorities and recommend positive action' and secondly in the fact that this involvement will 'deepen their understanding' of the nature of society. Thus, the importance of the venture lies not so much in the completion of tasks as in the growth of self-direction and understanding within the young people themselves, and in its appeal to that 75 per cent of the young population who do not join conventional, 'other-directed' youth clubs. The commitment to self-direction of groups is such that YVF expects to withdraw its own field-staff once groups become independent.

It is clear from the above summaries that differing emphases are given by different bodies, and that these discrepancies may well give rise to later conflict. The Trust Deed, for example, acknowledges both a broadly educational purpose and a quite specific task orientation, directed principally towards the needs of the aged and disabled. It does not claim that the young volunteers must be 'educated' solely by people themselves still young. The DES circular emphasizes principally the advisory and consultancy functions of the staff, and their role as liaison officers between the supply of youthful goodwill and the many (unspecified) tasks which young people might fulfil. It evisages that the salaried field teams will be young themselves, but specifically refuses to exclude older people from the volunteer force. The director's statement, however, excludes older people from both the salaried staffs of YVFF and from the volunteer force. It plays down the importance of the individual task, which it sees as an introduction to the education of the young in the nature of social structure and social need. It is concerned with community change rather than case-work.

Equally, there may well be discrepancies in the degree of autonomy claimed, both for YVFF itself and for the field teams and the volunteers within it, and the degree of autonomy to be expected from the constitution of YVFF. As for financial independence, certainly the Government's initial grant of £1,000,000 over three years had few strings attached, but it did have one important string, that renewal is, of course, at Government discretion. The £55,000 raised for the financial year 1969/70 from private and business sources was untied, but the £30,000 raised for the same period by the twelve local authorities who invited YVFF to set up centres in their areas was subject to the same control as the initial Government grant, that it was only renewable at discretion.

As for the independence of field teams and volunteers, it was seen from the outset that there may be difficulties. The director's statement claims that centres based themselves at 'street level' and that 'in this way the keen, the casually interested and the drop-out can get together on equal terms', but it was evident that the 'keen', and, more particularly,

the professional full-time field teams, would unavoidably be the chief
influences. It seemd clear that the foundation was necessarily faced with
certain possibilities of conflict by the very nature of its principles and its
constitution.

After a total of six uneven years of support from national and local
funds, YVF was relaunched in April 1974 with government support of
£626,000 — £192,000 a year for three years and £50,000 to pay for a
new out-of-London HQ. A further £43,000 has been reserved for two
resource centres. Money allocated by local authorities and raised from
other sources means that YVF will spend around £390,000 a year.

Following the election of its first director to Parliament, Geoffrey
Clarkson has taken charge of the Foundation, and will execute Steen's
policy of radical rather than gap filling approaches to social problems — a
policy strongly endorsed by the Home Office. Not only should the 22
field projects experiment with new ideas for reviving the depressed
communities they are in, but they should, says the Home Office,
concentrate on new approaches that are most likely to be adaptable to
other parts of the country.

Des Wilson, writing in the *Observer* (31 March 1974) commented:

> Before making the grant, the Home Office had to swallow a paper
> from YVF complaining about the imbalance 'in the structures,
> functions and values of society as a whole' and describing part of the
> YVF role as 'to redress this balance by conscious and skilful
> intervention' — words that a few years back would have caused a fit
> of apoplexy in any civil servant worthy of the name. Either there has
> been a revolution at the Home Office or (more probably) they have
> learned that such words from the new breed of radical social worker
> are inevitable but rarely frightening in practice.

> After the relaunch YVF should have a much more confident,
> permanent feel about it. It is here to stay. Harold Wilson's baby has
> survived its crisis-ridden childhood to reach affluent, influential
> adolescence; much of the rest of the country's community develop-
> ment work can be expected over the years to regroup around it.

The Establishment of the YVFF in Stoke-on-Trent

It is clear from the publications issued by the central organization of the
YVFF that it aims to penetrate to the most deprived areas of the country
but it imposes one very severe limitation on its own choice of area —
it sets up centres only where it is invited by local authorities, and where
some, at least of its funds come from the local authority. Viewed as a
concession to political realities the restriction is undestandable, but it is

as well to bear in mind that this may mean that YVFF centres are not always set up in the area of greatest social need. However, the individual workers bear no responsibility for the choice of local authority areas to which they are sent, (though once delegated to a particular area they do claim complete choice as to where they set up shop).

In September, 1969 two YVFF field workers arrived in Stoke, with a brief to set up headquarters at their own discretion anywhere within the local authority area, and with an initial estimate that the project would be funded for three years within a total budget of £20,000, half of which was to be provided by the foundation out of Government funds. One of the workers had already worked with YVFF in Chesterfield and Shirebrook in Derbyshire. The other field worker was new to the work, but had attended a month's training course in London. Both were in their mid-twenties. They saw their first task as the investigation of needs within the area, so that they might decide where their centre should be. They were realistically convinced that wherever they founded their physical centre it would, in fact, prove to be the central point of their community influence, and that they could not hope to penetrate directly to all areas of the community. The most important single criterion was to be the needs of the area; resources available (in money, personnel, abilities) were to be a limiting factor only when needs were established. They realized from the first that Stoke-on-Trent was an uneasy agglomeration of quite separate communities — not merely of the original six towns which had become, by federation, 'Stoke-on-Trent' but also of much smaller communities within and beyond these towns — since they accepted the definition of a community as any geographically defined area where the people felt themselves, or were felt by others, to be a separate community.

They chose to investigate needs both at the level of individual deprivation (as indicated by figures on mental health, suicide, marital problems, loneliness, incidence of disability or old age) and at the level of community deprivation (as indicated by lack of community identity, poor facilities for play or social activity, lack of shops). Any comprehensive survey of needs was clearly beyond their resources in manpower, given that they wished to be in operation rapidly. Personal impressions were likely to be both superficial and subjectively slanted by the workers' own dominant interests. They decided, therefore, to seek advice from social workers, local councillors, informal community leaders, and such interested parties as the Citizens Advice Bureau and the Social Work and other Departments of the University of Keele. It is clear, however, from their weekly reports that though they made a conscious decision to base their choice on the third method (the gathering and assessment of expert, interested opinion) they were, in fact, much influenced by personal impressions gathered as they wandered about the city. This first part of their investigations lasted a month and was taken up with meetings with officials from statutory and voluntary organizations in the area. Despite obvious pressures from interested parties, the field-workers insisted on holding aloof from commitment to specific locations or to specific tasks, even when they were sympathetic to the hardships which might be caused by such events as the imminent demise of the Stoke Council for Social Service. This refusal to commit themselves was partly due to a tactful wish not to offend existing organizations (statutory or otherwise), but chiefly it was because the fieldworkers saw this period as a time for the absorption of information from all sides. As a result of these meetings they identified 23 viably separate communities in Stoke-on-Trent. They then set out to co-ordinate the information they now had available about these areas.

Several of the officials to whom they had talked had distinguished two types of area within the city boundaries — the decaying centres of the old towns, and the 'soulless' new housing estates. The types of deprivation involved are implicit in the terms of description — the newer areas were not badly off in terms of housing, and some, for example Bentilee, had specifically provided community centres, but they were less well provided with miscellaneous existing premises adaptable for community purposes and lacked any focus (often indeed physically lacked a central point); the decaying centres were short of community premises and their centres, though well defined, were increasingly dilapidated. Any one of these 23 areas might benefit from YVFF support; the field-workers felt that the work they could best do would require close involvement with the chosen community and that they must, therefore, choose just one. They decided, therefore, to add to their exiting information any statistical data they could find about what they considered to be relevant indices of need, centered around population statistics; numbers of families with children under supervision by Children's Department (not made available); mental health figures, educational provision (including 'early leaving' numbers), housing (including eviction orders, arrears, old people's homes, length of waiting lists), statutory and voluntary youth provision social clubs (sports, drama, old people's clubs, working-men's clubs etc.), numbers on probation, community amenities (shops, commercially operated clubs, cinemas, park and play facilities), local transport facilities. Much of this information was available only in the form of returns for particular political wards (24 in all) whose boundaries were by no means co-terminous with the 'communities' as identified above by the YVFF field workers. However, they did their best to apportion these data, and the results of these investigations, when added to the personal opinions expressed by relevant officials, left them with six areas of relative deprivation, in any one of which they might feel there was need. These areas were: Stoke and Fenton of the 'decaying town centres' variety; Chell Heath, Norton, Abbey Hulton and Bentilee of the 'soulless new housing estates' variety.

This list made some concession to pressures which the workers define as political in that it eliminated areas which the City Council might regard as unacceptably small for a Council-financed enterprise, and also areas so near the edge of the city and so inaccessible to other areas as to be difficult to justify in terms of a whole city enterprise.

At this point the workers felt that they had gone as far as they could with contacts at the 'first level', this is at the level of those whose concern was with the whole city. Now they decided to move to what they considered the 'second level', that is the level of interested parties whose concern was more particularly with one of these specific selected communities — such people as teachers, social workers, youth workers. In order to save time they now operated separately, not as a pair. But the most important difference in their activities arose from a deliberate change in point of view. Up to this stage they had considered only needs; from now onwards they felt that they must consider also resources, both personal (in terms of their own interests and abilities) and economic. They also felt that they must make a realistic assessment of the chosen community's ability to provide its own resources, and of the possibility of a community's finding suitable premises. The second month after arrival in Stoke was spent, therefore, in discussion with people influential within these six essentially local communities — such people as local representatives on the council, headmasters, youth leaders, church leaders. One of the six areas under investigation, Norton, was eliminated fairly early as having already a fair degree of the kind of coverage which YVFF might hope to provide.

It is interesting to see the grounds on which the final choice was made from the remaining five areas. The criterion of choice had quite suddenly ceased to be need and become one of ability to satisfy need. Two factors must be borne in mind here: first that the field workers had quite consciously chosen to allow resources (both their own and those of the communnity chosen) to become one added criterion; secondly that they had already established that there was a fair degree of need in all six communities on their short list. However, too much weight must not be given to these factors, first, since a decision to use ability to satisfy need as *one* criterion is very different from a decision to use it as *the* criterion; and second, since they had been rapidly able to prove to their own satisfaction that one of their original six communities was not, in fact, in need in the sense in which they felt they must define the term. As far as need was concerned, it was obvious from the contacts that the field workers made that Chell Heath must come first, as a 'problem estate' with a high rate of eviction, a high rate of crime, a high rate of referral to statutory agencies, and a young population notably wild and uncatered for. But it was rejected on the grounds 'that it would not respond to [a YVFF] kind of programme very quickly.' 'We bow to the pressure to produce some visible results fairly quickly, and so reject Chell', is how the workers explain their rejection.

Fenton and Stoke, which were places with obvious needs, were rejected largely on the grounds that they were subject to depopulation, and that 'if one has limited resources it seems more sensible to work in a place with a long future.' The grounds for rejection seem debatable, since it is obvious that Stoke and Fenton both have futures likely to be as long lived as that of YVFF, and that it may well be that such areas of depopulation are ones of greatest community need. The reasons for rejecting Abbey Hulton are not made clear, except that it 'would be a grind' to work there.

Bentilee, then, was chosen in spite (or perhaps because) of the fact that conditions were not so bad as in three of the other four areas then under consideration. The area is not physically run down — it has a new estate of houses built about fifteen years ago, with a very adequately equipped community centre and a centre well supplied with shops for day-to-day supplies. The field workers had been given some indication of need in that a larger than average number of children were referred to the Mental Health Officer in the city, and in their information that there had at one time been a gang of youths who had indulged in acts of petty destruction. However, once this gang had been 'busted' by the police it had not reformed. Two youth clubs already existed. There was an active Old People's Welfare Committee, who had visted every house on the estate, and the Roman Catholic and Methodist Churches ran a visiting service to old people. The Bucknall Amenities Association were also helping old people on the estate. One youth leader had already seen to it that some school playing fields should be open to the local community during the summer holidays. One might, therefore, question the choice of area in which to work. It appears not to satisfy as well as other areas might have done the conditions envisaged in the Trust Deed of YVFF, where young people were to serve particularly 'the aged and the disabled'; nor does it seem a particularly appropriate area for the setting up an 'advisory and consultancy service' as envisaged in the DES circular, as this might be expected to work better from some central location.

The Project in Bentilee

Establishing a Base

Once these reservations have been made, however, it is only fair to say that whatever its position may be in any order of relative deprivation, Bentilee is undoubtedly a place where there is ample justification for the application of new resources. Interestingly enough, it had been the subject in 1967 of an academic study demonstrating the importance of

'Space Relationships in Neighbourhood Planning'. (Herbert and Rodgers, 1967.) The authors of this study had pointed out that the shape (long and narrow) of the estate, and the lack of direct roads to the centre from some directions had meant that the comparatively well-provided centre of the estate (where the shops, community centre, health centre, hotel, post office are) was used, as one might expect, only by those with easy access. As many as 69% of tenants on the eastern periphery of the estate (from which access was most difficult) went into Hanley or Longton even for day-to-day shopping. The report concluded that an estate of this size (3,580 houses, population over 14,000) might well be too large to form a coherent community, at least with the type of spatial planning employed in Bentilee.

By the time YVFF came to Bentilee there were admittedly two youth clubs and branches of such national bodies as Brownies, Boys Brigade and Scouts, but for 'unclubbable' youth there was only a weekly dance in the community hall, and even that had been stopped for a time on police recommendation after an outbreak of teenage hooliganism. There were no commercially provided facilities of any kind. Consequently, young people (of whom there were more than on any other city estate) often roamed the streets to the annoyance of the populace, particularly the old people. Pre-school childern were also uncatered for, except for a half day a week play-group scheme in the community hall: attempts to start a proper nursery school had all foundered for lack of money. Yet the estate was one of the largest in the country and unofficial estimates suggested that nine out of ten mothers on the estate were working. There were few playgrounds and mothers were reported to be anxious about the lack of facilities for children in the school holidays (perhaps because so many of them were out of the home working).

The YVFF field workers saw their instrusion into Stoke as a dual one: an intrusion into the chosen small community in Bentilee, and an intrusion into the larger community whose interests the city council might be seen to represent. Of these they regarded the former as by far the more important. They set about getting themselves accepted by the local community first by continual face-to-face contact with local leaders, formal and informal. In their search for appropriate premises they were concerned more with the attitude that the small community might take up if they seemed to be usurping local rights than they were with the mechanics of getting local government permission to take over suitable premises. They were, therefore, reluctant to use a council house or flat as premises, since they felt they might be thought to be depriving the community of one of its most important resources — housing. They were relieved, therefore, to find one of the local, centrally placed shops coming vacant, and more than happy when they were granted the tenancy of it by the local council in January, 1970.

The shop satisfied the immediate need for central and prominent premises. The field workers now made a two-fold approach to getting themselves accepted by the local community. Firstly, they made official (though personal) approaches to the heads of those agencies — Welfare Department, Public Health, Children's Department, Departments of Health and Social Security, Probation, Housing — from whom they expected referrals to come. In these meetings they were careful not to promise too much, and to establish that any work undertaken by their foundation would have to have an educational element for the volunteer as well as being useful in itself. Anxious to offset the obvious uncertainty towards voluntary organizations which they found among some of the professionals (who clearly regarded such associations as likely to be 'amateur' in the worst sense and yet clearly felt uneasy towards their 'dynamic' approaches) they made their approach as businesslike as possible. They did not, however, hesitate to gain permission to approach actual field workers where they felt that these would be more aware of need than their office based superiors, and they were quite explicit in their request that these agencies should not associate them, in potential clients' eyes, with officialdom. In general they appear to have convinced the officials both of their seriousness of purpose and of their probable efficiency.

Their second approach was to the local community itself. Their first step had been a negative, but undoubtedly important one. They had avoided any press or local radio publicity (despite the natural pressure on a body partly financed by the local authority to explain itself.) Partly this was because of the bad image which the publicity given to other YVFF ventures had created in the minds of some local officials; partly it was because the field-workers wished to avoid the almost inevitable focussing on themselves and YVFF (perhaps in the guise of miracle workers), which was bound to arise if the publicity came before the foundation was actually operational; partly it was because they were anxious not to be forced into any premature specific definition of tasks. Once in their shop, the field workers felt justified in allowing the local press and the local radio to give them some coverage. They still went warily, however, and their first press coverage was devoted not to the possibilities of community development work in Bentilee (which they felt would be marred by publicity) but to the advisory service which, backed by the national organization of YVFF, they had offered to the wider Stoke community in a circular which they had sent to interested groups about a month before.

The second step in the field-workers' approach to the local community was also a tentative one, again designed to minimise the sense of intrusion which their arrival might arouse. They set to work to clean and decorate their new shop premises and simply made welcome, and talked to, people who stopped to enquire why they were there. They made use, in other words, of the simple fact that they were there but made no specific claims as to their objects, so as to leave themselves still receptive to the community and its apparent needs.

The First Months

During the first week of March 1970 the field workers opened up their YVFF shop in Bentilee, almost six months after their arrival in Stoke-on-Trent. There was no need to wait for referrals from statutory agencies since within a couple of weeks the shop had attracted a large group of young people.

The shop had been open at varying times of day and the young people had come in when it was open in the evening. However, many of these youngsters were in the main very young — from the six to twelve age group — and were using the shop largely as a play centre, a purpose for which it was neither intended nor adequate. (The fact did, of course, indicate a need for play provision for this age group, which was a confirmation of what the YVFF field workers had already realized.) The children up to thirteen were gradually eased out and an older group took their place. Many of these were deliquent, already in trouble with the law. The workers wished to convey, without being too directive, that the scheme was work-orientated, and the young people themselves seemed to have plenty of ideas about what might be done.

The first suggested project to get under way was the clearing of a local brook. This was followed in the Easter holidays by a successful play-day held around the brook, which made use of the now clear stream for matchbox races and the like. However, a second play-day where the organization was left largely in the hands of the young people themselves was not nearly so successful.

At the same time the field workers were becoming increasingly dissatisfied with their arrangements in the shop. They had no wish to be judgemental, indeed they felt that such an attitude would make impossible the kind of work they wished to do. Nonetheless, they could hardly ignore the strain caused by a large group of immature young people gathered in a small shop with little of a physical nature to occupy them. The occasion came in May, 1970 when they were forced to evict some of the more uncontrolled members of the group in the shop. This incident led the field workers to a careful consideration of what they were actually doing, and of what might usefully be done. They analysed various factors in their present situation:

1. The dual nature of the work they were doing with the young people who came into the shop: (a) They were trying to direct them towards community service, and (b) They were acting as informal counsellors — a service into which they were unavoidably drawn by their contact

with young people. (The outsider is tempted to add a third function — since they seem also to have been a play therapy group.)

2. The fact that adults (with whom they had hoped to be involved in community development projects) were keeping out of the YVFF shop because they associated it essentially with a young and rowdy clientele.

This analysis of the situation enabled the field workers to clarify their position and to decide which of these aspects of their work they wished (and were able) to develop, either with their own resources or with extra help from YVFF or grant aid from the local council. They decided on the following steps:

1. *Work with unattached youth* (basically the group who presently congregated in the shop) should be handed over to an extra worker to be appointed specifically for the task.

2. *Play schemes*, the need for which had been amply demonstrated, should also be handed over to another extra worker and be centred around the brook area.

3. *Community Service* projects, already slowly developing, were to continue, but the smaller number of volunteers left centred upon the shop were expected to be more efficient and independent once the younger and more agressive element were catered for by the 'unattached youth' scheme.

4. *Community development projects* were to stress (a) Work with adults and adult groups and (b) Welfare rights campaign.

5. *Advisory Service* Should be extended.

With the establishment of this list of objectives in May 1970 the YVF in Stoke may be said to have reached the state where its nature is defined.

The Work of Stoke YVF — June 1970 to June 1971

By June 1970 there had been two important shifts in emphasis from the original brief of the organization. The first involved a move away from the position where young people were regarded as the centre of any operation, to a position where the stress was on the needs of the whole community; the second involved a move from an operation devoted to community service (the provision of specific limited aids for specific limited needs) to one devoted to community development (the creation of groups and skills which will facilitate such social change as may eliminate the need for community service). These changes, although partly the result of the Stoke workers' experience on the job, were not peculiar to the Stoke group of YVFF alone, since there had already been a similar, though much less forceful, change in the thinking of the central organization away from a concentration on youth and from narrowly defined community service projects, presumably as a result of the combined experiences of their field teams.

The work that developed during YVFF's first full year in Stoke conformed closely to the analysis of needs and resources made in May 1970.

Community Service Projects: In so far as these are direct and self-contained small scale services (decorating or gardening for those unable to cope themselves etc.) they now scarcely exist. They have never, in fact, been found to contribute to the social education of young people, which had been the motive for introducing them. The one or two projects which have been undertaken on these lines have been used by the field workers rather as a form of therapy for individuals (an unemployed man, for example, or a deliquent boy) with whom they were able to make meaningful contact while engaged on such projects.

The larger scale project which might also be regarded as one of community service, that is the provision of a holiday play scheme for children on the Bentilee estate, provides, with its varying history, an interesting reflection on the thinking of the YVFF workers in Stoke. They had chosen to establish the centre of their activities in one large housing estate outside the city centre, in the confidence that this was a viably separate community, some of whose needs they might hope to meet. One of the first and most obvious needs to present itself to them was a need for play provision during the school holidays. After two months in Bentilee YVFF had run a 'clean up the brook' scheme on an area of neglected council land and had then run two play-days on the site. Despite the comparative failure of the second, which had been left quite largely to the local teenage helpers, such schemes were obviously locally popular.

For Summer 1970, therefore, YVFF appointed a new worker specifically to deal with play provision. He appointed further temporary paid and voluntary workers and a successful scheme was run in the Bentilee brook area during August 1970 with outdoor play provision and with indoor arts and crafts run by a local housewife. In Autumn 1970 this new YVFF worker, who had been expected to develop such play schemes, became first a part-time employee of YVFF and then, in December 1970, left. It looks at first merely opportunistic that this

resignation was accompanied by a change in the attitude towards
play schemes. Yet the resignation can, more persuasively, be regarded as
the occasion rather than the cause of such a change as it was accompanied
by a much more general change in the attitude of the field workers.
The original play scheme was (apart from the tentative move of the
second, unsuccessful, play-day) essentially a form of direct provision.
The decision to continue such schemes only with the help of local leaders
supported by the YVFF but without a YVFF worker to direct them
was part of a more general change from community service to community
development.

By March 1971 the workers point out, quite specifically, that
they do not intend to run such a project themselves and will do no
more than *support* the local community. However they are able to
make this otherwise fairly brutal statement only because they have,
by then, already demonstrated that such provision is both viable and
desirable, and developed a group of interested local people who have
now sufficient skill and interest to be able to run such a scheme themselves with a minimum of support. Moreover, the YVFF are then able
to use the worker appointed for four months with special responsibility
for play schemes more widely to help with three other new play
schemes. It is on the development of such groups, to be considered
below, that the two original workers have concentrated.

Community Development Schemes: The provision of help in cases of
immediate need has come to seem to YVFF workers in Stoke a
mere palliative that will only relieve any one of a constantly changing
series of symptoms, which will in turn be replaced by another requiring
a different palliative. None of these *ad hoc* measures will, they now
feel, cure the disease of economic deprivation and community apathy.
They see hope for a more fundamental change only if this apathy can
be dispelled, so that the community feels itself capable of making its
needs known, and so that new leaders emerge whose contacts with the
neighbourhood unit are unbroken, but whose skills are such that it is
worthwhile for them to engage themselves both in direct provision of
services, and in presenting a case for community help to the local council.
Put in this way the resemblance between the functions of the leaders
of these local groups and the theoretical function of such voluntary
members of local government machinery as local councillors is, of
course, obvious. However, in the setting up of such bodies as YVFF
is an implicit belief that local councillors have to some extent lost
touch either with the local populace or, less commonly, with
centres of local government power, or with both. This belief is made
quite explicit when the YVFF refer to 'a very unpopular local councillor';
theoretically the phrase should be a contradition in terms. The YVFF
workers in Stoke are implicitly concerned, as a community development

organization, in showing people how to make use of local government machinery, which they feel to be now remote, in the form of either councillors or of statutory bodies. Whether or not the YVFF workers in their turn, are in danger of losing their links with 'the people' will be considered below.

As part of their local community development programme the workers have further concerned themselves with the local take-up of welfare benefits, organizing two specific schemes (one on Rates Rebates and one on the Educational Welfare Benefits). It is interesting to note how these schemes, essentially community development ones, are closely linked with the 'Informal Citizens' Advice Bureau service that YVFF runs, which is essentially the direct provision of a service. This latter project arose from local demand. It informs local citizens, upon request, of their rights and obligations. The CAB were unable to set up an office in Bentilee for lack of funds.

Advisory Service: 'Advisory Service' is perhaps a misnomer for what has become during 1970/71 very much an extension of YVFF's community development work but upon a less narrow geographical basis. Demands upon the scheme were at first fewer than expected, despite the fact that 120 letters about the scheme had been sent out to the kind of people who were expected to be interested. However, once one or two projects had been set up with YVFF help, the work gathered momentum, and it now takes up about 50% of the field worker's time.

Much of the work has been done with already existing adult groups, or with groups that in any case had the initiative to form themselves. The YVFF workers see it as their function to facilitate the implementation of the declared aims of the group, by lending the expertise they have acquired both in defining achievable ends and in making use of existing statutory or voluntary provision to achieve them. The advice given by YVFF is usually refreshingly specific, and the work is important for the city-wide acceptance of YVFF since it covers many areas of the city from Chell Heath to Longton and to Stoke City Centre.

The service takes within its scope such things as broad community projects planned by students, surveys of local opinion on Skeffington-type land reclamation schemes for the local Planning Department to more restricted (though perhaps more important) schemes planned by such groups as the Stoke Adventure Playground Association set up on the initiative of YVFF.

Detached Youth Work: The informal 'counselling' service had set itself up as almost inadvertently in the YVFF shop in Bentilee as a spontaneous response to the demands of young people who found there two adults who were approachable but disinterested, knowledgeable but non-judgemental. This was so demanding of shop-space, time and emotional energy that it became impossible for the two original workers to run it, except to the detriment of their other work. In June 1970 they gathered together a group of local educationalists and social service personnel who formed an advisory committee to supervise a Bentilee Youth Project, whose terms of reference were not closely defined, but which appeared to wish to combine a counselling service and detached work with local young people. YVFF agreed to finance a full-time worker for this project, and a new worker was engaged to work in Stoke. For lack of other premises the Bentilee shop continued to be used for this work, even after the introduction of this new worker in September 1970.

This arrangement proved unsatisfactory, in part because the shop premises were not adequate for the combined demands of serving both as office for the adult projects which the original workers ran from the shop, and as a meeting place for a group of vigorous and socially disorganized young people that the new worker was engaged to help. This was not, however, the only reason for the breakdown of the arrangement, The decision of the third YVFF worker to leave, in December 1970, was partly due to personal dissatisfaction, which the original workers later hypothesized was the result of very nebulous job specification and of her anomalous position in being responsible both the YVFF workers in Stoke and to the youth project committee.

In the meantime the committee of interested people had taken on managerial status. They now claimed that there was not sufficient justification for centring such a project upon one housing estate (Bentilee) which in any case could not provide adequate premises and yet was not suitable for a detached work project proper, with no centre. In January 1971 they insisted on a move to the city centre in Hanley. The YVFF workers felt that if they prevented this move by refusing to finance a worker for the project then the development of detached youth work in the city would be considerably hampered. They thus agreed to the move on an experimental basis, reluctant though they were to lose a community project which might well have led to a creative debate on the role of youth within the local community, and have made possible a dialogue between adult and young groups about their conflicting interests.

The committee advertised in June 1971 for an action-research worker to run a project and simultaneously to evaluate the need for continuation. The evaluation and the continuation of YVFF activity in Stoke-on-Trent beyond the period of 1hr study is reported in Young Volunteers Force Foundation (1976).

Comments and Conclusions
The extent to which the work is not in accordance with the original national brief
It was suggested at the beginning of this chapter that the original brief was itself confused, as defined in three separate documents.

Certain principles were, however, agreed by all. Not all of these principles are upheld by the work of YVFF in Stoke.

All the documents are explicit about the fact the YVFF project is to depend chiefly on *young volunteers*. Most of the work in the Stoke scheme is based on adults, though many of the adults fall within the fifteen-thirty age group first suggested by YVFF.

There is a good deal of doubt as to whether the work done with the young volunteers in Bentilee was ever 'educational', however broadly the term may be interpreted. But this stricture does not apply to the detached youth work established in Hanley with the help of YVFF.

The aged and disabled were specifically indicated as groups to be helped. Much of the work in Bentilee is with old people — none of it is with the disabled in the normally accepted sense of the word; that is, it is not with the mentally or physically handicapped. The field workers do, however, make out a case suggesting that they are dealing with the economically disabled.

Community service projects have been few in number and by June 1971 have more or less dwindled to nothing. They have demanded much support and have not, in general, contributed to the social education of the participants. Their decline in importance (and that of the social education which they might be hoped to involve) has arisen from a change in YVFF's thinking which has shifted the emphasis from community service to comunity development.

The extent to which the preconceptions of the Stoke YVFF field workers have not been fulfilled

The need for specifically local community provision has been contradicted in two ways: by the setting-up of the detached youth work centre in Hanley, (reasons for this are given above) and by the fact that some of the Bentilee YVFF's most important and successful schemes (play-schemes, rent rebate schemes) have depended on bringing in volunteers, often sixth-formers or students from outside the local area. (It is important to bear in mind the smaller unit of the community accepted by the Bentilee field workers. The volunteers were not 'outsiders' in the sense of being outside the *city* community.)

Some projected and obviously desirable schemes have not been instituted — notably pre-school play provision. Further, the field workers had hoped and expected to make enough detailed studies of their volunteers to make some assessment of changes brought about by affiliation to YVFF. For wholly understandable reasons (lack of time and extent of personal commitment as well as change in the emphasis of the work) this has not proved possible. Also, the advisory service has become a more time-consuming (and valuable) part of the work than was originally envisaged.

The fact that the YVFF centre in Stoke has not always worked in accordance with its original brief should not be taken as implying that the project has failed. The very fact that the field workers were not obliged to stand by their preconceptions to the letter, as a statutory body could be obliged to, has allowed them to respond to local need. There already appeared to be in Stoke some provision for the disabled: The YVFF workers did not feel obliged to duplicate such provision. The Welfare Rights Scheme might have seemed to outsiders to duplicate the work of the Citizens Advice Bureau; the YVFF workers found, however, that the CAB could not extend its service to local provison in Bentilee, and they knew that local people who needed this advice would not (or could not) make the journey to Hanley to get it. The original brief called for 'young volunteers', and when their community development work needed more mature groups, the YVFF did not hesitate to call upon adults.

The YVFF Methods and their Implications

As far as relationships between the public and the foundation are concerned, the YVFF is unusual in that it comes into a local community from outside. This means that the arrival of the YVFF in Stoke was necessarily, in some sense, an intrusion however much this may have been played down by the tactful determination of the original field workers not to usurp existing functions. Intrusion may, however, bring its own benefits, namely that a fresh eye may well see truths to which local residents are inured by custom, and that outsiders are not bound by the claims of smaller local loyalties. Here, for example, it was the YVFF, not Stoke City Council, who insisted that such a group as theirs must be based on the local community, not on administrative boundaries. It would, indeed, be politically almost impossible for any city council to select one small community in the way in which the YVFF did. Yet the YVFF's demonstration might well allow the city council to proceed in this way.

It might, indeed, be argued that the YVFF in Stoke have not made as much use as they might have of the advantages which their partial independence of local official opinion and finance might give. This is, of course, partly a result of national YVFF policy, in its insistence on going only where it is invited, and partly a result of the dependence on discretionary grants. But the Stoke workers have sometimes proceeded with more caution than seems necessary. Projects like the Rent Rebates scheme are needed even if the statutory body concerned is not willing to cooperate. Similarly, the case made out for work based on the smaller local community is strong enough to have allowed the YVFF workers to fight for locally based detached youth work centres (not centrally based as in the new Hanley project). This careful avoidance of conflict may well weaken the YVFF's claim to be the advocate of the most needy sections of the community.

If one summarizes the present projects one sees a common link. Each group was originally distinct. Apart from the decreasing number of community service projects, the other three services (development projects proper, advisory service, counselling) have all become, in fact, either small-community based or city-wide development projects, where the YVFF workers operate through adult groups of interested parties. The YVFF in Stoke is no longer a youth organization at all (though some of their projects are concerned with young people) but essentially a resource organization devoted to fertilizing the aims of local groups and facilitating their fulfilment. One of their weekly reports (for March 1971) puts this quite specifically: 'Here is a microcosm of what I see YVFF being all about in the future, short-term demonstrations, feeding information and recommendations to local major agencies, helping new groupings to emerge, based geographically or issue oriented.'

So clear is this change in emphasis that it is difficult to see how the organization can continue to call itself the Young Volunteer Force Foundation. From this point of view it is interesting to note that the Stoke-on-Trent funding of the local branch of YVFF had been originally made as part of the education budget (all statutory youth work being so financed). In February 1971, however, the workers learned that the new Council with a Conservative majority had decided to discontinue the grant under the Education budget from May 1971, onwards. The YVFF, however, were able to get back into the budget under the umbrella of the Social Services estimates, and in the expectation that much of this expenditure would be recoverable from the central government under the Urban Air Programme. This change of financing reflects more or less exactly the changing nature of the work of the YVFF in Stoke, from the original preconception that it would be a youth service organization (though admittedly with a difference) to the reality two years later that it is, in fact, a form of general social service (though the workers would still claim that that too was with a difference).

This difference lies chiefly in the methods of operation both within the Foundation, and between the Foundation and the public which it serves. Relationships within the Young Volunteer Force Foundation appear to differ from those in contemporary bureaucratic organizations in that from the first they have been essentially charismatic. The director personally gathers together a small, carefully chosen group, who disperse in response to local authority invitations and themselves attract a small band of adherents. The members of each group appear to have exactly equal powers once an initial probationary/induction period has been successfully completed. The individual group then has a very large measure of autonomy, including financial autonomy for sums up to £100 and almost a free hand for budgeting within the prescribed limits of the annual grant. Agreement has to be reached with the central organization on the terms of a six-month plan, which is the chief organizational control, but each group makes its own plan, and can argue from a very strong position for its acceptance. Within these limits the group's autonomy extends to choice of a geographical base (though within given local authority areas); choice of project; choice of issues; choice of working method; choice of temporary paid help. Weekly reports have to be made to the Director of Field Work, who is an Assistant Director of the YVFF, but an examination of these reports for Stoke shows them to be somewhat sporadic and to embody complete freedom of choice as to what aspects of the work are reported in any given week. Subjects appear to be chosen according to the immediate interest of the writer, and (since no one person is officially in charge of any field unit) any worker may make the report, often without specific attribution. The chief constraint which the central organization has over the individual branch lies not in written rules but in the branch's expectations as to what will be acceptable to the centre. The fact, however, that these expectations are not embodied in rules means that the individual knows he has, at the least, the right to argue his case hopefully.

There is an equivalent lack of definition about the expected nature of the relationships between YVFF workers and the community. Essentially, as with relationships within the YVFF, these relationships are dependent often upon the chance of meeting or upon extremely personal choices as to whom to work with, and though the field-workers have, of course, deliberately set themselves up in an area of need, this area was also subject to personal choice.

There are certain advantages pertaining to this charismatic ordering of authority, and the YVFF has clearly been set up, in part, quite consciously to exploit these. If one may express the advantages negatively, they consist in an ability to avoid the drawbacks of official-dom, notably the remoteness of officials from the needs of the people they supposedly serve. Close involvement with the community means that the workers can provide a listening ear for local grumbles; the organizational freedom within the YVFF means that they can respond in whatever way seems best at that time, in that place, for those people, without being bound by rules which, because they have to be devised to fit the general case, may not always be most beneficial in the particular instance. The field workers, then living within the community, are, ideally, intimately aware of local needs and able to make rapid adjustments to them with no bureaucratic creaking at the joints. The rapidly changing nature of the work of the YVFF in Stoke is one manifestation of this readiness of response. Another direct benefit of the ability to avoid bureaucratic delay may be seen in research on the Hanley Youth Project. Yet another indication of this flexibility of response may be seen in the way in which the YVFF first made a rather controversial decision to work in one small community of the city, and now, as their work expands, are able partially to go back on that decision and have one of their workers engaged on city-wide projects and likely to move to the city centre. The fact that such decisions are, however, left to the necessarily personal choice of one or two workers may be seen as one of the dangers to be discussed below.

And there are, indeed, concomitant dangers in such a system; first, it is difficult for such a method of work to become a permanent one and secondly, such a method may be subject to abuse in that so much is dependent upon the choices made by one individual (or at most a few individuals) who may well be unable or unwilling to reflect exactly or impartially the choices of the people that he has chosen himself to serve. The YVFF seeks to avoid the first of these disadvantages, the impossibility of becoming permanent while still retaining the same methods and organization, by a built in commitment to 'temporariness', in that its workers are to be *young* (and, therefore, by implication can only be temporary) and in that its field teams are, theoretically, to be sent into an area for a specific limited term of three years. The YVFF is still a young organization, and it is difficult to estimate whether or not it will stand by these commitments.

Moreover, experience in Stoke seems to indicate that even a period of less than three years would be too 'permanent' for such an essentially temporary' method to survive. The further the work of YVFF spreads the more tenuous the charismatic links with the centre necessarily become, and the more difficult it must be to find workers both talented and in tune with the organization's aims and methods as were the original ones. For example, when, after a year, two new workers were introduced to the Stoke team they found it difficult to establish a place for themselves, and they both left fairly soon. Clearly, there were other causes as well as the difficulty they had in establishing themselves in such an informal set-up, where they could not hope for immediate equality with existing workers so well acquainted with the scene, and yet were given no specified place in the hierarchy. However, the fact that this was at least one cause may be seen in the tentative beginnings of a bureaucratic organization which arose during and after these experiences. There were, for example, at this time the first attempts to delimit areas of responsibility for specific team members, and it is notable, here, that it was the new workers whose areas were confined — to play schemes ('Play's your field, they say,' as one of the new workers rather sadly comments when he writes the weekly report) or to counselling — whereas the original workers retained a much less specific brief. The original workers themselves were conscious of a certain loss of simplicity, commenting that a two-man team has only the one personal relationship (A-B), whereas a four-man team has six (A-B), (A-C), (A-D), (B-C),

(B-D), and (C-D). But the problem remains; the number of field
workers returned to two, and the new extra YVFF-financed worker is
to be part of the more highly organized Hanley Youth Project.
Another YVFF worker who is to replace one of the original team has a
specific induction period and the original work load has been split in two
quite specifically on local/city-wide lines. A new temporary worker has
a well defined and restricted field — play schemes. One further bureaucratic manifestation arose as a direct consequence of the employment of
further YVFF workers. The different standards of behaviour in the
shop acceptable to four different individuals very quickly led to friction
(even earlier this had been something of a problem with only two workers)
and this led the workers to call a meeting at which the young people
suggested and accepted a set of rules for behaviour within the shop
instead of the former informal controls. The workers felt they had to
get such agreement also, in defence of their ability to establish relationships with the rest of the community, and they retained the right to
impose the sanction of excluding young people for limited (usually short)
periods of time if they broke these rules.

Moreover, it is clear from the weekly reports from Stoke that the
amount of administrative (i.e. 'bureaucratic') work tacitly demanded of
the Stoke workers has continuously increased. Both 1970/71 workers,
have, for example, been involved in central committees of the YVFF,
and though they obviously welcome the opportunity to contribute to the
central thinking of the organization and indeed, feel it necessary if they
are to get a fair share of resources and abilities for the area that they
represent, they have been quite conscious that this attention to both
national and local needs (even if only as a time-commitment) has
reduced the intimacy of their contact with the local area. They
mention, too, that the amount of paper work increasingly demanded of
them pushes out other work. Yet it is clear that any proper evaluation,
such as a permanent organization needs in order to work efficiently,
would demand more, rather than less, documentation. The workers'
own awareness of this danger and their attempt to offset it can be seen
in the initiative they have taken in involving the local university in a
projected evaluation of community work in the city.

The second characteristic of the YVFF's charismatic system which
may well be regarded as dangerous is that it gives a great deal of influence
in public affairs to people who are not, by the structure of their
organization, directly subject to public control. The central organization
of the YVFF has deliberately kept bureaucratic public control to a
minimum by providing quite substantial private funds, and by accepting
block grants from the DES and the local authorities which are not
subject to direct control but only to the control mechanism of periodic
optional renewal. This is, of course, an important control (and Stoke
YVFF's very existence was threatened by it when their block grant

was cut from the Stoke Education Committee's estimates for 1971/72) but it does not carry with it the ability to supervise the day-to-day working of any particular YVFF field team. Moreover, the YVFF is not subject to the kinds of electoral constraints that bind local councillors. Largely then, the YVFF makes its own choices as to what is 'good' for the public, despite the fact that it is, paradoxically, committed by its ideology to furthering what the public wants. At one level the workers set out sensitively to assess public need (interestingly, part of their in-service training has been some form of sensitivity training) but inevitably conflicts arise, both between the conflicting needs of varying groups and between what people want and what the YVFF sees as their needs. The Stoke weekly reports show that the field team there is essentially directive, resolving these conflicts in ways which the YVFF workers feel to be best, whatever the wishes of the public may be. So, despite the claim in one report that the workers have set a goal of maximum local involvement', there are frequently descriptions of work done which show that, whether or not this may be an end, it is certainly not the means used. To quote from these reports: 'Thus, although one would like to be completely open with a group, and to make it a complete learning process for them, I do not feel this will be possible in general, given limited time and resources.' Or even more appositely: 'There seemed no realistic alternative if the group was to continue to function at the level *we* wanted (as opposed to *them*).'

With such a structure, therefore, the workers may become as directive as they wish, and one sees this directiveness at work in such incidents as one where a YVFF worker invites one social service group to seek to set up an adventure playground, though this was not their original aim; or one where a secretary of a local association is set up against a rival and is persuaded by YVFF workers, against his better judgement, not to resign. The worker can, of course, claim with some justice that such things can only be done within the limits of public acceptability, but, then, the decision as to what is and what is not acceptable is also left to them. That the workers are aware of the problem may be seen in their attempts to counter it by such schemes as getting a student (placed with them for supervision) to run a survey on the public's views as to what should be done on local community premises, or by their attempts to assess public wishes in the case of a Skeffington reclamation project. Such attempts, however, are both infrequent and, ingenious as they may be, essentially limited in scope; — inevitably so in view of the resources available to the two Stoke workers.

In this way, therefore, an association which is set up to provide a *response* to local need, may well become the *arbiter* of such need, since it is subject only in the most attenuated way to the bureaucratic constraints which normally bear upon the legislature, and not at all to the commercial restraints which normally bear upon market supplies. Its remoteness from such sources of control means that response to public need is not built into its structure, but is, rather, dependent on the goodwill of the individuals who constitute the YVFF.

An interesting commentary on these conclusions is provided by Housden (1971) in his conclusion to a *New Society* article on YVF. He writes:

> YVF's work has developed to such an extent that its success can only be measured in general terms: has it done anything itself to improve the quality of life in the areas it works? And has it been able to spur other institutions and individuals to action? If — as I believe it to be — the quality of life is directly related to the control a person has over his own situation, then the recent shifts in YVF's role towards community development and non-authoritarian youth projects can only be steps in a positive direction. Its effect on existing organizations — as I have indicated — has varied from catalytic to catastrophic.

> YVF is probably responding to the contemporary mood as far as any institution is able. Yet for all its flexibility and diversity of role, it remains a government-sponsored institution and its performance suffers from the organizational difficulties inherent in any bureaucratic frame- work. It also suffers by being confined to a name that no longer fits what it really is.

> And in the final analysis, for all its energy, YVF can never extend itself too far beyond the official seal of approval — for it is the government of the day that, in fact, calls its tune.

10 A youth and community service for the future?

The Present Situation

In the preceeding nine chapters we have examined the Youth and Community Service in the 70s — the present state of one of the most fascinating and complex of British institutions. We have considered its history, rooted in the industrialization of the nineteenth century and the voluntary initiatives that attempted to alleviate the social problems to which industrialization gave rise. We have seen the development of the Service, still retaining the social conscience with which it was born, continuing through the first half of the present century: reinforced since 1939 by a growing statutory provision to achieve the dual system that has characterized the service since the 1950s. We have recorded the preoccupation with 'the clubs' in the 50s and with the 'unclubbables' in the early 60s spreading to a wider concern with the 'unattached' in the late 60s and with community action and the 'disadvantaged' in the 1970s.[1] Throughout there has been considerable evidence that at all stages of the development of the Service there has been and still is an impressive relevance to the needs of very large numbers of young people.

If we take a preliminary view of our evidence there is a *prima facie* case for the relevance of the three perspectives we outlined in chapter 2. The socialization, conflict and interpretative perspectives all offer valuable explanations of workings of various areas of the Service; certainly the dominance of the socialization frame of reference in the years before the *Albemarle Report* and the flowering of interpretative approaches in the 1970s are unmistakable. The current diversity of approaches, methodology and structure within the service has been noted by many writers; the current enthusiasm for a de-structured service

[1] The identity of the Youth Service within the Education service has been seen through the close parallel between events in the service and in the schools. The developments in the schools — increased flexibility, client decision making, and concern for community and social problems have been matched in the Service; and the coincidence of *Youth and Community Work in the 70s* with the raising of the school leaving age is worthy of note.

by a number of theoreticians (and a rather fewer number of practitioners) is striking if only for its rarity in the history of any established institution. All this is not to say, of course, that the service has passed from one perspective to another, rather that it has added others to the original and still dominant concern with socialization.

But it is clear that such a simple analysis though useful, is insufficient. It does no more than alert us to complexities such as the apparent co-existence of socialization and interpetative approaches often within the same organization. In order to illuminate the many complexities of the Service and some of their implications we have drawn our conclusions together into a number of sections that, intentionally, cut across the chapter divisions of the book. We now proceed to present them.

The Organizational Structure of the Service

Despite the complexity of the Service and the lack of parameters a number of general trends were visible, most notably the move from organization centred to client centred work; from institutional to individual approaches. We also recorded the successive waves of Service development in recent years — the establishment phase (1939-44) the reconstruction and development phase (1944-60), the expansionist era (1960-1965), the experimental phase (1965-72) and the community phase (1972-).

Yet perhaps not surprisingly the most visible differences in styles of organization were discernable between the two major components of the Youth Service — the statutory and the voluntary organizations. The statutory organizations tended to display a bureaucratic pattern of administration in which critical decisions were taken by largely full-time officers clearly aware of their position in an administrative hierarchy. Conversely the voluntary side tended to show a greater autonomy in its local units — the move towards uniformity of practice, even though sometimes keenly sought, was at times limited by the capacity of the lay workers, in whom considerable power rested, to devote time and energy to the control of the Service. But the diversity also at times appeared to arise because the leaders, as former members of the Service, wanted to keep things as they were.

Yet notwithstanding the superficial divergences in structure, it was notable that both statutory and voluntary bodies displayed strikingly traditional patterns of organization in that longstanding practice was seen to be an important determinant of present day arrangements. There appear to be three main reasons for this:

1. The apparent dependence of promotion to decision making rank, whether as a member, a lay-worker or a professional worker, upon a capacity to conform to the norms of the organization.

2. a strongly held belief that the most effective way to seek governmental or local authority support was by reference to precedence; that it was difficult and even hazardous to seek central funds for radically changed policies.

3. a belief that non-public funds were more readily obtainable from benefactors or the general public in support of the activities for which the organization is traditionally known. Thus, one of the major fund raising initiatives — the Scouts 'bob-a-job' week — was presented to the public in a way calculated to remind them of the Scout 'good deed' concept, even though evidence suggests that at least a majority of the 'bobs' were paid for not doing the job. As we have already noted, we encountered a frequent ambiguity between expressed innovative aims and traditional 'survival' activities.

A notable feature of the Service was the undoubted strength of the influential pressure groups which represented the voluntary organizations singly or collectively. Several workers drew attention to what they considered to be the irrelevance of distinguished 'lay' members on committees, yet during the project we were made fully aware of the strength and effectiveness of the representation of the Service, often at the level of national politics and administration.

Yet such pressure groups are not only divisive in that they sharpen competition for scarce resources, they are also only infrequently innovative. It was put to us on a number of occasions that a more innovative organizational structure might be encouraged by the existence of a small consultative body in which both government and the members of the Youth Service, adult and adolescent, could further develop co-ordination at the national level and explore new administrative strategies in relation to existing and prospective organizations. The suggestions of Ewen in *Towards a Youth Policy* (1972) and of Ewen and others for a 'thinking' group at Cabinet Office level, and PEP's suggestion (1974) for a Youth Organizations Grant Committee are relevant in this context. It could be desirable for such a body to be able to indicate that, with adequate notice, it did not feel obliged to recommend the perpetuation of longstanding administrative forms and also to find ways to make it possible for new organizations, perhaps not necessarily 'pure' Youth Service organizations, to participate more readily in government funding. These new organizations could well be ones in which young people themselves play a greater role in determining and presenting the case for public funding. The DES has recognized the strength of the arguments in a discussion document suggesting that future reappraisal of work with young people should include 'the creation of suitable machinery for regular and continuing consultation among the various interests, including young people themselves' (DES, 1975.)

But it is probably at a more local level that new strategies for co-ordination and planning are most urgently needed. Such a move may well be associated with a broadening of local responsibility for the Service and here the consideration being given by some of the new local authorities towards involving their Social Service Departments more fully in the Youth and Community Service appears worthy of exploration. Certainly many of the new community action and welfare approaches that we have reviewed would appear to be more closely aligned with the Social Services rather than the Education Departments. There are, however, a number of impediments to any formal transfer. A major difficulty is the legislative position of the Service, as local authorities were reminded by DES Circular 8/73. Another is the publicly expressed unhappiness of many of the professional and voluntary bodies towards a move from an 'educational' identity. None of these problems present a barrier to greatly improved co-ordination of relevant services at local level or even to the appointment of inter-departmentally based officers with some such title as 'Director of Youth Services' in the larger urban authorities[2]. Certainly the profusion of community action projects in such authorities, often short lived and frequently staffed with newly qualified or unqualified workers, many with little knowledge of the area or its resources, calls for a breadth and seniority of oversight and guidance that is not always available at the present time. In whatever form it may take place, there seems to be a very strong case for more effective and more broadly based local co-ordination and support of Youth and Community Service activities in areas with a high incidence of community development projects. Without it there is likely to be an increasing duplication and waste of effort which can lead only to frustration and an intensification of the very alienation of young people which is being combated. Recently proposed legislation (the proposed *Youth and Community Work Bill 1974)* offered a number of suggestions for improved local co-ordination and achieved a notable level of interest.

This study suggests that in the long run the 'mainstream' organizations will be surrounded by (and, in many cases, give rise to) a far less structured and institutionalized periphery; that the present structure is already being augmented by a more immediately responsive, often ephemeral, frequently local pattern of institutions, some responding to short-term needs. With effective local oversight and support, such organizations could have available to them a cadre of professional services including not only appropriately qualified Youth Service workers, but also other educational and social workers with a contribution to make to young people — particularly those with employment, housing and the other

[2]The concept of a Youth Affairs Co-ordinator within the Liverpool Authority's Chief Executive's office was an early example of such an initiative.

social and personal problems for whom the new approaches are
frequently designed. In such a context the 'ephemeral workers' to whom
we refer could enjoy a more effective support and a considerably enhanced
role.

The Values of the Youth Service

Our evidence here was drawn from a range of sources. Overall it suggests
that there has been very little change in the values that underlie the
provision of the Youth Service; that the long standing conformist and
high status orientations prevail almost intact. Both statutory and
voluntary organizations have remarkably similar sets of values that are
presented to members. Though there is evidence of change and
adaptability in all branches of the Service, notably in some of the
voluntary bodies (without it organizations would perish), it is also
clear that many of these changes serve to perpetuate rather than modify
the basic values. There is little doubt that the latent if not the manifest
objective of almost all Youth organizations, including many of the new
experimental ones, is that members identify themselves with their
values and, in so doing, become the kind of adult envisaged by the
organization and epitomized to a greater or lesser extent, by the adult
leaders within the organization. The values of course differ according to
the organization; the models of the Church organization, the Scouts,
the Guides, the Cadet Corps, the Boys' Brigade and a number of
other organizations are clearly visible. But beyond these organizations, as
well as within them, it is possible to discern more general values that have
to do with such matters as citizenship, the healthy way of life, the right
mixture of competitiveness and co-operation, respect, loyalty and so on.
The illustrations as well as the text of many of the promotional leaflets
of the clubs convey this message very clearly — even when allowance is
made for the difference between external characteristics and basic values.

The actual activities provided for members of the club can be seen to
fall into two categories: those that are devised to further the personal
qualities and values for which the club or organization stands and those
that provide an incentive to members to attend the club that is sufficiently powerful to encourage them to accept (or to tolerate) the values as
part of the price for participation.[3]

The important feature of the values of the organizations is that in
general they are either imposed or, at least, taken as given. Often they
appear to be unnoticed for much of the time. Democratic decision
making in the club or unit, even where it exists, characteristically takes

---

[3]To use somewhat harsh labels, which would be unacceptable to many, we could
say that the activities are those which reinforce social control and those that keep
the members happy while it is happening.

place within, rather than about, those values which are both determined and preserved by the organizations' adult leaders.

The 'socialization' aspect of the clubs that we have been speaking about is indeed seen by many of the leaders of the statutory and voluntary organizations as an important 'social control' function, a set of arrangements whereby the kind of adult values, whether they be moral, religious or political, which they believe to be appropriate to society at large may be preserved and perpetuated and, often, re-invigorated in the process. Indeed, it is clear that without such a commitment a very great deal of the leadership of the movements would cease to be available.

The Membership of the Clubs

The study did not undertake an overall survey of membership of youth organizations, this task was performed by the Office of Population Censuses and Surveys study that has already been published (Bone and Ross, 1972). Our project was much more concerned with the membership of individual clubs. A notable feature of many of the clubs studied were the tightly drawn territorial boundaries from which membership came. Almost in the manner of the Glasgow gangs studied by Patrick (1973), there was little overlap of membership and in a real sense many represented the range of local interests with remarkable precision.[4]

A particular feature of the project was the study of the 'life cycle' of membership of the five clubs selected for detailed analysis. The ways in which members found themselves able to participate fully in the life of the club and the ways in which they eventually removed themselves, or were removed, from it provided a wealth of interesting material. In general it was possible to divide participation into three categories:

1. members who were initially attracted by the programme and activities of the club or organization, but who found the required commitment to the values or discipline of the club unacceptable and withdrew, or who found the club unattractive or unrewarding in comparison with other leisure opportunities. The Bone and Ross study (1972) indicates clearly how large a group this is, particularly over the age of sixteen. We illustrated this group with the profile of Terry, the 'alienated' member.

[4]This was, as Bone and Ross (1972) have shown, less true in middle class areas in which there was a substantial middle class population. A notable feature of the middle class groups was the tendency for them to be junior members of adult interest groups — sporting clubs, natural history, railway preservation, gliding, caving and similar activity clubs. We argue later that a number of societies of this nature may, through a modest extension of public financed support, be able to open their membership at a more modest subscription to a far wider social cross-section of young people.

2. members who were attracted by the programme and who, though not finding themselves in agreement or sympathy with the expected commitment to the organization, nonetheless found themselves able to go along with it, or at least to tolerate it, and still be able to enjoy the programme. Here we portrayed Kevin, the 'non-committed' member, as representative of this, the largest group.

3. a smaller but significant group of members who were attracted by both the programme and the commitment and usually went on to embrace in a very full way the values of the organization. Such members were characterized by Sybil, the 'committed member'.

Members of this third group tended to become senior members, committee members, junior leaders and similar senior member ranks. It is in part a consequence of the predominance of this latter type of member on the club committees that little radical initiative tends to arise from such bodies. By and large in most of the 'mainstream' clubs investigated, the club committee exercised only a very limited range of decision making and in these areas its decisions tended to be conformist and orthodox. The short space of time in which members of the first two categories came to perceive what they regarded as the 'real' nature of the club tended to make them either disinterested or even hostile to the committee and certainly deterred them from using the committee in any way to challenge the organization — a response which was frequently, and we feel inaccurately, labelled as apathy and indifference by the senior members and adult leaders. It may be that our evidence here points to some general deficiency in leader training in the nature of democratic discussion in different areas of the social system.

The Aims of the Members

The foregoing findings may suggest that members brought a largely negative attitude to the club; this is not the case. Extensive interviews with members suggested that many came to the Service with real needs and an unclear but certainly real hope that the club could enable them to realize them. One overriding response of members interviewed was a deeply held desire to 'count for something' in society, to be able to take part in the decisions that determined the kind and quality of life they would lead at home, in work and in the community, in short to achieve some form of personal 'power'. Coupled with this was a perceptive realization that their often average or lowly position in school had in

[5] Sociologists have drawn attention on many occasions that the socialization offered by schools has commonly been for 'success' roles that can, by definition, only be achieved by a limited number of pupils. In consequence the result for the majority is not only a feeling of failure but also of alienation (Hargreaves, 1967).

many cases already defined them as 'failures' and made it likely that
occupationally they were already destined to be 'on the receiving end'.
Indeed, a number regarded their school experience as an education for
acceptance and conformity.[5] A minority felt that their only hope of
counting for something was to engage in deviant or even anti-social
behaviour. A few looked for their identity to the Hell's Angels, collective
vandalism, football violence and other law-breaking of various kinds in
which at least some kind of social power could be experienced, however
negative. But many cherished a hope that the youth club or organization
would offer power in more acceptable ways. For some this proved to be
the case. These were the young people who found themselves able to
embrace the values of the organization and who, as we have seen,
developed themselves in its image.

But for many, if not a majority, this was seen as yet another process of
being 'fitted in' and offered little solution to their need to express themselves, to be able to achieve their own self-image and through it obtain a
meaningful place in society. In seeking such an individual identity, of
course, these young people were probably expressing, unconsciously,
their realization that present day society, for a variety of social and
economic reasons, has come to value individuality and initiative more
highly than conformity and acceptance and yet frequently fails to help
them to achieve such goals. This was by no means always appreciated
by the leaders or the part-time workers who for the most part had
achieved some level of participation in the power structure of society —
even if only within the club itself.

It was notable that some of the more successful responses to demands
of this nature were visible in some of the more experimental areas of the
Youth Service, particularly those in which some kind of community
action was taking place. Interestingly, these were usually focused on the
young people who were likely to be most powerless in society — those
with problems of employment, housing, poverty, health, race and personality. The measure of achievement with such young people, though
uneven, was often impressive. In projects of this kind it was often
possible for them to identify themselves with an active and important
role and a voice that counted for something not only within the project
but within the community. It was also notable that many young people
found themselves actively involved in movements outside the Youth
Service, such as Child Poverty Action, Release, Shelter, Claimants' Unions
and a number of other spontaneous local groups working with and for
the under privileged. It is possible that in such areas lies one of the
greatest opportunities for working with and for young people and that
many of the present resources of the Youth Service are well placed to
further it. But such approaches are likely to require a new kind of
professionalism in the Youth Service — a kind that, sensitive and
humanitarian, can help young people to negotiate, obtain information,

find words and arguments with which to talk with experts, professionals, politicians and administrators. In achieving this they may help their members not only find a role and a capacity to play in society, but above all the kind of self-image that will enable them to become fully adult. But of course the organization of the Service itself must reflect such changing roles and capacities of its members.

The rapid turnover of workers, their relative inexperience, the expressed disregard for professional qualifications in a number of the new projects and the reluctance of many 'mainstream' workers to join them seems to be hazardous in view of the complex, difficult and responsible tasks being undertaken. There seems to be a strong case not only for 'ephemeral leaders' but also for equipping more workers with a wider range of social work and interpersonal skills and requiring at least an availability of appropriately qualified workers in any publicly financed project. Our earlier suggestion for stronger and more broadly based institutional support at the local level in urban areas where there is a high incidence of experimental projects is relevant here. There is, however, a more general problem for the adult worker in the new approaches. If he is to help his members to achieve an effective decision making role in the community he will find himself involved with members in action that is essentially political in nature. Indeed he must act as their political advocate. Our case study of the work of YVFF effectively demonstrated this. But if he is to do this he is likely to find himself 'confronting' the existing power structure of which he himself is part. If the worker is not to lose faith — and face — with his members he requires a measure of integrity, political awareness and maturity that may be considerably in excess of that required in more 'traditional' situations.

It will be seen from all this that in one sense the aims of the young people are remarkably similar to the aims of the providers of the service. Both see the Youth Service as an opportunity to achieve adult role and status. Yet the similarity is dangerously misleading, for the providers commonly see adult status as being defined in their terms, whereas the clients seek, in most cases, a chance to define their own. To respond to the clients calls for subtle yet fundamental differences in organization and adult participation. The change required seems to be no less than a change to relationships of 'contract' rather than 'commitment' with all the implications for power and control that this raises.

Yet it is important to notice that our evidence does not support the sophisticated radicalism of young people that is often assumed to exist by many contemporary writers on the 'Youth scene'. While there is unquestionably a strong desire to 'change society' in fundamental ways by a number of young people our evidence suggests that this is not a majority view, rather that it is confined to a politically conscious minority and is more likely to characterize the adult workers, particularly those engaged in community action projects, rather than the members. Our evidence suggests that the majority of members are well aware of the nature of contemporary society and are well disposed to accept it as it is. Most are content to find a meaningful place within it that is consistent with a satisfying self-image; to be able to make decisions within the present society rather than refashion it. It is this that we mean by 'counting for something' rather than any capacity for social revolution. Indeed our evidence showed that there was widespread respect for structure, ordered relationships and a stable framework of social organization, and a desire to maintain and develop them both within the club or organization and the community. The most radical position of the 'average' member seemed to be the desire for some redistribution of power in which he and others could share more readily in a largely unchanged society. Often he may not wish to exercise power, only to know that he could if he wished through his trade union or the various community groups to which he has access.

It may well be that many of the more radical workers in the Service are attempting to move too rapidly and that the slower response of the 'mainstream' bulk of the Service may, almost inadvertently, serve as a useful brake to prevent them getting too far ahead of the members. Certainly the image of a de-structured 'permissive' Service may be unattractive to many young people — we have indicated in our discussion of immigrant youth that the Youth Service's move from earlier structured approaches that might have been more acceptable to the cultural patterns of immigrant families appears to have made the Service less attractive to them by intensifying rather than diminishing 'culture shock'. And our discussion of the persistent and effective pressure by immigrants for provision that is *de facto* segregated has shown clearly what we have glimpsed on many occasions — that the Service is not usually an instrument of social change; rather it is a response to social needs that are independently and usually previously formed. We detected no major evidence of attitude change as a result of Youth Service activity, though there was frequent evidence of attitude reinforcement.

Ways Forward

The evidence of the study suggests that, increasingly, the main thrust of the Youth Service would lie in the development of the participative identity through which the young may achieve meaningful adult roles in the sort of society in which they are likely to live; a society of which most of them are well aware and willing to accept if the community will accept them.

There is little doubt that the fundamental issues are to do with power — its availability and distribution — and are political in nature. Of course they always have been, the new feature is that they are now somewhat more explicit and often more urgent than before. To date, the experimental organizations seem to have been more successful in providing such facilities particularly for those most lacking in social and political power, but there is no reason why most existing youth organizations could not adapt to make an even more effective contribution to this end. There is indeed considerable recognition that they can (Davidson, 1973). And in those parts of the service that are linked closely to the schools, the new school curriculum approaches in community involvement and the development of individual judgement are capable of offering important reinforcement.

But it may well be that in focusing on this area the Service may wish, or even need, to place less emphasis on some existing areas of provision. The concept of the Youth Service as being able to provide most things for most young people is possibly something of an anachronism. It may be that we no longer need to try to serve the needs of, say, many of the young people who are successful and well catered for in schools.[6]

It may also be that the Service need not try to replicate in its clubs those facilities that appear to be better provided commercially, especially when the commercial provision is not only more flexible and popular but also self-supporting while that of the Youth Service is less popular and subsidized. Instead it may be that the major focus of activity needs to be for those who need the service most, identifying, like the schools, 'Youth Service priority areas' that pinpoint where effort shall be concentrated. In doing this we may well find that we can also develop what is at present a somewhat uneven professionalism in the Service, offering improvements not only in the sheer expertise of providing the new kinds of activities we wish to provide, but also in areas such as counselling and guidance and the range of social work skills that are probably most helpful in the development of identity and participation, particularly for those in greatest need.

What forms may such a Youth Community service take in the future? To answer this question we must go beyond our evidence into the field of speculation — though it is speculation guided by five years of intensive experience of the service gained during the production of this report. Our surmises may be set out as follows:

The continuance of a considerable amount of existing 'mainstream' provision. There is little doubt that many of the existing 'purpose built' voluntary organizations will survive largely intact with only gradual modifications of their programmes and values. Here we include the uniformed bodies, the church organizations and the other predominantly

[6]This is not to say that they too may not have other needs not catered for by the schools.

voluntary bodies with an established identity that satisfy long standing needs of substantial groups of young people. It is clear that there will also be a continuing need for many of the more successful general purpose clubs and organizations that can provide relaxed, relatively undemanding leisure activities and a social meeting ground at an acceptably mature level for young people for whom alternative facilities are unavailable because of cost or distance or simply indifference.

But beyond this continuing core of voluntary and statutory provision, and in part springing from it, we might expect to see the bifurcation of the predominantly general purpose provision into two forms:

1. Junior clubs predominantly for those at school providing a range of activities appropriate for the fourteen to sixteen age range using, in the main, the facilities of the school campus and recognizing, instead of denying, the links between school and Youth Service provision, links that already exist in the growing similarity between school and 'club' curricula and methodology. Our evidence, like that of Bone and Ross (1972), suggests that young people of this age keenly wish to use the Service and that their needs are clearly different from those of older adolescents. It could well be that attendance at the club, like attendance at the link course in the college of further education, could be seen as an appropriate 'school attendance' by the 15 year old 'ROSLA', children providing an acceptable alternative to the full scale continuation of formal schooling and an alleviation of the problems often associated with this group in the schools.

2. A gradual running down of specific 'segregated' provision for older adolescents. Some provision is already occuring in the context of community and leisure centres where the young are joined by adults in activity-focussed programmes. But for the majority it is arguable that general purpose recreational activities can often not only be better provided by commercial organizations that are well structured yet highly flexible, but also that such provision is increasingly accessible and acceptable to a majority of older adolescents. It may even be that appropriate arrangements could be made to subsidize participation in such commercially provided leisure by adolescents who are unable, on economic grounds, to finance themselves. Such an arrangement, though unprecedented in the Service, has precedents elsewhere in the social services and may well be a considerably less costly facility than the widespread and often under-used current provision for older adolescents within the Service.

The further development of largely short term, exploratory 'non-established' predominantly local projects of varying size and scale for young people in need', those experiencing social, economic and physical difficulty. The experience of the late 60s and early 70s of a wide range of national and local initiatives such as Community Industry, Community Service Volunteers, YVFF and many others has indicated the general viability and relevance of such projects — a viability and relevance that may be enhanced in the later 70s with improved training and local co-ordination and guidance.

A number of developments of this kind could well fall within the context of the Government proposals for a national Community Development Project involving experiments in community development in selected areas of high social need which envisage a 'co-ordinated approach by an inter-service team to the total personal needs of individuals and families and of the community as a whole'. Yet it is interesting that, in the list of 'relevant services' that follow the proposals, the Youth Service is one of the few services that is not included in the 'inter-service team' suggested for each area. Clearly the potential role of the Youth Service in such fundamental proposals for community welfare has by no means been fully recognized; this is also the case in other areas such as the development of Intermediate Treatment strategies. Our suggestions for improved training and more effective local supervision and co-ordination may hasten such recognition.

The further development of special interest groups with open membership but with special opportunity for participation by young people of 'Youth Service age'. These include at one end of the spectrum the groups concerned with matters such as sport, archaeology, railway preservation, theatre, music and the like, to those concerned with pressure groups for community action both at the national level such as Shelter, Release and Child Poverty Action and at the more spontaneous local level in play groups, claimants' unions and so forth. There is abundant evidence of the demand for participation in such activities from young people of all levels of society. The well known report (DOE, 1972) of the *50 Million Volunteers* working party offers some indication of the potential support for activities in the area of community action, conservation and welfare. In a revised Service it may well be that ways might be found to provide appropriate financial support on a broader and more regular basis than now to such organizations. Again the recommendations of *50 Million Volunteers* are relevant. As has been suggested, such a service may well be less formalized, less 'permanent', more client determined, and in consequence more responsive than many of the present arrangements often are. It may even be possible for it to become both less expensive and more effective at the same time. Certainly such a revised service might minimize some of the weaknesses that arise from the present efforts to try to do too much over too wide an area. The Youth Service, like its members, needs to achieve identity and status in contemporary society; to become politically and professionally mature. A sharper focus may offer considerable assistance in reaching these goals.

How may we evaluate the kind of Youth and Community Service that might spring, in the late 1970s, from the evidence we have considered? The question of evaluation is indeed central to the service — as we have seen, it lies at the heart of almost all the difficulties, conflicts and uncertainties. Yet the very process of evaluation is itself surrounded by conflict. One school of thought appears to say 'if you cannot measure it, it's not worth doing', its opponents appear to claim 'if you can measure it, it's too trivial to be worthwhile.'

In practice evaluation is in part a consequence of the culture of the evaluator; sociologists of the phenomenological school show us that our perceptions and interpretations of social situations — our view of what is 'really happening' — may be determined by the way our social background has led us to 'understand' what we see. Is then the whole process of evaluation a subjective one, unamenable to any statement of general principle or practice? Our experience within the five years of the project suggests that such a conclusion, though in part true, is not a necessary one. There appear to be a number of questions that one can apply to contemporary practice in the Service; and though these questions may not be researchable ones, they are certainly ones that can be answered with considerable clarity by any competent, sensitive practitioner. They are, in our view, unquestionably more important that records of buildings, attendance, parades and fund raising. These questions appear to us to include:

1. Do young people join and leave the organization or the club when they are ready to and, in particular, is care taken to ensure that they are not held back from reaching the latter stage?

2. Similarly are projects, activities and programmes initiated and continued because there is evidence that they are serving a useful purpose for members or the community or both and not primarily because they are keeping the organization in being or the workers in work?

3. Is the provision of a kind that could not have been available to the members at all or only with considerable hardship without the Youth and Community Service, rather than just replicating in a more conveniently available form other public and commercial provisions?

4. Is the initiative and motivation increasingly springing from the minds of the members or those they are serving and is the adult worker not in the driving seat for the whole time? Are the outcomes unpredictable because the spontaneity or initiative of the members cannot be foreseen rather than wholly predictable because of the adults' capacity to manipulate the situation?

5. Has the experience of the Service effectively brought members into relationships with adults in the community as equals or near equals and not caused them to be labelled or even to label themselves as segregated and different? Are community issues seen as differences of ideas rather than differences between young and old?

6. Finally, and perhaps most fundamentally, has the existence of Youth and Community Service provision led members to achieve and experience power; to develop judgement in its use and understanding of its nature and to construct or reconstruct their own self-image in the process?

Our experience suggests that these questions are often implicit in general evaluations — for example in Hart's evaluation of YVFF: 'We see real value in this sort of very different field work and we think it's good value for money.' (quoted in Moorehead, 1974.)

We are of the opinion that where all or most of the questions can be answered in the affirmative with regard to any specific aspect of Youth and Community Service provision then it is likely to be right and proper for some branch of the Service to be there and to be in receipt of public funds for the purpose. The evidence of our report suggests that there are many such cases and that there will be many more in the kind of future Youth and Community Services we have considered — a future in which, however integrated and co-ordinated our diagnosis and responses become, there are likely still to be clearly identifiable 'youth' needs and a Youth Service. Yet however certain the need, it is equally certain that discussion, debate and controversy about the way it is to be met will continue, as the DES Discussion Paper (1975) has recognised. We hoped that the information assembled in this report will be of continuing assistance in the debate.

Appendix 1
Description of the clubs

The description of each club falls into four sections: a general description of buildings, facilities, personnel and availability; an account of the general nature of the club; the leadership and, finally, an impression of the club's atmosphere. Each description is prefaced by a 'short account of the locality in which the club was situated.

Colliery Bank

Club Setting

The club, run jointly by the National Coal Board and the Local Education Authority, was situated on a National Coal Board housing estate on the outskirts of a large Midland city. The estate had been built during the 1950s to house miners transferred from areas where the industry was declining: largely Wales and the North East.

There had been much local opposition to the erection of the estate and the social barrier between the estate residents and the people living in the adjacent private houses and on the nearby Council estate was still much in evidence. Additionally, because the estate still suffered from the reputation it had acquired in the early days of its existence, the aim or aspiration of many people on the estate was to move off as soon as possible and buy houses of their own.

Interestingly, while non-estate people saw estate residents as a group apart (immigrants with their own customs) who 'kept themselves to themselves', the people on the Coal Board estate felt that the rest of the community excluded them.

General Description of the Club

a) Type of building, facilities, personnel, availability The club was housed in a large hut on the perimeter of the estate at the end of a cul-de-sac.

Behind was open countryside and in front a small paved area. Facilities were limited. It was open three nights a week.

The major part of the activity took place in one large room. A glass-panelled office, used by the leader, was set in the corner of this room. There was, in addition, a smaller room and a kitchen.

As well as the youth club, a Sunday School was also held on the premises and once a week, on a non-youth club night, there was a ladies' sewing class. The club had a part-time male youth leader who had been at the club since its inception about eight years previously.

There were two female helpers known as 'coffee ladies', one of whom collected the nightly fees at the door as members entered and also kept general vigilance over the club during the course of the evening.

b) Nature of the club Although, locally, the club was called and actually thought to be the 'miners' club' and, in practice, membership was drawn solely from the Coal Board estate, technically membership was open. Despite members' complaints about the lack of people from outside, on the rare occasions when outsiders had ventured into the club they had met with a somewhat stormy and unfriendly reception and consequently never returned.

An average night's attendance was about seventeen, while thirty was considered a good night's attendance. There was a tendency for the same group of people (approximately 60% boys) to be in the club each evening. The age range was wide: from about eight to nineteen years. The typical member, however, was male and thirteen to fourteen years of age. The wide age range was due to the fact that children went along in family groups. When parents left an older child in charge of younger children, the young ones were brought along to the club as well.

The club was predominantly a social club. Most attenders joined in some kind of game: football on the floodlit area, tabletennis, billiards, snooker, darts or board games. There was a background of pop music from a record player, but only a few of the girls present ever danced. There was no specialist activity of any kind although classes and discussions had been tried. There was a club football team. Rotation for table-tennis was organized by the members, but as few ever wanted to play at the same time this presented no real problem. The remaining members sat around and talked or ran about.

There were no club rules as such, but there was emphasis on the care of equipment and property. It was also generally understood that there was to be no 'messing about'. The club had a committee but this was largely composed of adults.

c) Leadership The leader, approximately in his late forties, was a paternalistic figure. He closely identified with the members in two ways. In the first place he lived on the Coal Board estate. Secondly, his full-time occupation was teaching apprentices at the local National Coal Board Training Centre. Consequently he knew a great deal about the members and because of his close connections with mining he made attempts to discourage boys from going into the pits.

He managed to make his presence felt without any undue show of authority and was obviously liked and respected by the members. He spent most of his time in the main room talking with members and generally making himself available. He was nominally in charge of the football team but in actual fact this was run by the members.

General Atmosphere

Barren and unprepossessing, at first glance the club appeared riotous. In fact any disturbance was generally due to high spirits and lack of space in which to move without disturbing others' games. There was no violence or organized vandalism. The atmosphere was free but members knew that breaking equipment would lead to banning for a period.

Older members tended to become bored and eventually drifted away. In many ways the club could be said to provide a temporary shelter for the younger people who were more tied to the locality. Although it was within walking distance of other neighbourhoods and other clubs, the defining characteristic of this club was that it served a closed and well defined group.

Coronation Estate

Club Setting

The club was situated on a pre-war housing estate about one mile from the centre of a Midland borough. The area had been designated as an Educational Priority Area and although there were a few well cared for pockets, the general atmosphere was one of poverty and neglect.

Because of access to an independent study[1], more detail was available for this area. The area was generally seen as the most undesirable in the borough. In fact the area contained a high proportion of unskilled workers (95% of the male population) and had the highest delinquency and probation rate in the entire borough. There were 23 offences between May and July 1970 and the club itself had suffered from vandalism. There was a large under fourteen age group and social amenities on the estate were few.

[1] A social area analysis carried out by the local College of Education.

General Description of the Club

a) Type of building, facilities, personnel, availability The club was established with money from the National Association of Boys' Clubs and the Local Education Authority. In consequence the club faced the problem of having to raise much of the necessary money for repairs, for example, for damage caused by vandalism.

The club was built about fifteen years ago: a purpose built modern brick building. There were five rooms plus an office for the leader. These rooms comprised of a coffee bar, dance floor, table-tennis room, billiards room and a spare room which in the past was used for canoe construction and other craft work.

The club was open every weekday evening. No other group used the building at the same time although parts of some evenings were devoted to different age groups. For example, on Tuesdays and Thursdays of each week children from five to fourteen could attend on payment of 2½p per session. This attracted about 50 children. In addition the first part of Friday night was juniors' night, the purpose of which was 'to keep them off the streets'.

The club had a history of leadership difficulties and continuity was provided by the current part-time leader and his wife, both of whom had previously been members and then voluntary helpers. There were also two other young assistants, male and female.

b) Nature of the club There was a membership list of 47: sixteen girls and thirty-one boys. There was also a system which enabled people to 'drop in' for an evening. Average attendance ranged from ten to twenty except on disco night (Wednesday) when attendance rose to fifty or sixty. Not many people made regular use of the club on non-disco nights. It appeared to be confined to a small group which was untypical of the majority of young people in the area. Of actual attenders the sex ratio was roughly equal. The only limit on membership was age: fourteen to twenty-one years. People coming along to the club signed in and paid a small entrance fee (5p) except on disco night when the entrance fee was higher.

On a typical evening members played table-tennis or billiards. Others listened to records or chatted in the coffee bar. A few did general football training and there was an enthusiastic football team. The club was predominantly a social club and there was no compulsion to take part in any organized activity. There was a certain amount of member participation in the organization of the club.

Members ran the coffee bar, arranged the equipment for the discotheque and helped to run it.

c) Leadership From Wednesdays to Friday the club was run by the husband and wife who had been former members and had the interests of

the club at heart. They themselves lived on the estate. On Monday and
Tuesday evenings the club was run by the other two assistants. All were
young (mid-twenties) and were paid part-time workers. The leader
seemed to supervise, rather than organize, in a very informal atmosphere.

General Atmosphere

Considering the large number of young people in the area, club attendance
was very low and the interviewer felt that those attending the club were
not representative of the young people in the area. The general atmosphere was rather apathetic. There were a few people in the fairly large
space and they came to enjoy a quiet game of billiards or table-tennis.
There was quite a large proportion of steady courting couples.

The leaders were conscious that the club needed more members but,
because of the area, people from outside were not attracted. In addition,
as the over-fifteens left there were not enough young people joining to
take their place. The leader felt that unless something could be done to
give the club a better image it would die. One of them felt that the only
future for the club was for it to become a community hall.

Colourview Rise

Club Setting

The club was situated at one end of a private housing estate on the outskirts of a prosperous and expanding Midland city. Open countryside was
within a few minutes walking distance. The impression of the area was
one of well kept detached and semi-detached housing on a fairly well
established estate.

General Description of the Club

a) Type of building, facilities, personnel, availability This Local Authority
youth and community centre was housed in one half of a war-time
building, the other half of which was used by an infant school. The
reorganization which had taken place when the area had been incorporated within the city had resulted in this space being made available to the
Youth Service. The club had been open for one year. There was a large
open area plus a coffee bar, table-tennis area, three small rooms, corridors
and an office for the leader. During the day the centre was used by old
age pensioners and a play group.

There was a full-time leader who was in charge of daytime as well as
evening use of the premises. She was, approximately, in her mid-forties.

There was also a female adult helper and several activities were organized by older members.

The club was open on Monday, Wednesday and Friday evenings. The early part of the evening was devoted to younger members between the ages of nine and thirteen. Older members, technically fourteen to twenty-one year olds, although in reality few over eighteen attended, came from 7:30 to 10:00 p.m.

b) Nature of the club There were 50 members of the club although a visitors system sometimes raised the attendance figures to over 80. On the whole the same people went each week, roughly two thirds of whom were male, and attenders signed in at the door. Membership was not restricted in any way although the rasing of the fees to 75p earlier in the year had affected membership to some extent. Many of the members were children of families who had moved into the area for jobs. On a typical evening the girls sat around chatting and the boys took part in football and other sporting activities. The leader felt that members did not persevere with an activity once started. On the suggestion of members a disco was run once a week and this was very popular. The club was predominantly social rather than activity orientated, although this tended to fluctuate with the membership.

c) Leadership Although she organized the occasional outing the leader was largely non-directive. Members found her approachable although she was certainly respected. She usually spent the evening moving round the club chatting with the members.

General Atmosphere

The atmosphere was quite disciplined but at times bordered on the apathetic. Although the facilities were quite good several said they were bored. On the other hand many thought this was the best club in the city.

Uptown Grammar

Club Setting

The Boys' Grammar School, where the club was held, was near the centre of a Midland borough in a street of detached and semi-detached modern housing. Because it was a selective school and a club with membership restricted to its own pupils and those of the neighbouring girls' grammar school, the area in which the club was situated was not of the same order of importance as in the case of the other clubs.

General Description of the Club

a) Type of building, facilities, personnel, availability The youth club used parts of the school premises, both old and new. Five rooms were available: the discotheque, gymnasium, table-tennis room, coffee bar and committee room. The discotheque and gymnasium were apart from the rest of the club area. There was a male leader in charge (probably in his mid-thirties) and twelve adult helpers. All were teachers in either the girls' or the boys' grammar schools. The club was held once a week on Friday evenings and had been open for about seven years. The disco, which was to some extent independent of the rest of the club and had a separate entrance fee, had been running for four years.

b) Nature of the club Membership was restricted[2] to the fourth year and upwards of the local boys' and girls' grammar school, i.e. fourteen to eighteen year olds. Consequently it drew its members from the whole borough and had a cross section of social classes.

The membership was about 250 and the sex ratio approximately equal. An average night's attendance was between 150 and 200 and many of the same people attended each time. The highest attendance in the previous year had been 207. A committee member took names at the door as people entered and there was a guest system whereby names were recorded and cards issued. There were very few guests. On one particular evening out of a total of 226 attenders, from which the sample was drawn, there were six guests. Partaking in organized activity was not compulsory, in fact the club was becoming predominantly a social club rather than one that extended education. Activities included football in the gym, table-tennis, the disco and general socializing in the coffee bar area, which was always full.

According to the leader, members did belong to other local authority clubs but they always came to this club on Friday nights. The attraction was their own school friends and friends from the girls' school.

The club committee was appointed by the staff. They were in charge of the 'door' and the coffee bar; with help from the staff, and anyone else who was interested, the committee organized celebrations for special

---

[2] Consideration was given to the choice of the term 'restricted' as opposed to 'open'. Both terms described the same phenomenon, but their implications differ. The essential features of this club were its exclusiveness, high status and the envy it induced in outsiders. During one visit there was an attempted raid by a gang from a nearby council estate. The police were called and they and the teachers dispersed it. One police officer said he could appreciate the club's attractiveness to the outsiders and felt sympathy for them. The exclusive nature of the club was again emphasized by the remark of a member of the school staff who observed that the people who really could have benefited from the club were discouraged in the early days because the club did not want any trouble.

occasions such as Christmas and also ran the discotheque. The committee also made the rules and saw that they were carried out. A no-smoking rule, for example, had been agreed by the committee.

c) Leadership The leader was the most active of the adults. He chatted with the members and generally moved from activity to activity. While being friendly he was always approached in a respectful way and was always addressed formally. Although no reprimands were seen to be given he was obviously a vigilant presence.

General Atmosphere

The atmosphere was lively. Although the discotheque was noisy and dark there was an overall consciousness of discipline which would prevent any riotous behaviour. There were always sufficient members of the staff about to give the club a generally controlled atmosphere, although this was done in a friendly way.[3]

Ambridge Green

Club setting

The club served a scattered rural area characterized by valley and moorland farming, quarrying and a very limited range of agriculturally based light industry. The village of Ambridge Green provided the focus for the area.

General Description of the Club

a) Type of building, facilities, personnel, availability This was a Methodist youth club and had use of the church hall, a building about 100 years old situated at one end of the village. There were four rooms available for use. The club was run by a male voluntary leader, a farmer in his late thirties, who was assisted by his wife. He had a separate office but did not stay in this for any length of time during the course of the evening. The club was held on one evening each week, although practices for table-tennis matches were held on non-club evenings.

b) Nature of the club This was a mixed club with a membership of 80 roughly half of which were girls. Attendance on a 'good night' was about 70. The same group appeared to attend each session, although there was a sizable floating fringe of several groups who attended infrequently.

---

[3] The fact that this was a school club run by school staff meant that control within the club was reinforced by the possibility of supportive control by staff during school hours.

Membership did not appear to be restricted in any way. On joining, a form was signed and, when established, members bought a badge.

On a typical evening there was table-tennis, darts, (say 10% of attenders participated) music, dancing, sitting and talking.

All this was quite unorganized except occasional practices for table-tennis although, as noted, these usually took place on non-club nights. Most people spent the evening in a small music room with loud music and low lights. There was no coffee bar but coke and crisps could be bought. This was predominantly a social club and there was no compulsion to take part in any organized activity.

c) Leadership The leader was an ex-member of the club. His home was 'open house' to members and everyone was on Christian name terms and very friendly and jovial. The leader spent his time mingling with members, chatting and making them feel at home and relaxed. He occasionally organized hikes and country rambles.

General Atmosphere

The premises were very cold and uninviting but the general atmosphere was relaxed and friendly and one of general enjoyment. Some members found the club boring but there was never any unpleasantness of any kind.

Apparently there was little else to do in the area. There were three or four branches of 'The Young Farmers' and some of the club members were also members of these groups, but on the whole the 'Young Farmers' tended to be older, even married. They met for a few special occasions each year. Consequently Ambridge Green club had virtually no competition and thus there was no great necessity to think of different ways of attracting people.

Appendix 2
Club questionnaire

Name of Youth Club

1. Approximate average attendance
2. What constitutes a good night's attendance?
3. How many times does it meet each week?
4. Sex ratio
5. Did it seem to be the same group who came each evening or were there, on the whole, different faces each time you went?
6. Did they sign in:

   have membership cards
   have membership slips
   have membership badges
   have membership ties
   or anything else?

7. Were you aware of membership being restricted in any way? Did people just drop in?
8. How would you describe a typical club member?
9. Were there any club rules, e.g. from notices on the board or what the leader or members said?
10. If yes, did the leader reprimand at all excessively and make his/her presence felt?
11. How would you describe the general atmosphere of the club, e.g. disciplined, apathetic, riotous (could you be as full as possible) or anything else?
12. What went on, on a typical evening?

    Type of activity
    What proportion of attenders took part?
    Was there just general messing about?

13. Had people to take part in some organized activity?

14.   If yes, did the leader insist on this?

Would you say the club/group is:

Predominantly an activity club 1
Predominantly a social club 2
About half and half 3
Fluctuates according to the membership 4

Leader

1.   Sex
2.   Approximate age
3.   Was youth work the leader's

full-time paid occupation 1
part-time paid 2
full-time non-paid 3
part-time non-paid 4

4.   What was the leader's full-time job if not youth work?
5.   How long had the leader been at the club?
6.   Did he have his own office?
7.   How did people approach him/her, e.g. did they have to knock on the door; were they on Christian name terms?
8.   Did he involve himself with the members or distance himself/herself in some way?
9.   How did he/she spend his/her time on a typical evening, e.g. prowl about, sit in his office, instruct in any activity?
10.   Did the leader run any group, team or anything of that nature?
11.   What was the leadership turnover rate?
12.   Were there any other adult helpers in the club, e.g. assistant leaders, outside instructors, coffee ladies?
13.   Were they paid or unpaid?
14.   Did any members act as helpers, e.g. run the coffee bar, take entrance money?

Type of Building and Use

1.   Does the youth club/group have sole use of the building?
2.   About how old is the building?

3.   What is the *main* use of the building today?

Youth club/group 1
School 2
Community Association 3
Church 4
Other 5

4.   What other clubs/groups use the building, if any?

Other youth clubs/groups 1
Pre-school play group 2
Young mothers 3
Old age pensioners 4
School 5
Church members 6
Other (write in) ....
.... 7
None 8

5.   What purpose was it built for?

Youth club 1
School 2
Community Centre 3
Church Hall 4
Village Hall 5
Other (write in) ....
.... 6

6.   How many rooms are available for use on club night including kitchen, gymnasium, etc.?

7.   Is there usually some other group using the building at the same time?

8.   If yes, what is it and how much does it interfere with the youth club?

9.   What type of club, judging from what goes on there, would you say it was, e.g. predominantly sports, athletic, social, disco?

Were there any teams or regular activities?

10.   Is there anything else you could say about the club which would bring out its essential characteristics in a descriptive report?

Appendix 3
Intensive
club questionnaire

Serial No. [   ]

Interviewer's Name [   ]

Date of interview [   ]

| 1. | Sex of respondent | Male | 1 |
| | | Female | 2 |

2.	Age last birthday	14 or under	1
		15	2
		16	3
		17	4
		18	5
		19	6
		20 or over	7

| 3. | Are you at school or doing any sort of studying? | Yes | 1 ask 4 |
| | | No | 2 ask 5 |

4.	What sort of school (or what sort of studying)?	Secondary modern	1
		Comprehensive School incl. bi-lateral or multi-lateral schools	2
		State grammar	3
	QUERY SANDWICH	Technical school	4
		Independent/Direct Grant	5
		Schools abroad	6
		Other types of school (Specify)	7
		College (specify)	8
		University	9
		Apprenticeship	10
		Sandwich course	11
		Other (specify)	12

PROBE mixed or single sex Institution	Mixed	13
	Boys only	14
GO TO 9	Girls only	15

5.	What kind of school did you last go to?		
	PROBE mixed or single sex Institution	Secondary modern	1
		Comprehensive school incl. bi-lateral or multi-lateral schools	2
		State grammar	3
	QUERY SANDWICH	Technical school	4
		Independent/Direct Grant	5
		Schools abroad	6
		Other types of school (specify)	7
		Mixed	8
		Boys only	9
		Girls only	10

6.	Are you at work?	Yes	1 ask 7
		No	2 ask 8

7.	What sort of job?	In a full-time paid job (incl. self-employed)	1
		On a sandwich course — currently in a job	2
	Occupation:	Currently in college	3
		Apprenticeship	4
	Industry:	Other (specify)	5

8.	TO THOSE NOT AT SCHOOL OR NOT AT WORK		
	What are you doing then?	Looking after house/family (and not working or studying full time	1
		Waiting to start job for which you have been accepted	2
		Waiting to take up place at college/university for which you have been accepted (but not in temporary full time paid job	3
		Unemployed, looking for work	4
		Dropped out	5
		Other (specify)	6

	TO ALL SHOW CARD A		
9.	Are you doing any of these now or have you done any of them since you left school?		
	PROMPT AS NECESSARY	A full-time course	1
		A sandwich course	2
		A part-time course you attend during the day time only	3
		A part-time course you attend during some days and evenings	4
		A course you attend in the evenings only	5
		An apprenticeship	6
		Some other course (specify)	7
		None of these	8
10.	Will you (or did you) stay on at school after a time when you *could* have left?		
		Yes	1
		No	2
11.	At what age will you (or did) you leave?		
	PROBE IF R SAYS 16: WAS THIS AT THE EARLIEST OPPORTUNITY?	15 or under	1
		16	2
		17	3
		18 or over	4
		Over 15, but exact age not known	5
	AVOID USING THIS IF POSSIBLE	D.K.	6
	CHECK WITH RESPONSE TO 10		
12.	Are you taking any CSE or GCE O or A level exams?		
	RECORD NUMBER	CSE	1
		GCE O Level	2
	No. of subjects being taken at present	GCE A Level	3
		None of these but other exam mentioned	4
	CSE O Level A Level	None of these	5

13.	Have you ever taken any CSE or GCE O or A level exams in the past?		
	RECORD NUMBER	CSE	1
		GCE O Level	2
		GCE A Level	3
	No. of subjects taken in past	None of these but other exam mentioned	4
		None of these	5
	CSE O Level A Level		
14.	What do you (did you) hope to do when you leave (left school?)		
	PROMPT	Get a job	1 ask 15
		Continue as a full time student	2 ask 16
	IF RESPONSE DISCREPANT WITH 3, 6 and 8, PROBE	Do something else	3 ask 17
15.	What kind of job?		
	GO TO 18		
16.	Where do you (did you) hope to study?		
		Technical college/ Polytechnic/Commercial College	1
		Art/Music/Drama college/ school	2
		College of education	3
		University	4
		Other (specify)	5
		D.K./haven't decided	6
17.	What do you (did you) hope to do?		
		Get married	1
		Voluntary Service Overseas	2
		Other (specify)	3

18. Now I'd like to ask you something about the area round here.
What I'd like you to do is to
describe the different areas
round here.

ASK WITHOUT PROMPT, USE
PROMPT ONLY IF RESPONSE
IS MINIMAL AFTER PROBE.
RECORD WHETHER PROMP-
TED OR NOT' UNDERLINE
PROMPTED RESPONSES.

PROMPTED: Yes   1
No   2

PROBE: ANYTHING ELSE

THEN PROMPT: FOR
INSTANCE, WHAT SORT OF
HOUSES THERE ARE IN
EACH PART, WHAT SORT
OF PEOPLE LIVE THERE,
WHAT SORT OF JOBS
THEY DO, OR ANYTHING ELSE
YOU MAY BE ABLE TO
THINK OF TO DESCRIBE
THEM.

Areas

1.

2.

3.

4.

5.

6.

19.	Could you put these places in any order? Like the way people think about them or talk about them?	
	TRY TO GET AS MUCH AS POSSIBLE HERE. TRY TO PICK UP CLUES ABOUT SOCIAL CATEGORIES, RANK— RANKING ORDER ETC. TRY TO PUSH R AS TO WHAT EXACTLY HE MEANS.	
	1st	
	2nd	
	3rd	
	4th	
	5th	
20.	Where would you say you and your family fitted in?	
	PROBE: SORT OF AREA LIVED IN	
21.	How would you describe people like you and your family?	
22.	Do you think everybody is like that?	
	Yes	1 ask 24
	No	2
	DK	3 ask 24
23.	How would you say some people are different?	

24.	What sort of things are important to you?	
25.	You may have heard people, at home or on TV for example, talk about class, working class, class distinctions. Have you heard of such things? Yes No	 1 2 go to 27.
26.	Where have you heard it mentioned?	
27.	What do you think 'class' means? PROBE IF D.K. GO TO 36	
28.	How many classes do you think there are?	
29.	What would you say they are? TRY TO GET R TO PUT THEM IN ORDER AND LIST THEM ACCORDINGLY 1. 2. 3. 4. 5.	
30.	What class would you say you were in?	

31. Can you say some more about
class? For example how do you
think you can tell that people
belong to a certain class? i.e.
what makes them different from
each other?

LIST WHAT R STATES AS
DIFFERENCES

1.

2.

3.

4.

32. You've just described some ways
in which people are different.
Could you give me a bit more
detail about these differences in
each of the classes you mentioned.

WORK THROUGH R'S LIST OF
CLASSES AND DIFFERENCES.
DO NOT ACCEPT ONE WORD
ANSWERS. PROMPT IF
NECESSARY AFTER PROBE.
RECORD WHETHER PROMPTED
OR NOT. UNDERLINE PROMPTED
RESPONSES'

PROMPTED: Yes   1
No   2

PROBE: COULD YOU EXPLAIN
A BIT MORE?

THEN PROMPT: JOBS,
POSSESSIONS, BEHAVIOUR

R's 1st class:

R's 2nd class:

R's 3rd class:

R's 4th class:

R's 5th class:

33.	Do you think it is possible to be born into one class and move into another?		
		Yes	1
		No	2 ask 35
		D.K.	3 ask 35
34.	How? GO TO 36		
35.	Why do you say that?		
36.	What do you think about people who try to get on?		
37.	Are you going to try?		
		Yes	1 ask 38 & 40
		No	2 ask 39 only
		D.K.	3 go to 41
38.	Why? PROBE		
39.	Why not? PROBE GO TO 41		
40.	How will you go about it?		
41.	Why do you think some people are well off? IF R SAYS DO YOU MEAN MONEY, SAY, WELL MONEY OR ANY OTHER WAY YOU CAN THINK OF.		
42.	Why do you think some people are badly off?		

43.	Now I'd like to ask you some more personal questions. What do you think your *parents* want your life to be like? PROBE FOR: JOB, HOUSING MARRIAGE, FURTHER EDUCATION/TRAINING FINANCIAL SITUATION	
44.	What do *you* want your life to be like? PROBE FOR COMPARISON WITH PARENTS' LIFE JOB, HOUSING, MARRIAGE, FURTHER EDUCATION/TRAINING FINANCIAL SITUATION	

45.	Do you think it will be like that?
	
	                                  Yes
	                                  No
	                                  D.K.
		1
		2 ask 47
		3 ask 48

46.	Why? THOSE IN FULL TIME JOB TO GO TO 48 OTHERS GO TO 49	
47.	Why not?	
48.	ASK THOSE IN FULL TIME JOB NOW — OTHERS GO TO 50 What is your 'take home' pay? AMOUNT GO TO 50	
49.	ASK THOSE NOT IN FULL TIME JOB NOW How much spending money do you usually get each week, including any money you get for spare-time jobs? AMOUNT	

50.	Apart from this club are there any other clubs, societies, or other groups you could go along to or join if you wanted to: things like school clubs, works club, students union, football teams, political groups, drama clubs, scouts/guides or church and social groups for example?		
		Yes	1
		No	2
		D.K.	3
51.	Do you go to any other sort of club that I've just mentioned?/ So you don't go along to any other sort of club that I've just mentioned.		
	BEWARE OF DOUBLE NEGATIVES		
		Yes	1
		No	2

Could you tell me what you go to? (So you just come to this club?)

Name or description of club etc.	Off. Use	Name or description of club etc.	Off. Use
1.		6.	
2.		7.	
3.		8.	
4.		9.	
5.		10.	

So could I just check, altogether you go to   clubs, including this one?

RECORD TOTAL NUMBER OF CLUBS ETC. R GOES TO. IF R NOW OR LATER RECALLS ANOTHER CLUB HE GOES TO' RECORD HERE

THOSE WHO GO TO MORE THAN 3 CLUBS OTHERS GO TO 54

Of the clubs you go to *now* which two do you most enjoy?

1. This club
2.
3.

ASK ASK (i) — (x) FOR EACH CLUB ATTENDED OR EACH CLUB LISTED IN 53

Name of this club	Off. Use	Name of second club	Off. Use	Name of third club	Off. Use

(i) What do you do there (here)?

(ii) What made you decide to go (come) along to   in the first place?

(iii) What did you expect to find?

(iv) What do you think about the club now?

USE NAME OF CLUBS

(v) Did you go (come) along the first time or with someone else?	THIS CLUB	2nd CLUB	3rd CLUB
Went alone	1	1	1
With 1 or 2 friends	2	2	2
In a group	3	3	3
With a relative	4	4	4
Or with someone else	5	5	5
(vi) Is it for boys/males/girls/female only. or is it mixed?			
Boys/males only	1	1	1
Girls/females only	2	2	2
Mixed	3	3	3
(vii) What are the ages of the other people who go?			
Lower limit			
Upper limit			

	THIS CLUB	2nd CLUB	3rd CLUB
(viii) About how often do you go there (come here)?			
More than twice a week	1	1	1
About twice a week	2	2	2
About once a week	3	3	3
Less than once a week	4	4	4
but at least once a month	4	4	4
Or more than once a month.	5	5	5
(ix) And about how long is it since you started going there (coming along)?			
4 weeks or less	1	1	1
Up to 6 months	2	2	2
Up to a year	3	3	3
Up to 2 years	4	3	3
Up to 4 years	5	5	5
4 years or more	6	6	6
(x) How long is it since you last went there (last time you came here)?			
A week or less	1	1	1
Up to 4 weeks	2	2	2
Up to 3 months	3	3	3
Up to 6 months	4	4	4
Up to a year	5	5	5
Up to 2 years	6	6	6
2 years or more	7	7	7

55.	Have you ever in the past been to any Club or group which you no longer to go to?		
	Yes	1	
	No	2 ask 58	

56.	What were they?	
	RECORD NAME OF CLUB ETC. OR DESCRIPTION OF GROUP	
	1.	
	2.	
	3.	
	4.	
	5.	

57.	Why did you stop going there?	
	1.	
	2.	
	3.	
	4.	
	5.	

58.	Thinking about this club, would you say that most members:		
	RUNNING PROMPT	Come from within ¼ mile of the club	1 ask 60
		Come from within a mile of the club	2 ask 60
		Come from a wide area	3
		D.K.	4 ask 60

59.	Why do you think this is?	

60.	How far away do you live?		
		come from within ¼ mile of the club	1
		Come from within a mile of the club	2
		Come from further away (Specify how far)	3
		D.K.	4

61.	How do you get here?		
		Walk	1
		Bus	2
		Bicycle	3
		Motorbike	4
		Scooter	5
		Car	6
		Transport provide by club	7
		Other (specify)	8
62.	Thinking of the sort of area round the club, how would you describe it?		
63.	Would you say you lived in the same sort of area?		
		Yes	1
		No	2
		D.K.	3
64.	Does this club have a committee DO NOT PROMPT		
		Yes	1
		No	2
		D.K.	3
		Several	4
65.	Are you a member of the/a committee		
		Yes (specify)	1
		No	2
66.	Would you like to be a member of the/a club committee		
		Yes	1
		No	2
		Other (specify)	3
67.	Why?		
68.	Do groups of members ever organize activities etc. off their own bat in this club?		
		Yes	1
		No	2 ask 72
		Other (specify)	3

69.	Is this successful on the whole or does it usually collapse before it achieves anything?		
		Usually successful	1
		Usually collapses	2
		Other (specify)	
			3
70.	About how many times *in the last year* have members tried to get something going in this way, whether or not it was successful?		
71.	Can you tell me about *the last time* you remember this happenning? PROBE IF NECESSARY: Who initiated, who took part, whether committee members were involved, what activity etc. was aimed at, whether leaders helped — and how, whether successful — and why.		
72.	Do you think an adult leader is necessary?		
		Yes	1
		No	2 ask 74
73.	Why?		
74.	Why Not?		
75.	What do you think of the job of a youth leader? PROBE IF NECESSARY: is it A JOB THAT ANYONE COULD DO? WHAT DO YOU HAVE TO BE LIKE TO BE ONE?		

76.	SHOW CARD C		
	Which of these do you think is the most important part of a leaders work?		
		Look after club and order equipment	1
		Be available as a helpful adult	2
		Arrange lots of activities	3
		Keep people in order	4
		Other (specify)	5
		D.K.	6
77.	If a friend of yours was banned from the club for breaking the rules — for example for bullying younger members or throwing darts about — would you leave too or stay in the club or what?		
		Leave	1
		Stay	2
		Other (specify)	3
		D.K.	4 go to 79
78.	Why		
79.	What if one of your friends was banned for something you didn't think was important — or you thought the banning wasn't fair. would you leave or stay or what?		
		Leave for good	1
		Leave for a short time	2
		Stay	3
		Other (specify)	4
		D.K.	5
80.	Why?		

81.   If there was any real trouble in
the club what do you think
would happen?

PROBE FOR R's DEFINITION
OF REAL TROUBLE

PROBE FOR LEADER'S
REACTION OTHER MEMBERS'
REACTION R'S REACTION
OFFENDER'S REACTION e.g.
MEMBERS COMPLAIN TO
LEADER, TROUBLEMAKERS
THREATENED BY OTHER
MEMBERS, BANNED FROM
CLUB, REPORTED TO
PARENTS, SENT TO COVENTRY
WHETHER RECENT OR NOT

82. Here is a list of things which some people have said about Youth Clubs, and I'd like you to say for each remark whether or not you agree with it, as far as this club is concerned.

PROBE IF NECESSARY 'ON THE WHOLE' GET AN ANSWER TO EACH ITEM BEFORE GOING ON TO NEXT, AVOID CODE 4 IF POSSIBLE

	Agree	Neither D/K	Disagree	Depends on on the Individual
1. On the whole people are friendly here	1	2	3	4
2. You see fights and violence	1	2	3	4
3. You get bored here	1	2	3	4
4. You can please yourself what you do here	1	2	3	4
5. You get bossed around by the leader	1	2	3	4
6. You get bossed around by other members	1	2	3	4
7. There are lots of interesting things to do	1	2	3	4
8. You feel you have to come regularly	1	2	3	4
9. There are too many young people here	1	2	3	4
10. You are treated as an adult	1	2	3	4
11. You feel lonely and out of it	1	2	3	4

PERSONAL DETAILS

1.	Sex of respondent		
		Male	1
		Female	2
2.	Age last birthday		
	CHECK THIS	14 or under	1
		15	2
		16	3
		17	4
		18	5
		19	6
		20 or over	7
3.	Date of birth in figures		
4.	Place of birth		
5.	Marital status		
		Single	1
		Engaged	2
		Married	3
		Widowed/Divorced/	
		Separated	4
6.	Residence: Do you live with your parents for 4 days a week or more?		
		Yes	1 ask 8
		No	2 ask 7
7.	Where do you live then?		
8.	How many bedrooms has your house/flat etc?		

9.	Who are all the people who live in your house/flat?									
Person No	Relationship to Respondent	Sex M.F.	Age last birth	Marital Status M.S.W/D/S		Working Status Full Time Part Time Not Work			Member of this club Past Present	
1.	Respondent	1 2		1 2	3	5	6	7	8	9
2.		1 2		1 2	3	5	6	7	8	9
3.		1 2		1 2	3	5	6	7	8	9
4.		1 2		1 2	3	5	6	7	8	9
5.		1 2		1 2	3	5	6	7	8	9
6.		1 2		1 2	3	5	6	7	8	9
7.		1 2		1 2	3	5	6	7	8	9
8.		1 2		1 2	3	5	6	7	8	9
9.		1 2		1 2	3	5	6	7	8	9
10.		1 2		1 2	3	5	6	7	8	9
11.		1 2		1 2	3	5	6	7	8	9
12.		1 2		1 2	3	5	6	7	8	9
13.		1 2		1 2	3	5	6	7	8	9
14.		1 2		1 2	3	5	6	7	8	9
15.		1 2		1 2	3	5	6	7	8	9

10. Who would you say is head of your household?

RECORD PERSON No. FROM 9

11. Have you any brothers or sisters not living in the same house/flat as you?

Yes   ask 12
No   ask 13

12.	SEX M.F.	AGE LAST BIRTHDAY	MEMBERS OF THIS CLUB PAST OR PRESENT		WHERE LIVING	
	1 2		3	4		
	1 2		3	4		
	1 2		3	4		
	1 2		3	4		
	1 2		3	4		
	1 2		3	4		

13. So how many brothers and sisters have you altogether?

+R

14.	Where was your mother born? Where was your father born?		
		Mother	Father
	U.K. incl. N. Ireland	1	1
	Channel I's, I.O.M.	2	2
	Eire (S. Ireland).	3	3
	Other (specify)	4	4

15.	What is your father's occupation	
	IF FATHER HAS RETIRED OR DIED ETC. NOTE AND RECORD LAST OCCUPATION	
	Occupation:	
	Industry:	

16.	What is your mother's occupation	
	Occupation:	
	Industry:	

17.	IF R IS A MARRIED WOMAN	
	What is your husband's occupation?	
	Occupation:	
	Industry:	

18.	How old was your mother when she left school?		
	How old was your father when he left school?		
		Mother	Father
	14 and under	1	1
	15 but under 16	2	2
	16 but under 17	3	3
	17 but under 18	4	4
	18 and over	5	5
	D.K.	6	6

19.	Length of interview		
		Less than ¾ hour	1
		¾ hour but less than 1 hour	2
		1 hour but less than 1¼ hrs.	3
		1¼ hrs. but less than 1½ hrs.	4
		1½ hrs. but less than 2 hrs.	5
		2 hrs. or longer	6

References

This list must necessarily exclude the countless pamphlets and leaflets that provided a large part of the research material.

Aalto, R. 1970: The Goals of Youth Organizations and the Wishes of Young People and Youth Workers Concerning Youth Work, *Bulletin for Sociology of Leisure Education and Culture*, No. 3, pp. 7-24.

Abrams, M. 1959: *The Adolescent Consumer*, London: London Press Exchange.

Adeney, M. 1971: Club Trumps, *Guardian*, 26 May.

Albemarle Report 1960: *The Youth Service in England and Wales*, Report of the Committee on the Youth Service in England and Wales, London: HMSO Cmnd. 929.

All London Squatters Federation, 1974: *The Squatters' Handbook*, London.

Allatt, P. 1973: The Use of Social Area Analysis in the Examination of Young People's Formal Social Activity, unpublished M.Sc. thesis, University of Keele.

Anon. 1973a: A School and Youth Service Project, *Forum*, 15 February, 1973b: Youth Problem Advice Centre Serves as a Model, *Education* vol. 141, 16 p. 461.

Bailey, C. 1962: £ s d in Voluntary Youth Clubs, London: NAYC.

Bath and Wells Diocesan Youth Office and Somerset Youth Service, 1971: Minehead Detached Project: job details and reports.

Belstead, Lord 1972: Speech to the Standing Conference of National Voluntary Youth Organizations, 15 September, *Times Educational Supplement*, 22 September.

Berger, P.L. and Luckman, T. 1967: *Social Construction of Reality: Treatise in the Sociology of Knowledge*, London: Allen Lane.

Bernstein, B. 1970: Education cannot compensate for Society, *New Society*, 15, pp. 344-7.

Bernstein B., Elvin, H.L. and Peters, R.S. 1966: Ritual in Education, *Philosophical Transactions of the Royal Society of London*, vvli, pp. 429-36.

Bessey Report 1962: *Training of Part-time Youth Leaders and Assistants* Report of the Youth Service Development Council, London: HMSO. 1965: *Service by Youth,* Report of the Youth Service Development Council, London: HMSO.

Bettelheim, B. 1963: The Problem of Generations, in Erikson, E.H., editor, *The Challenge of Youth,* New York: Doubleday.

Birnbaum, N. 1970: *Crisis of Industrial Society,* New York: Oxford University Press.

Bishop, N.H. 1970: The Youth Service in Leek: an investigation into the membership and attendance of young people at clubs and organizations in Leek, unpublished Diploma dissertation, University of Keele.

BIT, 1973-4: Bitman, London.

Bolton, F. and Laishley, J. 1972: *Education for a Multi-racial Britain,* Fabian and Research Series 303, London: Fabian Society.

Bone, M. and Ross. E. 1972: *The Youth Service and Similar Provision for Young people,* London: HMSO.

Bottomore, T. 1954: Social Stratification in Voluntary Organizations, in Glass, D.V., editor, *Social Mobility in Britain,* London: Routledge and Kegan Paul.

Bourdieu, P. 1971: The Thinkable and the Unthinkable, *Times Literary Supplement,* 15 October, pp. 1255-6.

Brighton Archways Venture, 1968: *General Report,* Brighton.

Bristow, M.H. 1970: The Role of the Youth Worker in Contemporary Society, unpublished M.Ed. thesis, University of Leicester.

Caspari, I.E. and Eggleston, S.J. 1965: A New Approach to the Supervision of Teaching Practice, *Education for Teaching,* Autumn.

Chekki, D.A. 1973: Youth and Social Change: Student Activism in the US and Canada, unpublished paper, Department of Sociology, University of Winnipeg.

Cheltenham Youth Trust, 1972: *Young People at Risk: A Study of the 17-24 age Group.*

Chisnall, A. 1970: A BIT of Help, *Youth Service,* 4 April.

Cicourel, A.V. and Kitsuse, J.T. 1963: *The Education Decision Makers,* Indianapolis: Bobbs-Merrill.

Clark, M. and Clark, J.P. (editors) 1972: *Youth in Modern Society,* New York: Holt, Rinehart and Winston.

Clernans, M. 1966: Youth Work in Teacher Training, *Trends in Education,* 1:2, pp. 9-13, London: HMSO.

Coleman, J. 1961: *The Adolescent Society,* Glencoe, Ill.: the Free Press.

Coleman, T. 1969: *The Railway Navvies,* London: Hutchison.

Commonwealth Secretariat, 1970: *Youth and Development in the Caribbean,* London: HMSO.

Cottle, T.J. (editor) 1972: *The Prospect of Youth: Contexts for Sociological Inquiry,* Boston: Little, Brown.

Cox, D.M. 1970: *A Community Approach to Youth Work in East London 'Avenues Unlimited'*, London: YWCA.

Crowther Report 1959/60: *Fifteen to Eighteen*, Report of the Central Advisory Council for Education (England)Vols. 1 and 2, London: HMSO

Cruickshank, M.A.C. 1963: *Church and State in English Education, 1870 to the present day*, London: Macmillan.

Davidson, C. 1973: *Last but not Least: essentials for a creative community service in Liverpool*, Liverpool: Council of Social Services.

Davis, K. 1940: The Sociology of Parent-Youth Conflict, *American Sociological Review*, 5:4.

Dearling, A. 1973: The Theory and Practice of Youth Work in One Large Centre, *Hard Cheese*, 2.

Department of Education and Science, 1961: *Youth Service Buildings: General Mixed Clubs*, London: HMSO.

1971: *The Education of Immigrants,*London: HMSO.

1972: *Education: A Framework for Expansion*, London: HMSO Cmnd. 5174.

1975: *Provision for Youth — a discussion document*, London: DES.

Department of the Environment, 1972: *50 Million Volunteers*, Report of the 50 million Volunteers Working Party, London: HMSO.

Documentation Centre for Education in Europe, 1970: *European Youth Research 1960-1970*, Strasbourg: Council of Europe.

Durkheim, E. translated by Fox, S.D. 1956: *Education and Sociology*, Glencoe, Ill.: the Free Press.

Eggleston, J. 1974: *Contemporary Research in the Sociology of Education*, London: Methuen.

Eisenstadt, S.N. 1956: *From Generation to Generation*, New York: The Free Press.

1971: Generational Conflict and Intellectual Antinomianism, *The Annals of the American Academy of Political and Social Science*, vol. 395.

Elias, N. and Scotson, J.L. 1965: *The Established and the Outsider*, London: Frank Cass.

Evans, P. 1971: *Attitudes of Young Immigrants*, London: Runnymede Trust.

Ewen, J. 1972a: *Towards a Youth Policy*, Leicester: National Youth Bureau.

1972b: *Youth Service Provision for Young Immigrants*, Leicester: YSIC.

1972c: Should Youth Workers be Peaceful Revolutionaries or Agents of Conformity? *Youth Review*, No. 24.

1974: Introduction, in Gardner, M. *Developmental Work with Young People*, Leicester: National Youth Bureau.

1975: *The Freebooter Coffee Bar and Club, Report of an Exploratory Project*, Cambridge: Freebooter Club.

Farrant, M. and Marchant, H. 1970: *Making Contact with Unreached*

Youth, London: Youth Development Trust.

Feuer, L.S. 1969: *The Conflict of Generations,* New York: Basic Books.

Fleming, C.M. 1963: *Adolescence: its Social Psychology (2nd. edition),* London: Routledge and Kegan Paul.

Freire, P. 1972: *Pedagogy of the Oppressed,* Harmondsworth: Penguin.
1974: *Education for Critical Consciousness,* Dublin: Sheed and Ward.

Gardner, M. 1974: *Developmental Work with Young People,* Leicester: National Youth Bureau.

Goetschius, G.W. and Tash, J.M. 1967: *Working with Unattached Youth,* London: Routledge and Kegan Paul.

Goldhammer, H. 1964: Some Factors affecting Social Participation in Voluntary Associations (Abstract from Ph.D. Dissertation, 1942) in Burgess, F.W. and Bogue, D.J.M. editors, *Contributions to Urban Sociology,* Chicago: The University Press.

Goldthorpe, J.H. 1969: *The Affluent Worker in the Class Structure,* Cambridge: The University Press.

Goldthorpe, J.J., Lockwood, D., Bechhofer, F., and Platt, J. 1969: *The Affluent Worker: Industrial Attitudes and Behaviour,* Cambridge: The University Press.

Gouldner, A.W. 1957-8: Cosmopolitans and Locals: Towards an Analysis of Latent Social Roles I and II, *Administrative Science Quarterly,* 2:3 pp 281-306, 2:4, pp. 444-80.

Hall, S. 1967: The Young Englanders, London: Community Relations Commission.

Hall, S. and Jones, H. 1950:'The Social Grading of Occupations', *British Journal of Sociology* 1(7).

Hargreaves, D. 1967: *Social Relationships in a Secondary School,* London: Routledge and Kegan Paul.

Hartley, B. 1969: *The Multi-racial Youth Club: Evidence to the Select Committee on Race Relations and Immigration,* London: National Association of Youth Clubs
1971: *They say we're too Soft with Them,* London: National Association of Youth Clubs.

Herbert, D.T. and Rogers, B. 1967: Space Relationships in Neighbourhood Planning, *Town and Country Planning.* April.

Hitchin, K.H. 1971: Contact — Counselling by Young Voluntary Workers in a Pub Situation, Liverpool: Merseyside Youth Association, mimeo.

Hollingshead, A.B. 1949: *Elmtown's Youth,* New York: Wiley; paperback New York: Science Editions.

Housden, R. 1971: Model Force, *New Society,* 18 August.

House of Commons (Chairman: Arthur Bottomley) 1969: *Report of the Select Committee on Race Relations and Immigration,* London: HMSO, HC 58, p.523.
1971: (Chairman: William Deedes) *Report of the Select Committee*

on Race Relations and Immigration — Housing, London: HMSO, HC 228.

Hunt Report 1967: *Immigrants and the Youth Service*, Report of the Youth Service Development Council, London: HMSO.

Jahoda, M. and Warren. N. 1965: The Myth of Youth, *Sociology of Education*, xxxviii pp. 138-49.

John, G. 1970: The Churches and Race Today, *Race Today*, October.

Johnstone, M. (editor) 1974: *A Bibliography of Youth Social Work including Intermediate Treatment*, Leicester: National Youth Bureau

Keniston, K. 1963: Social Change and Youth in America, in Erikson, E.H., editor, *The Challenge of Youth*, New York: Doubleday.

Kuper, L., (editor) 1953: *Living in Towns*, London: The Cresset Press.

Latey Report 1967: Report of the Committee on the Age of Majority, London: HMSO.

Lindsay, K. 1975: What went wrong with the Youth Service, *Times Educational Supplement*, 1 August.

Lister, R. 1974: *Justice for the claimant*, London: Child Poverty Action Group.

Lockwood, D. 1966: Sources of Variation in Working Class Images of Society. *Sociological Review*, 14.3, November.

Lowe, J. 1973: *The Managers; a Survey of Youth Club Management, its structure, function and effectiveness*, London: National Association of Mixed Clubs.

MacDonald, M., McGuire, C. and Havighurst, R.J. 1949: Leisure Activities and the Socioeconomic Status of Children, *American Journal of Sociology*, 54.6 pp. 505-19.

McGill, A. 1969: The Youth Service and the Social and Educational Development of Young Immigrants, *Youth Review*, 14, Spring.

Manchester Youth Development Trust 1967: *Young and Coloured in Manchester.*

Mannheim, K. 1952: The Problem of Generations, in Kacskemeti,P., editor, *Essays in the Sociology of Knowledge*, London: Routledge and Kegan Paul.

Matthews, J.E. 1960: *Professional Skill: Functions of Club Organizers in Social Group Work* (reprinted 1963), London: National Association of Youth Clubs.

Mead, M. 1942: *Growing Up in New Guinea: A Study of Adolescence and Sex in Primitive Societies*, Harmondsworth: Penguin.

1943: *Coming of Age in Samoa: A Study of Adolescence and Sex in Primitive Societies*, Harmondsworth: Penguin.

Methodist Association of Youth Clubs 1970a: *Anniversary Report on MAYC Development in the 1970s*, London: MAYC.

1970b: *Report on Hemsby*, London: MAYC.

Milson, F. 1972: *Youth in a Changing Society*, London: Routledge and Kegan Paul.

Moore, R. 1971: From one of them to one of us, *Youth Review*, Spring.

Moorhead, C. 1974: Helping People to Help Themselves, *The Times*, 8 April.

Morse, M. 1965: *The Unattached*, Harmondsworth: Penguin.

Murdock, G. and Phelps, G. 1972: Youth Culture and the School Revisited, *The British Journal of Sociology*, xxiii.4, December.

Musgrove, F. 1964: *Youth and the Social Order*, London: Routledge and Kegan Paul.

National Council of Social Service 1945: *Partnership in the Youth Service*.

Nicholson, S. 1972: Theory of Loose Parts, *Studies in Design Education and Craft*, 3.2.

Office of Population Censuses and Surveys, 1972: *Youth Service and Similar Provision for Young People*, London: HMSO.

Parlett, M. and Hamilton, D. 1972: Evaluation as Illumination, Edinburgh: Centre for Research in the Social Sciences, mimeo.

Parsons, T. 1961: The School Class as a Social System, in Halsey, A.H., Floud, J. and Anderson, C.A., editors, *Education, Economy and Society*, Glencoe, Ill.: The Free Press, pp. 434-55.

1965: General Theory in Sociology, in Merton, R.K., Broom, L. and Cotrell, L.S., editors, *Sociology Today*, New York: Harper and Row, pp. 3-38.

Patrick, J. 1973: *A Glasgow Gang Observed*, London: Eyre Methuen.

Plowden Report 1967: *Children and Their Primary Schools*, Report of the Central Advisory Council for Education, volumes 1 and 2, London: HMSO.

Political and Economic Planning 1975: see Thomas & Perry, 1975

Reich, C.A. 1971: *The Greening of America*, London: Allen Lane.

Report of the Standing Consultative Council on Youth and Community Service 1968: *Community of Interests*, Edinburgh: HMSO.

Rex, J. 1961: *Key Problems in Sociological Theory*, London: Routledge and Kegan Paul.

Riesman, D. 1969: *The Lonely Crowd*, New York: Doubleday.

Robbins Report 1963; *Higher Education*, Report of the Committee on Higher Education London: HMSO.

Robinson, N.M. and Fox, B.V. 1967: *Girls in Two Cities*, London: National Association of Youth Clubs.

Rose, E.J.B. (revised Deakin, N.) 1970: *Colour Citizenship and Social Class*, London: Tavistock.

Roszak, T. 1970: *Making of a Counter Culture: Reflections of the Technocratic Society and its Useful Opposition*, London: Faber.

Schools Council Working Paper No. 28 1970: *Youth Service in the Schools*, London: Evans-Methuen.

Schools Council, Nuffield Foundation 1970: *The Humanities Project: An Introduction*, London: Heinemann Educational.

Smith, C.S., Farrant, M.R. and Marchant, H.J. 1972: *The Wincroft Youth Project,* London: Tavistock.

Steen, A. 1968: *This Service is Alive,* London: YVFF.

Stevenson, T. and Wallis, S. 1970: The Prospects for Immigrants, *Youth Digest,* October.

Seebohm Report 1968: Report of the Committee on Local Authority and Allied Personal Social Services London: HMSO Cmnd. 3703.

Silverstein, H. (editor) 1973: *The Sociology of Youth: Evolution and Revolution,* New York: Macmillan.

Skeffington Report 1969: *People and Planning,* Report of the Committee on Public Participation and Planning, London: HMSO.

Swannell, R. and Muir L. 1973: More Help Needed for Neglected Community and Youth Workers, *Times Educational Supplement,* 6 May.

Thatcher, M. 1971: quoted in *Hansard* 29 March.

1972: quoted in *Education* 21 April, 139.16, p.372.

Thomas, N. and Perry, J. 1975: *National Voluntary Youth Organizations,* London: PEP.

Thrasher, F.M. 1927: *The Gang,* Chicago: The University Press.

Ward, B. 1970: The Soho Project, *Youth Review,* Spring.

Watkins, O. 1972: *Professional Training for Youth Work,* Leicester: Youth Service Information Centre.

Webb, J. 1962, The Sociology of a School, *British Journal of Sociology,* xiii.3, pp. 264-72.

Whyte, W.F. 1955: *Street Corner Society,* (2nd edition), Chicago: The University Press.

YMCA National Commission 1970: *Changing Needs and New Perspectives,*

Youth Service Development Council 1967: *Immigrants and the Youth Service,* London: HMSO.

1969: *Youth and Community Work in the 70s* London: HMSO.

Youth Service Information Centre (annually) *Year Book of the Youth Service in England and Wales.* Leicester: YSIC.

1972: *Occasional Paper No. 6: Structures for Supervision,* Leicester: YSIC.

Young Volunteer Force Foundation 1976: *Evaluation Theory and Community Work* (Armstrong, J., Hudson, P. and Key, M.) volume 1 and 2, London: YVFF, n.y.p. *UBB — Towards a Critical Appraisal of a Community Newspaper* (Armstrong J., Hudson, P. and Key, M.) London: YVFF, n.y.p. *UBB — The Voice of the People? An Appraisal of the Role of YVF in a Community Newspaper* (Whittaker, J. and M.) London: YVFF, n.y.p.

Zald, M.M. 1970: *The Political Economy of the YMCA,* Chicago: The University Press.

Index